Group Therapy with Sexual Abusers

Copyright © 2016 by the Safer Society Press, Brandon, Vermont
First Edition
All rights reserved. No part of this book may be reproduced in any form or by any electronic or mechanical means, including information storage and retrieval systems, without permission in writing from the publisher, except by a reviewer who may quote brief passages.

Printed in the United States of America
August 2020

Library of Congress Cataloging-in-Publication Data
Names: Sawyer, Steven, 1954- author. | Jennings, Jerry L., author.
Title: Group therapy with sexual abusers : engaging the full potential of the
  group experience / Steven Sawyer and Jerry L. Jennings.
Description: First edition. | Brandon, Vermont : Safer Society Press, 2016. |
  Includes bibliographical references.
Identifiers: LCCN 2016021530 | ISBN 9781940234045
Subjects: LCSH: Sex offenders--Rehabilitation. | Sex offenders--Treatment. |
  Group psychotherapy.
Classification: LCC RC560.S47 S29 2016 | DDC 616.85/83--dc23
LC record available at https://lccn.loc.gov/2016021530

P.O. Box 340
Brandon, Vermont 05733
(802) 247-3132
www.safersocietypress.org

Safer Society Press is a program of the Safer Society Foundation, a 501(c)3 nonprofit dedicated to the prevention and treatment of sexual abuse. For more information, visit our website.

Group Therapy with Sexual Abusers: Engaging the Full Potential of the Group Experience
Order # WP174

Group Therapy with Sexual Abusers

Engaging the Full Potential of the Group Experience

Steven Sawyer • Jerry L. Jennings

Brandon, Vermont

Contents

Preface: Why This Book? xi
    Terms and Conventions Used in the Book xiii

Chapter 1: The Theoretical Foundations of Group Therapy 1
    What's Been Missing in Group Therapy for Sexual Abusers? 2
    Group Therapy Is About Relating and Relationships 4
    Different Types of Groups—But They Are All Groups 6
    Group-Centered Therapy Versus Therapy-in-a-Group 8
    Yalom's Group Therapeutic Factors 9
    Mechanisms of Change 13
    RNR and Group Therapy with Sexual Abusers 13
    Drawing from Other Psychological Theories 15
        Maslow's Hierarchy of Needs 15
        Erikson's Stages of Development 16
        Developmental Theory and Attachment Theory 17
    Summary and Conclusions 18

Chapter 2: Guidance from the Research 19
    The Increase in Research and Knowledge
        About Sexual Offenders 19
    Knowledge from the General Group Therapy Literature 21
        Group Is as Effective as Individual in Treating Multiple Disorders 22
        Group Therapy Works Across Different Theoretical Orientations 23
        Cohesion Is the Key Therapeutic Factor 23
        Group Composition Affects Cohesion and Outcome 24
        The Group Therapist Is the Most Essential Agent 24
        Other Guidance from the General Group Therapy Literature 25

- RESEARCH SPECIFIC TO GROUP THERAPY WITH SEXUAL ABUSERS 27
  - *Group Therapist Qualities That Promote Good Outcomes* 27
  - *Confrontation Is Counter-Therapeutic* 29
  - *Cohesion and Therapeutic Climate* 30
  - *Therapeutic Factors Impacting Group Engagement* 32
  - *Clinical Advantages and Client Preference for Group Over Individual Therapy* 36
  - *Sexual Offender Perceptions of Therapeutic Factors* 39
  - *Mixed Versus Specific Sexual Offender Types in Groups* 42
- SUMMARY AND CONCLUSIONS 43

Chapter 3: Ethical and Professional Challenges of Group Therapy with Sexual Abusers 45
- SOURCES OF PROFESSIONAL STANDARDS AND GUIDELINES 45
  - *Behavioral Health Licensing Boards* 45
  - *Professional Association Standards* 47
- PROFESSIONAL CHALLENGES CREATED BY CRIMINAL JUSTICE INVOLVEMENT 50
  - *Limits to Confidentiality May Impact Upon Openness* 50
  - *Avoiding Multiple Relationships* 51
  - *Maintaining Professional Boundaries* 52
  - *Balancing the Dual Roles of Therapist and Authority* 54
  - *Outside Influences That May Impact Upon Group Therapy* 55
  - *Balancing Curricular Demands with Dynamic Group Process* 57
- SUMMARY AND CONCLUSIONS 59

Chapter 4: Composition and the Essentials of Group Structure 61
- PRINCIPLES OF GROUP COMPOSITION 62
  - *The Challenges of Group Composition with Sexual Abusers* 62
- FOUR GUIDELINES FOR MEMBER SELECTION AND GROUP COMPOSITION 65
  - *Composition and the Question of Mixing Offense Types* 67
- PRINCIPLES OF GROUP STRUCTURE 68
  - *The Group Agreement* 68
  - *Preparing Members for Group* 69
  - *Setting Norms in Early Sessions* 70
  - *Establishing Group Structure* 70
  - *Maintaining an Equidistant Circle* 71
  - *Start on Time* 71
  - *Close the Door* 72

Everyone Stays Until the Session Is Finished 72
End on Time 72
SUMMARY AND CONCLUSIONS 72

Chapter 5: Understanding Group Dynamics and Developmental Stages ... 75
PROCESS, CONTENT, AND STRUCTURE 75
Using Structure as an Intervention 77
Integrating and Interweaving Structure, Process, and Content 78
UNDERSTANDING DEVELOPMENTAL STAGES IN GROUPS 80
Models of Group Developmental Stages 81
Applying Knowledge of Group Developmental Stages 85
SUMMARY AND CONCLUSIONS 89

Chapter 6: Facilitating the Group 91
LEAD, RUN, OR FACILITATE? 91
Include Everyone and Get All to Participate 92
Greeting New Members 93
Saying Good-Bye to Departing Members 93
Facilitate Member-to-Member Interaction and Shared Goals 95
Roving Eye Contact 95
Active Facilitation 96
Facilitate to Manage Six Deficits in Group Composition 96
*Applying Five Established Group Principles to
   Sexual Offender Groups* 101
Facilitating Silence in Groups 109
Co-Facilitation 114
SUMMARY AND CONCLUSIONS 117

Chapter 7: Using Group Therapy to Treat Insecure Attachment 119
MARSHALL'S THEORY OF THE INSECURE ATTACHMENT
   OF SEXUAL ABUSERS 119
Biological Basis of Attachment Theory 120
Secure and Insecure Attachment Styles 121
RESEARCH SUPPORTING THE THEORY OF INSECURE ATTACHMENT 122
Rates of Insecure Attachment 122
Loneliness 123
Intimacy Deficits 124
Isolation 124

Negative Family Upbringing......................................125
Attachment Style Corresponds to Sexual Offender Type..................126
Summary of Sexual Abuser Attachment Research......................128
CASE STUDIES SHOWING THE THREE ATTACHMENT TYPES...................128
Determining Attachment Styles...................................130
Using Self-Report Attachment-Style Measures......................131
THE IMPACT OF ATTACHMENT STYLE ON GROUP THERAPY..................131
Impact of Attachment Style on Perception
of Therapeutic Climate.......................................132
Knowing What to Expect......................................133
Adjusting Interventions to Different Attachment Styles..................133
How Your Attachment Style May Interact with Other Styles...............133
USING GROUP THERAPY TO TREAT INSECURE ATTACHMENT.................134
Facilitate Cohesion as the Secure Base..............................134
Group Must Be a Safe and Protected Place........................135
Highlight the Occurrence of Connection...........................135
Reframing Negative Expressions of Connection.....................135
INTERVENTIONS SPECIFIC TO INSECURE ATTACHMENT STYLES...............136
Avoidant-Dismissive Attachment Style.............................136
Preoccupied-Anxious Attachment Style............................137
Avoidant-Fearful Attachment Style................................138
SUMMARY AND CONCLUSIONS...139

Chapter 8: Managing Resistance and Other Common Problems in Sexual Offender Groups 141

RESISTANCE 141
Expressions of Resistance..142
Resistance as a Normal Expected Response........................143
Blaming the System..144
Higher Levels of Resistance Expected in Early Stages of Group.............144
Missed Sessions as Resistance....................................145
MANAGING OTHER COMMON PROBLEMS IN SEXUAL ABUSER GROUPS..........146
Subgrouping...146
Scapegoating..148
Boundary Violations—In and Out of Group.........................149

    Facilitating Difficult Groups 151
        The Passive Group 151
        The Anti-Group: Managing the Dark Side of Groups 153
        The Stuck Group 155
    Managing Our Own Issues 157
        The "Ick" Factor—Countertransference 157
        Burnout 157
        Raising (or Lowering) Expectations 158
        Changing Leadership Style for an Advanced Group 159
    Summary and Conclusions 160

Chapter 9: Tools for Measuring Group Processes 161
    Why Assess What Is Happening in Your Groups? .161
        Group Mapping 162
        Multiple Benefits of Group Assessment 163
    Measures of Group Functioning 164
        The GES (Group Environment Scale) 164
        The GCQ (Group Climate Questionnaire) 165
        The TFI-8 (Therapeutic Factor Inventory–8) 166
        Cohesiveness Subscale 167
        Group Session Rating Scale (GSRS) 168
        The GEM (Group Engagement Measure) 169
        Group Member Satisfaction Questionnaire 169
        RSQ (Relationship Scales Questionnaire) 170
    Tools for Assessing Therapist Facilitation Skills 170
        GPIRS 170
        IC-SWG 171
    Summary and Conclusions 172

References 175

About the Authors 193

Preface: Why This Book?

Our goal in writing this book was to blend current knowledge from the general group therapy literature and sexual offender-specific treatment into sound, practical principles and guidelines for conducting highly effective group-based therapy to treat individuals who have sexually abused. Even though the great majority of sexual offender-specific treatment is currently delivered in a group format, and even though this has been true since the beginning of the field more than 50 years ago, this is the first book to be dedicated specifically to group therapy with sexual abusers.

The purpose and timing of this book reflect, first, a long-standing need in the field for a clear understanding of, and appreciation for, the value of group therapy as a fundamental modality in itself. Second, we believe that this book is crucial because most of the sexual offender-specific treatment being delivered today is weakened and impoverished by its continuing failure to utilize the power of the group for therapeutic growth.

This is not the first time that we have challenged the field to reconsider how it can improve its application of group therapy. The authors first met after Steve (Sawyer) posted a challenge to the field in the *ATSA Forum* in 2000 (Sawyer, 2000). Steve was intrigued by how most sexual abuser treatment programs used group therapy, and yet very little attention had been paid to the rationale, techniques, and efficacy of the treatment group processes. In a review of 60 issues of *Sexual Abuse*, the official journal of the Association for the Treatment of Sexual Abusers, we found that only 7 of 375 articles (1.8 percent) focused on group therapy in the years 1998 to 2013 (Sawyer & Jennings, 2014, p. 127).

Inspired by Steve's question, *Why do we believe group therapy is the preferred modality for treating sexual offenders,* Jerry (Jennings) wrote to him and we shared our dissatisfaction with the field's apparent lack of appreciation for the full potential of the group modality to make treatment more effective. We joined together to write "Principles and Techniques for Maximizing the Effectiveness of Group Therapy with Sex Offenders," which was published in *Sexual Abuse* three years later (Jennings & Sawyer, 2003). Today, a dozen years later, we are close friends, and the field has been evolving in ways that suggest that a paradigm shift has been happening. The field has gradually been moving away from a narrow cognitive-behavioral focus on offense behavior and relapse prevention toward more holistic, multi-modal treatment approaches (Bauman & Kopp, 2004; Longo, 2004; Marshall, Marshall, Serran, & Fernandez, 2006; Yates & Ward, 2008). For example, Marshall and his colleagues describe an integrated sexual offender program that is explicitly multi-modal and whose diverse targets of treatment include self-esteem, acceptance of responsibility, coping and social skills, offense pathways, and sexual interests (Marshall et al., 2006; Jennings & Deming, 2013). At the same time, we believe that these trends may signal a new openness to using proven principles of basic group therapy and group therapeutic process.

Our assertion is supported by the dramatic increase in the number of published studies that focus on group therapy. Our 2003 article relied almost entirely on an appeal to clinical practicality; we lacked empirical studies specific to sexual offender group treatment to support our assertion. But, as shown in the graph below, a veritable explosion of sexual abuse group articles occurred in the decade of 2000 to 2009, amounting to a total greater than the four previous decades combined.

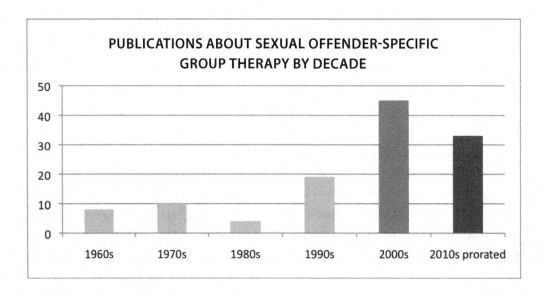

In particular, 27 empirical studies have been published in the years since our article in 2003. There is now solid research within the sexual abuse treatment field—not just research from the general group therapy literature—that can further support the special importance of group therapy as a primary modality with this clinical population. Later, in chapter 2, we'll review this new wave of empirical studies.

Terms and Conventions Used in the Book

Before beginning, it is important to provide a few points of clarification about the terms and conventions used in the book. First, we will reference sexual abusers and offenders as male and use the pronoun *he* throughout. We do this because the vast majority of sexual abusers are male. We recognize that some theories and concepts, such as chapter 7 on attachment theory, may not apply to females.

Second, we will use the terms *sexual offender* and *sexual abuser* interchangeably in the book. We do so to accommodate the language that is commonly used in the research literature in this field. We, of course, recognize that some clients are not adjudicated as "offenders" and are not involved in the criminal justice system. Moreover, the stigma of labeling someone as an offender or abuser is of even greater concern when talking about adolescents, persons with intellectual disabilities, and/or clients who have been victims of sexual abuse themselves. In this regard, we use the labels gently and need to acknowledge that this book is intended for the group treatment of young adult and adult male sexual abusers. Treating adolescents and persons with disabilities may call for alternative modifications of group practice and theory to accommodate their developmental differences.

Finally, the appearance of the following icon marks the beginning of a group therapy case example:

CHAPTER 1

The Theoretical Foundations of Group Therapy

I've been out of the group two and a half years but I still take it [the group] with me.
—Reflection from a former group member

The word *group* was first used in the 1700s to describe people with some common traits. The *Shorter Oxford English Dictionary* (2002) traces the early origins of the term to the French word *groupe*, Italian *gruppo*, and Spanish *grupo, gorupo,* and *grupa,* meaning "knot," "cluster," or "group." The definitions of *group* include: an assemblage of persons, animals, or material standing near together so as to form a collective unity; a knot (of people), a cluster (of things). These early definitions juxtaposed the individual against the group with the group representing a source of commonality or common bond. Early group therapy observers identified that not only does a group offer strength and solace, but it is also a support against which the individual may push to develop his own sense of identity, self-confidence, and self-esteem.

These definitions of the word *group* illustrate the essential, and often overlooked, basic human need to affiliate with others. The etymology of the word suggests affiliation with others with similar traits or interests. The practice of working therapeutically with people in groups has evolved over more than 100 years and is based on this fundamental social instinct to bond with others and belong to a common group. (The reader should note that in our field of treating those who sexually offend, we are often repulsed by the cruelties and exploitive behaviors of our clients. In dealing with such seemingly inhuman behavior, we can succumb to anger and revulsion, even despair, which can lead to the risk of dehumanizing our clients and forgetting their fundamental human need to affiliate. They have a fundamental need to affiliate, perhaps even more than most people, yet they also often lack the skills to effectively navigate the complexities of social relationships. We will return to this topic in later chapters.)

"Although groups devoted to healing are as old as mankind, the professionally guided helping group is an American invention" (Scheidlinger, 2000, p. 316). In 1905, Joseph Pratt, a Boston internist, first organized "classes" to teach proper home care to his indigent tubercular patients. He soon discovered, however, that the patients within the classes began bonding closely to one another. They were no longer individual classmates. They became a group with a shared problem and purpose, caring and supporting one another through the process. Notably, this unplanned phenomenon was viewed critically by contemporaries (Rutan & Stone, 1993). One critic named LeBon concluded that the group contributed to "a diminishing of human functioning," which was caused by the increased suggestibility and contagion experienced by individuals when in groups. Another critic, McDougal, agreed with this potential negative effect, but observed that the group had the potential to enhance the desired healthy behavior of the individual members.

Seventy years later, Rutan and Stone (1993, p. 11) noted the importance of this historical episode in revealing several crucial aspects of the group experience: "the power of groups to affect the behaviors of individuals; the presence of contagion or the capacity of groups to fill each of the members with affects; and the importance of organization, group agreements and goals." These early observers clearly recognized the significance of group interaction in changing the behavior of the individual members of the group.

What's Been Missing in Group Therapy for Sexual Abusers?

In the preface we observed that group therapy has been the predominant mode of treatment in the field of sexual offender-specific treatment for 50 years, and yet it has been virtually ignored as a topic of research until the beginning of the new millennium. The reasons, we believe, are that academic coursework about group therapy is usually generic in content (i.e., not specific to sexual abusers) and that many of our colleagues are untrained or undertrained in group therapy and lack appreciation for the unique therapeutic power of group as a modality in its own right. Simply put, many new and even some experienced group therapists fail to use the group relationships, which has the potential for increasing the effectiveness of treatment.

Much of the group work that we have observed in treatment programs for sexual offenders consists of what might be called individual therapy in front of an audience. This occurs when the group therapist begins a group discussion with a question directed to one group member, and the interaction becomes a dialogue between that member and the group leader. This phenomenon also occurs when one member takes his turn to present a treatment assignment; the other members may be invited to offer suggestions, but otherwise the group leader focuses all attention on each group member individually, one at a time. The leader focuses specifically on a group member's response and how it may have revealed some particular cognitive distortion or therapeutic issue. Then it is time to turn all the attention to another group member. Instead of promoting group therapy as a series of individual-centered interventions, we will emphasize how group-centered interventions can engage the entire group all at the same time and unleash the full therapeutic potential of the group experience—both for the individual and for all members of the group.

In 2003, we termed the individual-centered approach *spokes of the wheel therapy* (see figure 1.1). Without the unifying rim of the therapy circle, the members are discrete spokes that lack direct connections with one another; their relations with one another are governed entirely by the hub—the therapist. Such a wheel "rolls" awkwardly and can be easily fractured. In such a group, the interactive process is stilted or nonexistent. The result is an atmosphere of disengagement where group members feel disconnected and the group lacks cohesion.

Figure 1.1 Spokes of the Wheel Therapy

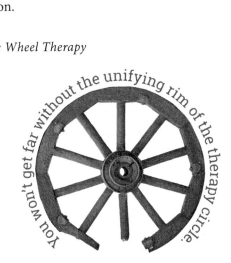

It takes a different mind-set and some practice to see a room of individuals as a *group* and not as a mere gathering of individuals. A group has its own personality, style, and dynamics; it is much more than the sum of its parts. In this book, we will show you how to facilitate groups in a manner that promotes greater interpersonal interaction and cohesion among the group members rather than focusing on the one-to-one interactions between you and each group member.

Steve remembers early in his career the first time that he let go of pursuing an individual issue with one group member and instead shifted his attention to the entire group by, quite simply, presenting a question to the *group* rather than the individual.

The difference was immediate and dramatic. Instead of the usual boredom and disinterest that came from each member waiting his turn, the room came alive as group members became interested, energized, and motivated. That was the moment Steve learned to trust the group process and let go of the burden of doing all the work.

Before this realization, Steve, like many therapists who treat sexual abusers, mistakenly felt like he was the only person in the room whose responsibility was to confront denial, correct cognitive distortions, challenge the minimizations and rationalizations, and manage the various character defects presented by each group member. Weighed down by the incessant pressure to take on all offender dynamics that emerge in group sessions, Steve was conditioned to lead the group in a way that was confrontational and analytical. He was, in effect, controlling the group and many of the interactions that occurred. He did not yet understand that the group is a bonded social system in which all members share the responsibility for supporting and challenging one another to grow. Learning to let go of that burden of responsibility brought immediate relief from a work style of excessive and unnecessary stress and pressure. Better yet, it energized and freed Steve to observe, appreciate, and even enjoy the vital member-to-member interactions through which *the group members do the therapeutic work* of challenging and supporting one another. The art and fun of group therapy is appreciating the group experience (the music of the group) and the potential influence of the group in helping its members to find hope, escape loneliness, build self-esteem, learn compassion, and feel the musical harmony of genuine belonging. This chapter lays the foundation of the group experience and why we use groups as a primary treatment modality.

GROUP THERAPY IS ABOUT RELATING AND RELATIONSHIPS

When we think of a group today, we typically envision people sitting in a circle. Why do groups meet in a circle? Fehr (2002) observed that the circle is continuous and that it represents human connectedness. He went on to observe that "the circle or sphere is an entity that is self-contained, it has no beginning or end . . . It is the only symbol in which all points have parity and equivalency." The significance of the circle is a major theme in Jungian psychology. "In its many representations of culture, and relationships between peoples . . . [the circle] represents wholeness, it is used to represent all time, all possibilities" (Liungman, 1991). Thus, the simple act of sitting in a circle actually mirrors holistic, naturally occurring and primitive experiences that are deeply rooted in human existence.

There are also critical functional aspects of the circle. Sitting in a circle forms a physical space in which all of the group members can see one another. It allows members to be equally "exposed" and visible to all other members. There is no table or obstruction that can conceal nervous behavior from the sight of others. How often have you observed a group where members are fidgeting with their hands, picking at their shoelaces, or constantly moving their feet or legs? These manifestations of anxiety, which can hold important clues about a person's attachment issues or level of comfort in the group, would be hidden if the group were sitting at a table.

The group circle represents the larger outside community in microcosm. Group members' patterns of interacting in the social world of a group reflect and express their values and beliefs about the broader world and their place in that world. Some may argue that a group is an artificial creation, a temporary social laboratory, but there is no denying that it is populated by real people interacting with real people dealing with real problems and experiencing genuine feelings.

As summarized by Steve in an *ATSA Forum* article (Sawyer, 2000), each member's behavior in the circle of a therapy group provides a means of recognizing and understanding that individual's essential *patterns of relationship*:

1. Treatment seeks interpersonal *and* intrapersonal change. Interpersonal change occurs when behavioral, attitudinal, or affective changes occur in the context of *relationships*, not simply in the context of one's own thought processes.
2. As *relationships* form in the natural course of any group of significant duration, group therapy can elicit the reparative power of human caring and belonging.
3. Membership in a group naturally provides an opportunity for abusers to engage in *relationships*, which also helps to evoke and reveal the characterological and relational deficits that lead to interpersonal harm.
4. Treatment in a group allows for multiple *relationships*, with all sorts of variations in quality and closeness, which allows for multiple sources of feedback, emotional support, and insight.
5. The group experience reduces loneliness, alienation, and isolation through *relationships*. It facilitates belonging when group members can experience support and share common problems, and when they can experience the healing power of acceptance after risking the disclosure of shameful or frightening material.
6. The *relationships* within the group create a culture with new prosocial norms that encourage honest, meaningful disclosure, openness to multiple perspectives, and a safe place to constructively and respectfully challenge the problematic behaviors, thoughts, and affective states related to their offense.

DIFFERENT TYPES OF GROUPS—BUT THEY ARE ALL GROUPS

Just as there are reasons why we use group-based treatment methods, there are also different types of groups that are designed with different goals and expected outcomes (Jennings & Sawyer, 2003). Sexual offender treatment is conducted in groups that vary in terms of goals, topics, size, duration, membership, style, practitioner qualifications, and other factors. Groups also vary, and quite dramatically so, in their emphasis (or lack of emphasis) upon interaction and relationships. The following definitions help to clarify the various types of groups and their corresponding interventions.

- *Group-based interventions* are any interventions (educational, supportive, or therapeutic) that are delivered in a group format. Surveys and anecdotal information suggest that most sexual offender treatment programs primarily utilize group-based, as opposed to individual, interventions.
- *Group-focused interventions* are any interventions that are focused specifically on the group itself. This would include interventions that utilize group structure and interpersonal relations among group members to achieve therapeutic goals.
- *Educational groups* provide information pertaining to a specific topic to a group of individuals for a limited period, generally in a didactic fashion, and typically as part of a more comprehensive therapeutic regimen.
- *Psychoeducational groups* are groups that present psychological topics and concepts. Examples might include groups for assertiveness, anger management, criminal thinking, or stress management.
- *Group therapy or group psychotherapy* is the application of theory and therapeutic techniques pertaining to group relationships that further the therapeutic goals of the individual members. Many sexual abuse treatment programs use the term *process group* to distinguish groups of this type.

Why are these definitions important? The goals or purpose of a group will shape and define the character and style of the group as well as its size and format, primary topic or focus, expected outcome, and facilitation needs. But the most important feature that differentiates a group is whether or not interpersonal group processes are emphasized and facilitated. If we graphically represent the types of groups on a continuum of interaction and relationship, we would see educational groups at one extreme and group psychotherapy at the other (see figure 1.2).

Figure 1.2 Continuum of Group Types

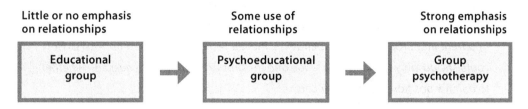

Since the primary goal of an educational group is to convey specific information to the members, the level of group interaction is generally expected to be minimal, and the group leader will not be focused on group interactions and relationships. Nevertheless, all groups have dynamic potential. Even though some groups may be designed explicitly for purely educational purposes—that is, to impart information to a "class"—our point is that *there is always potential for using member-to-member interactions and relationships*. Even in the historic example of Dr. Pratt's educational class for TB patients in 1905, the group naturally formed relationships of support and caring—which were valued more by the patients than the information that was imparted. We believe that group process interventions can be used to benefit all types of groups, and that the greatest human potential can be realized with what can be termed *group-focused* or *group therapy interventions*.

A Psychoeducational Group—An Unsafe Environment

Let's look at a difficult situation that occurred in a group in a residential treatment program. Since this was a psychoeducational group, there was little focus on facilitating group interactions or cohesive relationships. Nevertheless, it will illustrate the importance of relationship dynamics in groups—in both the creation of the problem and its potential resolution.

> *A female clinician was leading a psychoeducational group in which her role was to present a curriculum of didactic information, exercises, and related homework assignments. One group member, Joe, always tried to sit beside or near the group leader. Another group member, Tony, noticed that Joe would frequently drum his fingers on the inside of his leg. Tony complained, anonymously, to a supervisor that Joe appeared to be masturbating in the group.*

When this information was reported and processed with the therapist, she was understandably upset. She felt fear and intimidation regarding Joe and questioned her own competence for failing to observe Joe's pattern of sitting close, and especially his apparent inappropriate sexual behavior. She felt responsible and embarrassed. How could she possibly go back to face Joe and the group? She began to question whether to quit her position and even her career.

At first glance, this case appears to raise serious concerns about Joe as an individual, and our first impulse might be to pull Joe aside and confront him about his behavior. It might also result in dismissing Joe from the group, or even having to change the group leader.

But let's also consider the group dynamics in this scenario. As important as it is to stop Joe's individual deviant behavior, the *group* also has a treatment responsibility of maintaining its group norm of respect—by doing something to stop Joe's behavior. This is a treatment group problem, not just a problem for the therapist or a serious behavioral violation by Joe. It is just as important for the whole group to process this problem. Everyone in the group, including Joe, can learn from this event. Joe needs to get feedback from the group that they will not tolerate such behavior. But everyone in the group also needs to confront their own failure to speak up. What happened to the treatment contract/agreement and their shared fundamental rules and values of mutual respect? Was there covert support for Joe's inappropriate behavior? In addition to the damage done to the clinician, what about the damage to the group? Were group members also violated by Joe's behavior? Can this episode be used as a shared experience of empathy for a victim of sexual abuse?

In the end, after a review of the situation, it was determined that Joe was not masturbating. This result left the question of why Tony reported what he thought he saw, how Tony could have handled it differently, and what the therapist could learn about her own response to her observations in the room.

Group-Centered Therapy Versus Therapy-in-a-Group

The group is a social system that engages everyone in the room. We believe that the primary purpose and unique value of group therapy and group psychotherapy is to focus on relating and relationship. But there is a huge difference between group-centered group therapy and therapy-in-a-group (see figure 1.3).

Figure 1.3 Comparison of Therapist-Centered and Group-Centered Groups

Therapist-Centered Group **Group-Centered Group**

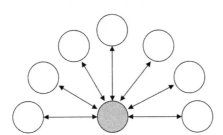
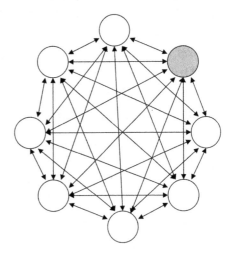

As stated earlier, group-centered therapy promotes interpersonal interaction and cohesion among the group members. Therapy-in-a-group, or therapist-centered group, occurs when the therapist knowingly or unknowingly focuses attention on one group member at a time. In effect, this produces a series of one-to-one therapy encounters between the therapist and individual members. It is like doing individual therapy in front of a group. In such a group, the interactive member-to-member process is stilted or nonexistent. The result is an atmosphere of disengagement where group members feel disconnected and the group lacks cohesion.

YALOM'S GROUP THERAPEUTIC FACTORS

Irving Yalom has probably had the single greatest impact on the field of group therapy. First published in 1970, Yalom's theory of the 10 curative factors of group therapy has shaped practice and research in the field of group therapy in a profound way. We still use the factors and terms that he first coined to conceptualize the specific processes that give group therapy its unique therapeutic power. His landmark book, *The Theory and Practice of Group Psychotherapy*, now in its fifth edition, still stands as a manual for all group therapists. Over time, Yalom has added to, renamed, and reconceptualized his original 10 "curative factors" into the following 12 "therapeutic factors" (Yalom & Leszcz, 2005).

1. **Universality** This is the recognition that one's feelings and problems are not unique and that one is not alone. The recognition of shared experiences and feelings among group members as reflecting common or universal human concerns serves to remove a group member's sense of isolation, validate his experiences, and raise his self-esteem.
2. **Altruism** The group is a place where members can help one another, and the experience of being able to give something to another person can lift a member's self-esteem and help him develop more adaptive coping styles and interpersonal skills.
3. **Instillation of hope** This factor refers to the sense of optimism that members gain from observing improvement in their peers. In a group that has members at various stages of development or recovery, a member can be inspired and encouraged by observing other members as they overcome the problems with which they are still struggling.
4. **Imparting of information (guidance)** While this is not strictly speaking a psychotherapeutic process, members often report that it is very helpful to learn factual information from other members in the group, such as information about their treatment, recovery, or gaining access to help. This factor was termed guidance in the third edition of Yalom's book. In the Yalom Q-sort measure (Yalom, Tinklenberg, & Gilula, 1968), the factor was defined as "accepting advice from other group members."
5. **Corrective recapitulation of the primary family experience (family reenactment)** Members often unconsciously identify the group therapist and other group members with their own parents and siblings in a form of transference specific to group psychotherapy. The therapist's interpretations can help group members gain an understanding of the impact of childhood experiences on their personality, and they may learn to avoid unconsciously repeating unhelpful past interactive patterns in present-day relationships. (This factor was termed family reenactment in the third edition of Yalom's book and in the Yalom Q-sort.)
6. **Development of socializing techniques** The group setting provides a safe and supportive environment for members to take risks by extending their repertoire of interpersonal behaviors and improving their social skills.
7. **Imitative behavior (identification)** Through simple observation and imitation, group members often learn to behave like the group therapist and others in the group that they admire. Group members can develop social skills

through observation and modeling, such as sharing personal feelings, showing concern, and supporting others. (The term *imitation* was replaced by *identification* in the third edition and in the Yalom Q-sort.)

8. **Group cohesiveness (cohesion)** This is the primary therapeutic factor from which all others flow. Humans are herd animals with an instinctive need to belong to groups, and personal development can only take place in an interpersonal context. A cohesive group is one in which all members feel a sense of belonging, acceptance, and validation.

9. **Existential factors** This factor is learning that one has to take responsibility for one's own life and the consequences of one's decisions. It is accepting the fact that the responsibility for change comes from within oneself.

10. **Catharsis** The experience of relief from emotional distress through the free and uninhibited expression of emotion. When members tell their stories to a supportive audience, they can obtain relief from feelings of shame and guilt.

11. **Interpersonal learning (input and output)** Group members achieve a greater level of self-awareness through the process of interacting with others in the group, who give feedback on each member's behavior and impact on others. This factor was split into two subcategories in the third edition and the Yalom Q-sort. *Interpersonal learning (input)* is receiving feedback from group members about one's behavior; *output* is learning effective ways to relate to other group members.

12. **Self-understanding** The achievement of greater levels of insight into the genesis of one's problems and the unconscious motivations that underlie one's behavior. It has also been defined as discovering and accepting unknown parts of oneself. This therapeutic factor was not added until the third edition of Yalom's book in 1995.

Each of Yalom's therapeutic factors evolves from the group process. As is often the case, groups that engage in member-to-member interaction and experience cohesion deepen their interpersonal experience spontaneously. Throughout the following chapters we will offer group examples of how these factors are experienced in groups and how to facilitate group process.

"You Have Us"—Therapeutic Factors in Action

Let's look at an actual group and see how some of Yalom's therapeutic factors might be expressed. Since this group was newly formed, the men were still getting to know one another and there were many moments of awkwardness and silence. Here, in just the third or fourth meeting, a powerful emotional event occurred:

> *The group was listening patiently as Joe, who was on probation for having sex with an underage girl, talked about the people in his life that he could turn to for social and emotional support. He was able to list a number of close friends and family members who knew about his sex offense and to whom he talked on a regular basis. As Joe finished, Dan looked upset and shifted uncomfortably in his chair. The other members looked toward Dan with concern. With tears in his eyes, Dan said, "I don't have any people like that in my life right now. I really wish I did." Mike turned to Dan and said, "You have us." The other group members nodded in agreement. Dan replied, "I know, and I appreciate that."*
>
> *This heartfelt exchange was followed by an outpouring from the other group members, who shared similar feelings of isolation and being unable to talk to anyone about their shameful behavior. Robert chimed in to say, "I'm so glad to know I'm not the only one going through this . . ."*

What therapeutic factors do you see in this moment? In this brief, but powerful moment, this group of strangers became unified as a group. In their shared despair, they experienced *instillation of hope* from the discovery of the *universality* of their common pain and loneliness. They found acceptance and empathy from others despite their shameful offending. *Altruism* was shown when Mike said "You have us" and continued as the men affirmed their appreciation for one another's support. Altogether, the experience strengthened the *cohesiveness* of the group as the men felt acceptance and belonging. This moment of bonding was a decisive moment in the life of this group, one that would carry forward. The phrase *You have us* became a motto and reference point for this group. The phrase could be used and summoned by the group therapist or any member at critical moments in the many weeks and months to come.

Mechanisms of Change

Let's look at another theory of how people learn and are moved to change in group therapy. Rutan and Stone (1993) describe three main mechanisms of change: imitation, identification, and internalization.

1. **Imitation** One of the main ways that group members gain new behavioral options is simply by directly observing how others in the group behave and change and trying it for themselves. For example, Sam noticed how, paradoxically, the other members appeared to show relief and feel better about themselves *after* they took the risk of revealing their shame and self-disgust. He decided to try it for himself. Imitating their behavior worked for him, too.
2. **Identification** Identification is a process in which a person feels an affinity with another group member because of a shared characteristic or experience. Often without clear conscious awareness, a group member sees himself in another person, or wants to be more like another person, and finds himself taking on those desired characteristics. This happened to Sam when he recognized that he was not the only one tormented by self-loathing. He identified with the other members and wanted to share in the relief they gained from disclosing their feelings and finding acceptance rather than rejection.
3. **Internalization** Internalized change is described by Rutan and Stone as the "most advanced and durable mechanism of change . . . not the result of something taken in from the outside . . . rather, due to a shift in the psychic structure of the individual." This change mechanism occurs at the deeper level as the person continues to imitate and try out new ways of behaving—until it no longer feels awkward or temporary and becomes internalized as true to the self.

What we like about this theory of behavior change is that integrates the intrapsychic change of the individual with the interpersonal social influence of the peer therapy group. It enriches and expands the traditional cognitive-behavioral perspective in sexual offender-specific treatment, which too often focuses on individual change and misses the impact of social factors in shaping behavior.

RNR and Group Therapy with Sexual Abusers

The research on sexual offender treatment includes both prison-based programs and community-based outpatient programs. Generally these programs operate groups that are open-ended and are considered therapy groups. Some programs also use didactic or educational modules. Conceptually, the theories of group interaction inform us that group processes and dynamics exist in all types of groups in all venues. That said, interpersonal and group dynamics are most discernible in group settings where there is member-to-member interaction, as opposed to didactic or educational groups.

There is debate in the field as to whether men with high scores on measures of psychopathic traits are able to effectively participate in a group and contribute to meaningful group interaction and outcome. Harkins, Beech, and Thornton (2013) found that psychopathy had less of a negative impact on therapeutic climate than hypothesized. This finding gives us reason to consider that even when working with men with significantly high scores on the Psychopathy Checklist–Revised (PCL-R), we can work toward engaging them in group processes and member-to-member interactions that contribute to positive group outcome.

It is not often stated in the literature that there are times when particular individuals are not able to benefit from, or contribute to, a group and *should not be placed* in a group or should be removed from the group to be treated on an individual basis (Maletsky, 1999). This raises the question of how to individualize treatment in a program that uses group-based modalities. We can begin answering that question by looking at the risk-need-responsivity model (RNR). Briefly, the three core RNR principles can be stated as follows (Andrews & Bonta, 2007):

- **Risk principle** Match the level of service to an offender's risk of reoffending by giving more treatment and more intensive treatment to higher-risk offenders and less to the lower-risk offenders.
- **Need principle** Assess criminogenic needs of the individual and then target those needs in treatment.
- **Responsivity principle** Maximize the offender's ability to learn from treatment by tailoring interventions to his learning style, motivation, abilities, and strengths.

There are two parts to the responsivity principle: general and specific responsivity. *General responsivity* calls for the use of cognitive-behavioral treatment methods to change behavior. *Specific responsivity* is a fine-tuning of the cognitive-behavioral intervention. It takes into account individual strengths, learning style, personality, motivation, and biosocial characteristics, such as gender, age, and ethnicity. (We will discuss group placement based on individual traits, strengths, and interpersonal skills in chapter 4.)

One of the most vexing challenges in a treatment program that has defined expectations and structured goals is to apply these RNR principles in a uniform manner while also individualizing the treatment to each member's criminogenic needs and level of cognitive and psychological functioning. This challenge becomes even more complex for the group therapist, who must balance program goals, treatment objectives, and RNR principles while maintaining a group environment that is perceived by the members as safe, accepting, respectful, and purposeful.

DRAWING FROM OTHER PSYCHOLOGICAL THEORIES

To the degree that the therapy group is a microcosm of real life, we believe that you can also draw from other mainstream psychological theories to gain a more holistic understanding of the dynamics and behavior of men who sexually abuse and their behavior in your treatment groups.

Maslow's Hierarchy of Needs

Maslow's (1954) theory of the hierarchy of human needs (see figure 1.4) reminds us that clients cannot attend to higher-order needs (e.g., the need to realize one's potential) until they have met their more basic needs (e.g., need to feel secure and safe).

Figure 1.4 Maslow's Hierarchy of Human Needs

We encounter clients at various developmental life stages, with varying degrees of cognitive abilities, and with significantly diverse personal, financial, and relational resources. Some are living day-to-day at the bottom of Maslow's hierarchy of needs, struggling to make ends meet, experiencing unemployment and homelessness caused by employers who embrace blanket policies that prohibit hiring felons and local residency restrictions and landlords who refuse to rent to felons.

When offenders are focused on gaining the most basic needs for food, shelter, and safety, and are ostracized and alienated from society, we cannot realistically expect them to have the psychological health to pursue higher levels of social belongingness and self-esteem. We have an obligation to adjust treatment to meet the individuals where they are, to use RNR to help them meet their treatment goals in a manner that does not create treatment barriers.

Erikson's Stages of Development

Erikson's (1968) theory of eight stages of psychosocial development (see figure 1.5) can also be useful in understanding our clients' limits and functional levels in the context of group therapy. Each stage is dominated by particular age-related challenges, beginning with the development of basic trust during infancy, then self-sufficient behavior as a toddler, basic independence as a preschooler, and so forth. The teen years, where many of our clients first get into trouble for maladaptive and aggressive sexual behavior, is the life stage where the healthy adolescent is forming friendships and developing a sense of personal and sexual identity. This is followed, in Erikson's stage theory, by the primary concern for romantic intimacy of young adulthood.

Figure 1.5 Erikson's Stages of Psychosexual Development

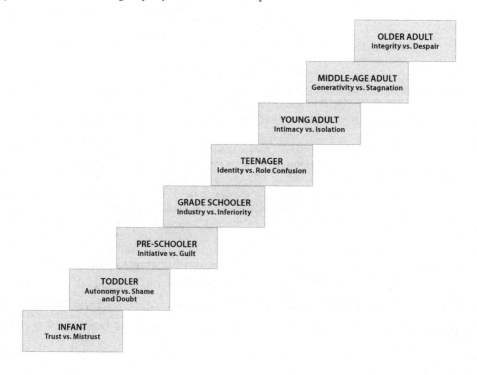

Let's look at how Erikson's theory of human development might apply to an actual sexual abuser in a group.

Developmental Theory in Action

Jimmy was a young man in his mid-20s, never married, who worked at a minimum-wage job. His offense involved a brief sexual relationship with a 15-year-old girl when he was 22. He displayed little motivation to pursue a career, describing how he rebelled against authority and, in particular, his father's expectations. When challenged by the group about setting goals in his life, he became angry, shut down emotionally, and did not want to continue talking about his goals.

In looking at Jimmy, we wonder whether he struggled to accomplish the essential tasks in his earlier developmental stages. His lack of basic trust and aimless lack of ambition may have been rooted in his insecure attachment to his parents and subsequent failure to develop autonomy and initiative during the early-childhood stages. He may have also adjusted poorly to adolescence, emerging with an incomplete sense of self and low self-esteem, and little experience with bonding or intimacy with peers to carry forward into adult relationships. Perhaps Jimmy was still fixated in the developmental challenges of childhood and adolescence as he pursued intimacy and competency with younger, immature girls?

Considering developmental questions such as these may give us clues about a client's level of maturity and psychological functioning and help understand his behavior in the group, such as Jimmy's rejection of any help from his peers. It can also suggest the problems and deficiencies that are holding him back from making progress in treatment—and, concurrently, suggest ways that group experience can directly address his needs for belonging, social competency, and purpose.

Developmental Theory and Attachment Theory

Erikson's developmental theory is very consistent with Marshall's well-known attachment theory of the development of sexual aggression, which is detailed in chapter 7. *Attachment* refers to how well the individual can form and maintain intimacy and connectedness with family, friends, peers, and others. Many sexual abusers have problems with trusting others (as in Erikson's stage one), while others struggle with self-doubt and self-esteem (stage two). For others, the sexual impulses of adolescence (stage five) can become confused, distorted, and displaced in maladaptive efforts as a young adult to find a sense of self and closeness to others. In fact, the research shows that, as a group, sexual offenders have extremely high rates of early trauma and familial disruption, report higher rates of loneliness and isolation, and show deficits in intimacy skills.

Summary and Conclusions

Humans have joined in groups of one form or another since the dawn of time. It is human nature to seek connection and form groups. The word *group* invokes the image of a circle. The circle is a symbol that implies meaning and completeness. We associate a circle with connectedness, integration, and equality among those who face one another. We "circle the wagons," we "gather around in a circle," and life "goes full circle."

We create different groups for different purposes—some are educational, some are supportive, some are task-oriented, and some are intimate and interpersonal. A treatment group is the experience of sitting in a circle, to see and be seen, symbolizing connection and the witnessing of other group members as they pursue their treatment goals. The goal of the group defines how it is facilitated and gives guidance to the expected interpersonal processes.

For some men, sitting in a long-term, open-ended therapy group for a year or more might be the most intense, meaningful, and intimate connection they have ever experienced with other people. It might be the most time they have spent with other adults, and for some it might be the longest relationship they have had in years. Even though the group therapy experience is frequently preceded by the traumatic and shameful process of arrest, prosecution, imprisonment, and court-mandated treatment. Group therapy is a unique opportunity to become more fully human and to find acceptance. The interpersonal experiences and bonding made possible in a therapy group can be the beginning of the therapeutic repair so desperately needed by men who have impaired social relations, fractured self-esteem, distorted views of sexuality, and patterns of failed relationships. The results can be profound when men are able to experience the safe and supportive relationships of a cohesive group, where they can take risks, find acceptance, and connect with others who have had similar lives and struggles.

As we will see in the next chapter, these ideas and concepts about the value of group therapy are not just feel-good generalizations. There is strong empirical research evidence, derived from both the general group therapy literature and the sexual offender-specific literature, that validates the importance of group therapeutic processes.

CHAPTER 2

Guidance from the Research

I feel like an odd piece looking for the right puzzle.

—Client in group therapy

Most group therapists have, at one time or another, had to lead a group that seemed particularly disjointed, disconnected, tense, hostile, or just plain draining to work with. Or just when a group was beginning to engage in meaningful and thoughtful interactions and therapeutic work, a new group member came in and derailed the entire group process. Common experiences like these reflect the potential negative impact of less-than-optimal group composition and remind us of the crucial importance of effective facilitation of the group therapeutic climate. Less-than-ideal composition is one factor that impacts upon the potential of any particular group. Particular member traits can contribute to or inhibit the group processes. The current stage of development of the group can also impact the level of engagement and disclosure in the group. Some groups can become "stuck" in the early developmental stages of hesitancy and distrust, and seem unable to progress in trust and cohesion. We can better identify and manage these common challenges if we know and apply some of the proven principles and key factors that have emerged from the work of researchers and theorists.

THE INCREASE IN RESEARCH AND KNOWLEDGE ABOUT SEXUAL OFFENDERS

Historically, sexual offender-specific treatment became well established as a specialized field in the early 1980s. At that time the supporting research was quite limited. Even though many programs had been in existence across the country for many years, we did not yet have a significant body of definitive research that guided us in how to assess and treat this heterogeneous population. Beginning with the dominant rise of cognitive-behavioral treatment, there has been tremendous growth in our knowledge of what works and what doesn't. Relapse prevention was then introduced, and although there were debates about how the approach applied to sexual and domestic violence, it was quickly embraced in the 1980s (Jennings, 1990). Groundbreaking research by Gene Abel's group (Abel, Becker, Mittelman, Cunningham-Rathner, Rouleau, & Murphy, 1987) generated vigorous discussions about the prevalence of cross-over offenders (those who engage in more than one type of sexually abusive behavior). William Marshall (1989; 1993) ignited a bonfire of research with his theory that attachment deficits may underlie the development and continuance of sexually abusive behavior. In the 1990s, the field continued to advance as actuarial studies were conducted, static and dynamic factors were identified, and risk assessment became increasingly reliable. Today, treatments have shifted to more comprehensive and multi-modal approaches that reflect our better understanding of the complexity of sexually abusive behavior (Marshall, Marshall, Serran, & Fernandez, 2006).

All of these developments were driven by an increasing demand for more information and more research on the prevalence, vicissitudes, and treatment of sexual abusers. Yet for all these advances in knowledge, one thing has remained constant throughout the history of the field: Group therapy continues to be the predominant modality used in the treatment of sexual abusers. This was true from the inception of the field in the late 1950s (Jennings & Deming, 2016). It was true 30 years later when Schwartz and Cellini (1988, p. 103) surveyed sexual offender programs across the country and observed that "group therapy was the one universal feature of every treatment program; in many instances, it was the only treatment provided."

More recently, the Safer Society 2009 North American Survey found that most community-based outpatient programs use group therapy in an open-ended, 90-minute, weekly session dosage (McGrath, Cumming, Burchard, Zeoli, & Ellerby, 2010). The survey distinguished programs by their primary theoretical approach, such as psychoeducational, psychodynamic, cognitive-behavioral, and relapse prevention, as well as their primary treatment targets, such as arousal control, victim empathy, relationship skills, and offense cycles/patterns. Unfortunately, the survey did not ask about the primary theory or treatment targets of the group therapy that they offer. The great majority of today's programs defined their theoretical basis as cognitive-behavioral (92 percent), followed by relapse prevention (80 percent), which suggests that their group approach is likely also cognitive-behavioral and offense-focused. We believe that the failure to ask *how* programs actually apply their most frequent treatment modality is another reflection of how little the field appreciates the importance of the interpersonal aspects of group therapy.

This was not always true. Historically, clinicians in the first few decades of sexual offender treatment had an appreciation for the unique potential of group therapy with this population (Jennings & Deming, 2016). Early pioneers clearly recognized that the peer group was especially powerful for breaking through the characteristic secrecy, shame, denial, and isolation of sexual offending—partly through confrontation, but also through mutual support and conformance with prosocial values. Ironically, they were using group methods with a full appreciation for their interpersonal impact, but were misguided in applying an impractical psychoanalytic approach that was not effective in addressing criminogenic issues and changing sexual offense behavior. For example, it was believed that pedophilia was caused by a fear of masculine competition, and exhibitionism was reassurance against castration anxiety (Costell & Yalom, 1972).

In the 1980s, cognitive-behavioral therapy surged into the practice of general psychotherapy and totally swept the field of sexual offender-specific treatment. Enamored with this new method, therapists began to hammer on the specifics of each individual's sexual offending behavior, deviant arousal, and cognitive distortions. But the field almost completely forgot the essential importance of the whole person, and that sexual abuse occurs within a social and interpersonal context. Along with this, they forgot the unique value of the group modality.

As discussed in the preface, a subtle but distinctive paradigm shift is occurring in this field, which has shifted attention back to a more holistic understanding and treatment of the sexual abuser, and to the general therapeutic factors that work with all clients, not just sexual abusers. With this shift, we have seen a resurgence of research on group therapy, which has significantly expanded our knowledge of group therapeutic factors in this field. Combined with the literature from general group therapy, there is a lot that we can now say with confidence about what works best in the group treatment of sexual abusers. There are also valid and reliable measures that can be used to evaluate the effectiveness of your group or the groups run by your organization. These measures will be discussed in chapter 9.

Knowledge from the General Group Therapy Literature

There is a rich body of research showing that group therapy is a highly effective modality with many disorders. This body of research also points to the key processes and factors that are most important to the success of group therapy.

Group Is as Effective as Individual in Treating Multiple Disorders

In a series of several large meta-analyses, Burlingame and his colleagues have shown group therapy is very effective and, in many instances, equally as effective as individual therapy. In their first review, McRoberts, Burlingame, and Hoag (1998) conducted a meta-analysis of 23 studies that compared group therapy and individual therapy across various settings and found no significant differences in effectiveness. In a second meta-analysis, Burlingame, Fuhriman, and Mosier (2003) analyzed 111 studies of group therapy that were published over a 20-year period. They concluded that recipients of group therapy were better off than 72 percent of untreated controls and that improvement was related to group composition, setting, and diagnosis. In a third large meta-analysis, Burlingame, Straus, and Joyce (2013) reviewed 250 studies of group therapy published in the decade 2000–2011. They identified five factors that contribute to patient improvement in group therapy: the group therapist, the patient, small-group processes, group structural issues, and formal change theory (i.e., the therapist's theoretical orientation and theory of the mechanisms of change). The first factor is key because the group therapist is the one who determines how the other four factors are integrated. It is the group therapist who determines whether the therapy group is used as a vehicle of change, or if the supposed "group therapy" is really just *individual* therapy being "conducted in a group setting without regard for group dynamic factors" (Burlingame et al., 2013, p. 641).

Observing that the most recent decade of research on group therapy has been more rigorous than ever, Burlingame et al. (2013) concluded that there is strong evidence that group therapy is valuable for a variety of disorders in a variety of settings, including inpatient and community-based treatment of substance abuse and mental health disorders (among them panic disorder, social phobia, OCD, eating disorders, depression, bipolar disorder, trauma-related disorders, schizophrenia, and personality disorders), as well as effective or promising for disorders in hospital- and community-based medical settings (such as breast cancer, pain, and somatoform disorders). Perhaps, if they had looked at the more recent research in our field, they would have added sexually abusive behavior disorders to this list as well.

Based on their review, Burlingame et al. (2013) proposed an anatomical model of group structure consisting of five components:

1. Imposed and emergent structure (e.g., group rules such as starting and ending times and attendance, as well as group expectations that evolve over time).
2. Foundational social processes and emergent processes (e.g., decision-making or developmental stages).

3. Formal change theory (e.g., theoretical understanding of the mechanisms of change).
4. Patient (e.g., patient variables such as motivation, resistance, capacity for change).
5. Therapist (e.g., style, rapport, engagement, warmth, empathy).

As concluded by Burlingame et al. (2013), comparisons between group and individual treatment often produced equivalent outcomes; when differences were shown, they were small. They therefore asserted that clinicians often have a choice of using either group or individual therapy because both show equivalent levels of effectiveness with many disorders. To the degree that both are equally effective, however, there is a clear economic advantage to using group therapy. Indeed, there are empirically derived estimates of cost-effectiveness that support the use of group over individual treatment.

Group Therapy Works Across Different Theoretical Orientations

Given the widespread use of group therapy across behavioral health settings, the group literature also encompasses a variety of theoretical approaches, including psychodynamic and cognitive-behavioral approaches, as well as all sorts of group formats, including open-ended, time-limited, long-term, and issue-specific groups. As a whole, the group psychotherapy literature has soundly demonstrated the efficacy of group therapy in diverse venues and clinical applications (Yalom, 1995; Tillitsky, 1990; Dies, 1986; Burlingame et al., 2013). Recognizing the compelling depth and strength of the empirical support for group therapy, Yalom (1995, p. 47) urged the field to move to the next level of "understanding of the necessary conditions for effective psychotherapy." In other words, we know group therapy works very well, but what are the specific processes and factors within group that are most important to its effectiveness?

Cohesion Is the Key Therapeutic Factor

In another comprehensive review, the Burlingame team looked specifically at the therapeutic factor that has been most often studied in group therapy: cohesion (Burlingame, McClendon, & Alonso, 2011). A cohesive group is defined as one in which members feel a sense of belonging, acceptance, and commitment. It can be defined as the accumulated and evolving emotional and psychological connection among members, between members and the group, and between members and the group leader. Based on an analysis of 40 studies published between 1969 and 2009, Burlingame et al. (2011) found a significant aggregate correlation of $r = .25$ between cohesion and outcome (a medium effect ranges from about .17 to .32). They concluded that cohesion and the therapeutic environment of the group are potent sources of change that is independent of theoretical orientation, whether cognitive-behavioral, psychodynamic, psychoanalytic, or other. Finally, they also distinguished five moderator variables—age of members, theoretical orientation, duration, group size, and use of interventions intended to enhance cohesion—that could significantly predict the magnitude of the correlation between cohesion and outcome.

Group Composition Affects Cohesion and Outcome

The importance of group composition is another major area of research and clinical practice guidelines in the field of general group therapy. Group composition is usually considered in terms of how individual member characteristics (e.g., gender, age, types of problems, psychological-mindedness, etc.) will affect group cohesion or compatibility and subsequently how the group interacts. The general wisdom in the field is that groups should, optimally, be composed *heterogeneously* with regard to the types of interpersonal difficulties of the members, but *homogeneously* with regard to the ego strength and level of functioning of the members. The therapist's goal is to bring together a mix of individuals who will both challenge and support one another and develop and maintain group cohesion.

Therefore, the group therapy field emphasizes the importance of carefully *selecting* members—as in applying criteria for both including and excluding individuals from the group—and then *preparing* the individual for entry into the group. For reasons that are unique to the field of sexual offender-specific treatment, however, we often have little say about who is referred and enrolled in our groups. We will discuss the challenges of selection and composition in detail in chapter 4, along with strategies to mitigate these issues.

The Group Therapist Is the Most Essential Agent

The general group therapy literature informs us that the composition of the group, creating and sustaining predictable structure, facilitating member-to-member interaction, timely and supportive interventions, and attention to group leader skills are the essential foundational concepts correlated with positive client outcome. As concluded by Burlingame's meta-analysis of 250 studies, however, the most essential agent is the group therapist, because he or she determines how well each of these components is applied (Burlingame et al., 2013, p. 641). Research regarding the impact of therapeutic factors and group processes across a variety of clinical venues and clinical populations all points to the primary importance of *the therapeutic alliance*, which encompasses the quality of the relationship between the group therapist and the group members, among the members of the group, and between the therapist and the group as a whole. When combined with member-to-member-interaction, the quality of the therapeutic alliance can promote more cohesive groups, which is correlated with goal attainment and positive client outcomes.

The crucial role of the group leader and the essential functions of effective leadership are explored further in chapter 6. This includes leadership skills such as starting a new group, establishing structure, the nature and timing of interventions, enhancing and sustaining emotional climate, facilitating engagement, balancing affirmation and confrontation, and utilizing facilitation skills that promote member-to-member cohesion.

Other Guidance from the General Group Therapy Literature
Character Disorders in Group

The general group therapy literature also offers valuable guidelines for managing the potentially negative impact of personality-disordered clients in a therapy group. Shields (2000), in particular, offers valuable ideas for how group therapists can redefine and understand the behavior of antisocial and character-disordered group members and thereby prevent disruption to the group. For example, his recommendation to "Cherish the troublesome as one road to the core of the self" is based on the need for engagement that feels real and is not merely compliant. When stressed by non-compliant clients, we may be tempted to respond with a punitive action or chastisement, such as "I'm reporting your behavior to your probation officer." Instead, Shields's guidance is to understand the nature of "the troublesome," that is, the meaning of the member's anti-group behavior, and find the opportunity for the group to learn from the behavior and avoid using reactive responses of rejection.

Obviously, in our field, we frequently encounter group members who suffer from severe characterological disorders, long-standing patterns of antisocial behavior, and, often, profound social deficits. Coming from a purely psychodynamic perspective, Shields's methods may lack the cognitive-behavioral framework of established sexual offender treatment, but he offers a unique perspective and practical ideas for addressing the characterological and attachment issues that contribute to an individual's offense pattern, dysfunctional relationships, low self-esteem, deviant attitudes, social alienation, and other common sexual offender issues. In fact, research has shown how the lack of interpersonal engagement is a problem shared by many sexual offenders, which can directly increase dynamic risk (Levenson & Macgowan, 2004).

Group Therapy with Non-Sexual Offender Populations

There have also been numerous papers and studies documenting group therapy with a variety of non-sexual offenders in correctional, outpatient parole, and inpatient forensic clinical settings (e.g., Stein & Brown, 1991). Long and Cope (1980) studied clients in an inpatient felony offender group by asking them to rank-order Yalom's (1995) list of 12 "curative" factors (as we described in chapter 1). Notably, the felons ranked catharsis, which is the relief of distress through open expression of emotion, and group cohesiveness as the most important and beneficial. The remaining factors, from the most to least important, were ranked as follows: interpersonal learning (input), interpersonal learning (output), self-understanding, existential factor, altruism, instillation of hope, guidance, corrective recapitulation of primary family experience, universality, and imitation.

MacDevitt and Stanislow (1987) compared the same curative factors across forensic groups. They found differences between the forensic groups studied by Long and Cope (1980) and outpatient groups studied by Yalom (1995). Catharsis was among the top four factors experienced as most beneficial in all groups studied, while family recapitulation and imitation were considered as being among the least beneficial. In another study of incarcerated chemically dependent inmates, Burtenshaw (1997) found that the offenders placed the most value on the therapeutic factors of self-understanding and catharsis.

While cohesion is typically given the most attention in group therapy research, it is interesting that catharsis is also highly ranked in all of these non-sexual offender clinical populations. But catharsis does *not* become therapeutic simply because the person is directly expressing anger or other strong emotions. Psychological research has shown that "venting anger" or "getting anger out" is more likely to reinforce aggressive responding. *The group climate is the essential ingredient in making catharsis into a therapeutic experience.* A safe, cohesive, and accepting group climate makes it possible for men to take the chance, often for the first time in their lives, to reveal and express vulnerable emotions that are typically forbidden, such as fear, hurt, loneliness, shame, or weakness (Jennings & Murphy, 2000). The new experience of peer acceptance in the group—as opposed to humiliation and rejection for weakness—is the element that makes catharsis into such a powerful therapeutic event.

Developmental Stages of Groups

As we will discuss in chapter 5, there are numerous models of the stages of normal group development, including a three-phase model created by Yalom. If a sexual offender-specific therapist knows what level of trust, openness, and conflict can be typically expected (or not expected) at the beginning, middle, and mature stages of group development, he or she can adjust interventions to be more effective.

Other Resources from the General Group Literature

In addition to Yalom's seminal work on therapeutic factors and group process, there are other major contributors from the general group therapy field from whom we can learn lessons to apply to sexually abusive clients. In particular, we recommend the following:

- Rutan and Stone (1993) provide guidelines for the management of negative dynamics in groups, and describe mechanisms of change in groups.
- Shields (2000) provides guidelines for managing character disorders in group therapy.
- Nitsun (1996) provides strategies to manage the destructive anti-group dynamics that are inherent in all groups and threaten therapeutic climate (chapter 8).
- Valid and reliable measures of therapeutic climate and group cohesion, including brief tools, are available to measure and monitor group treatment effectiveness (see chapter 9).
- The American Group Psychotherapy Association (AGPA) and Association for the Advancement of Social Work with Groups (AASWG) offer detailed guidelines for ethical and clinical group practice, covering everything from starting to ending a group (see chapter 3).

RESEARCH SPECIFIC TO GROUP THERAPY WITH SEXUAL ABUSERS

Until the 2000 decade, sexual offender-specific research has largely ignored the importance of group therapy as a primary modality of treatment. But there have been some significant research advances, particularly in the past decade, which enable us to make some conclusive statements about what works and doesn't work in group therapy with sexual abusers. In the first and only comprehensive review of research specific to group-based sexual abuse treatment, Jennings and Deming (2016) have organized the available research into the following seven areas.

Group Therapist Qualities That Promote Good Outcomes

In 2001, Marshall, Fernandez, Serran, Mulloy, Thornton, Mann, and Anderson (2003) made a major discovery when they had the opportunity to view videotapes of a psychoeducational, cognitive-behavioral treatment program for sexual offenders. At the time, administrators of the British prison system wanted to demonstrate the effectiveness of their new curriculum, which had been carefully manualized with every session and topic detailed and defined. Believing that greater compliance with the standardized program would maximize outcomes, the group therapists were videotaped to ensure that they were adhering closely to the set curriculum. However, despite this strong pressure to stick to the script, some groups had good outcomes and some groups had poor ones.

Under such controlled conditions, Marshall and his colleagues realized that the only factor that could vary was the style or way that each therapist delivered the curriculum. Interested in discerning the impact of specific process variables, they devised a rating system with 27 different therapist behaviors and qualities, which could be reliably observed from the videotapes. Three experienced clinicians then independently rated the videotapes. Of the 27 factors, they discovered that four therapist features were very highly correlated with the measures of positive behavior change: warm, empathic, rewarding, and directive. *Rewarding* was defined as "offering verbal encouragement to clients for small steps toward whatever goal was being sought." *Directive* was defined as "guidance from the therapist when necessary, such as 'Have you thought of trying . . . ?' and 'Did you consider . . . ?'"

They also found, as discussed below, that *confrontation* (defined as challenging the offender's beliefs and statements in front of his peers in a harsh, judgmental, rejecting, or unrelenting way) was highly negatively correlated with improvement. In fact, confrontation and the four positive factors accounted for 30 to 60 percent of the treatment effect, which was even higher than the strongest results reported in the general therapy effectiveness literature.

Enthused by the results, Marshall, Serran, Moulden, Mulloy, Fernandez, Mann, and Thornton (2002) conducted a second study. They changed the treatment program to emphasize the four positive factors, discourage the use of confrontation, and allow greater individual flexibility for the group therapists, which they regarded as equivalent to the responsivity principle in the risk-need-responsivity (RNR) model (Andrews & Bonta, 2007). Independent raters evaluated five videotapes for each group therapist—one at the beginning, three in the middle, and one near the end of treatment. The follow-up study replicated the findings of the first with even stronger effects.

Marshall and others continued to study the positive impact of group therapist qualities in sexual offender groups (Marshall & Burton, 2010; Marshall, Burton, & Marshall, 2013; Thornton, Mann, & Williams, 2000; Drapeau, 2005; Drapeau, Körner, Granger, Brunet, & Caspar, 2005). The huge importance of empathy and warmth is entirely consistent with what we know from the general literature of psychotherapy effectiveness. In fact, Marshall (2005, p. 109) is unequivocal in affirming that "displays of empathy and warmth by the therapist and provision of rewards for progress and some degree of directedness, maximize the benefits derived from the procedures employed in treating sexual offenders."

In their review of therapist qualities and group processes in sexual offender treatment, Marshall and Burton (2010) also pointed to the problem of overly rigid compliance with psychoeducational programs. They cited research showing that therapists who adhered most closely to manualized cognitive-behavioral group treatment for batterers were far less effective than those who emphasized the therapeutic alliance and flexibly adjusted the approach to individual needs. In fact, Jennings (1987; 1990) was early to recognize the shortcomings of overly manualized CBT group programs for male abusers and pushed for more "unstructured" group therapy that could focus more flexibly on treatment goals.

Confrontation Is Counter-Therapeutic

As shown in the same research on therapist qualities by Marshall and his colleagues, confrontational therapist behaviors were strongly negatively correlated with the effectiveness of sexual offender therapy groups (Marshall, 2005; Marshall et al., 2002, 2003, 2010, 2013; Thornton et al., 2000). Many other studies have also shown that confrontation is ineffective, if not counter-therapeutic. Beech and Fordham (1997) found that a confrontational style by therapists reduced treatment effectiveness, and Harkins and Beech (2007) found that confrontational approaches harmed group climate. Likewise, in their studies of child molesters, Drapeau (2005) and Drapeau et al. (2005) found that child molesters disengaged from therapists who were perceived as confrontational or not supportive.

There is also strong research support to show that sexual offenders themselves reject confrontational approaches. In their review, Jennings and Deming (2016) combined the satisfaction survey results from four different studies of sexual offenders by Jill Levenson and her colleagues and found that confrontation was always ranked lowest in importance and benefit. This was consistently true for 539 sexual offenders across outpatient and inpatient settings in four states (Levenson & Macgowan, 2004; Levenson, Macgowan, Morin, & Cotter, 2009; Levenson, Prescott, & D'Amora, 2010; Levenson, Prescott, & Jumper, 2014). Similarly, in their survey of sexual offenders' perceptions, Connor, Copes, and Tewksbury (2011) found that the most common complaint was the confrontational requirement of being forced to disclose details of their sexual offenses in the group.

These results raise the question of how group therapists can be more skilled in delivering interventions in a way that will be *perceived by clients* themselves as *supportive and challenging* rather than *judgmental and confrontational*. This is especially important in groups where challenging a client in front of his peers can heighten fear of public humiliation and social rejection. In chapters 6 and 8, we have provided some techniques and examples to help articulate interventions that engage clients in open consideration of their problematic behavior rather than evoking defensiveness and avoidance. In addition, the research against confrontational approaches suggests that motivational interviewing skills may be especially valuable for sexual abuse group therapists (e.g., Clark & Liddle, 2012; Prescott, 2008).

Cohesion and Therapeutic Climate

Cohesion is perhaps the most important of the therapeutic factors in group treatment defined by Yalom (1995; 2005) because cohesion is considered the primary therapeutic factor from which all others flow. Cohesion is the sense of belonging and acceptance that develops among group members, and it has been identified for its importance in group therapy with sexual offenders (Jennings & Sawyer, 2003; Marshall & Burton, 2009; Beech & Hamilton-Giachritsis, 2005). In the general group therapy literature, Moos (1994) developed the Group Environment Scale to measure various group processes, which includes a subscale for measuring group cohesion. Other group researchers have utilized objective behavioral measures of group cohesion, such as eye contact with persons speaking, member-to-member interaction, positive verbalizations by group members, disclosure of problems, ratings of trust in other members, and satisfaction with sessions and with the group itself (Upper & Flowers, 1994; Taube-Schiff, Suvak, Antony, Bieling, & McCabe, 2007).

Beech and his colleagues were the first to focus specifically on therapeutic climate as a crucial factor in the treatment effectiveness of sexual offender groups in a series of studies beginning in 1997. *Therapeutic climate* is conceived to "encompass a range of factors such as therapist characteristics, the therapeutic relationship, and *the interrelationships between individuals in a group*" (Harkins, Beech, & Thornton, 2013, p. 104, italics added). In their first study, Beech and Fordham (1997) employed Moos's Group Environment Scale to evaluate four prison-based and eight outpatient probation groups, finding that group therapy with strong cohesion showed superior outcomes on measures of cognitive distortion, denial, and disclosure of offense behaviors. Eight years later, Beech and Hamilton-Giachritsis (2005) replicated the study with seven outpatient groups and found that group involvement, commitment to and concern/friendship for one another, and the encouragement of emotional expressiveness within the group were significantly related to positive treatment outcomes for child abusers. Subsequently, Harkins, Beech, and Thornton (2013) put these strong outcomes to the presumably "hardest test" by measuring group process with psychopathic sexual offenders. They found promising evidence that group cohesion can be achieved with offenders with high psychopathy and that the quality of cohesion improved over the "three stages" of group treatment. Their findings were consistent with an earlier study by Houston, Wrench, and Hosking (1995), which showed that group process in two child abuser groups was consistent with Yalom's (1995) theory that groups develop from the first stage of hesitant participation and testing the waters; to the second stage of conflict, dominance, and rebellion; to the third stage of belonging and maximal cohesion (Tuckman, 1965).

Aylwin (2010) also observed a steady progressive rise in cohesion over the course of sexual offender group therapy. In an inpatient treatment program that exclusively used group therapy for a period of 12 to 15 months, Aylwin asked 95 group members to regularly rate the strength of their therapeutic alliance with the therapist, with their peers, and with the treatment program. In all three measures of alliance (collectively regarded as cohesion), the most rapid growth in cohesion was observed in the first four months and then grew steadily but more slowly through the 15 months. The same pattern was observed for *both* treatment completers and non-completers (i.e., those dropping out within seven months) except that the non-completers had consistently lower ratings of cohesion at all stages (see figure 2.1). Moreover, higher cohesion yielded positive treatment outcomes on multiple measures, including increased responsibility, more energy, improvements in conflict resolution and interpersonal relations, as well as reductions in anxiety and reduced behaviors defined as domineering, vindictive, cold, and intrusive

Figure 2.1 Group Cohesion Over the Course of Treatment

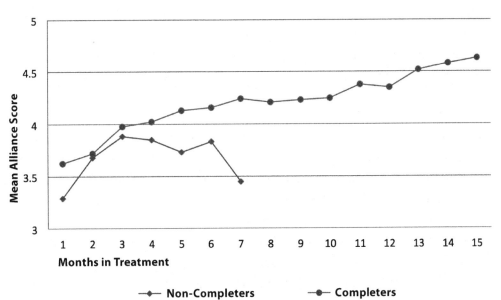

In another unpublished study, Davis, Marshall, Bradford, and Marshall (2008) used the Moos (1994) Group Environment Scale with seriously mentally ill sexual offenders in a prison and mental health center. They found that *cohesiveness* and *expressiveness*

were strong predictors of treatment goal attainment. Similarly, Levenson, Prescott, and D'Amora (2010) found that high cohesiveness within treatment groups contributed to reductions in antisocial beliefs.

In a study of 69 adolescent sexual offenders in residential treatment, Sribney and Reddon (2009) used the Yalom Card Sort and found that *cohesiveness*, along with *universality* and *family reenactment*, were ranked highest in importance. They also found that the importance of cohesion continued to increase over the length of treatment, while the family factor decreased. Compared with adult sexual offenders, the factors of *instillation of hope* and *universality* were rated three ranks higher and *interpersonal learning* was rated four ranks lower. Reimer and Mathieu (2006) used interviews and a questionnaire to directly assess adult sexual offenders' perceptions of the importance of Yalom's therapeutic factors in group settings. Defining cohesion as, "The group helps me because it is good to belong to a group of people that is together and cares about each person in the group," cohesion was ranked third in importance, while the therapeutic factors of *catharsis* (emotional expressiveness) and *self-understanding* were rated as most helpful.

In contrast, cohesiveness was *not* ranked as one of the most important therapeutic factors in a large survey of 159 group therapists (not specifically sexual offender therapists) working in 78 prisons (Morgan, Ferrell, & Winterowd, 1999). Instead the group therapists gave the most importance to Yalom's therapeutic factors of interpersonal learning, universality, and imparting information, and least importance to existential factors and corrective recapitulation of the primary family.

Therapeutic Factors Impacting Group Engagement

While not specifically focused on Yalom's theory of therapeutic factors or group process, two other researchers, Levenson and Frost, have independently published multiple studies on the issue of therapeutic climate in sexual offender groups—with a common focus on the issue of engagement. Levenson and Macgowan (2004) defined group member *engagement* as actively contributing to the group process, being connected to other members and to the therapist, and showing investment in the treatment contract.

Recognizing the profound social stigma that causes child molesters to feel shame and isolate themselves, Frost (2000) theorized that child molesters have a strong tendency to perceive threat in the group therapy environment. This, in turn, inhibits their ability to engage in treatment in general and their willingness to honestly disclose their offenses in particular. To test his theory, Frost (2004) videotaped group therapy sessions of 16 child molesters. Immediately after each group session, members identified three events that were "most personally salient." During a subsequent interview, the members viewed the video, identified the three salient episodes, and were questioned about their thoughts and feelings. Ultimately, Frost explained the reluctance to disclose in terms of four theorized *individual* styles of disclosure, three of which were *unfavorable* to engagement. He elaborated further on these four styles in a subsequent publication (Frost & Daniels, 2006). We believe, however, that Frost squandered a great opportunity to study the group therapy videotapes for how group process variables, such as cohesion and therapeutic climate, could have made it easier or harder for the members to disclose and engage, regardless of any hypothetical disclosure "styles."

In another study, Frost and Connolly (2004) found that the child molesters made significant movement toward or away from engagement in treatment during the out-of-group time between sessions. To explain this result, Frost cited a study from the general group therapy research, which showed that cohesiveness predicts the amount of between-session work, as well as the degree of participation (i.e., engagement) during group sessions (Budman, Soldz, Demby, Davis, & Merry, 1993). Similarly, in their clinical practice article, Clark and Erooga (1994) asserted that group therapy is the ideal modality for counteracting the characteristic isolation, secretiveness, and shame of child molesters and also reported that group cohesiveness promotes higher levels of engagement in treatment and optimism about future recovery.

In a series of six studies, Levenson and her colleagues also focused on engagement, but looked more directly at the role of the therapeutic climate in sexual offender groups. Macgowan and Levenson (2003) first developed the psychometrics for reliably measuring group process and engagement. They created a 37-item instrument called the Group Engagement Measure (GEM) with both therapist- and client-rated versions. The GEM rated seven group engagement factors: attending, contributing, relating to worker, relating with members, contracting, working on own problems, and working on others' problems. They also established correlations among the GEM, Group Attitude Scale, Sex Offender Treatment Rating Scale, and Facets of Sexual Offender Denial measure at the scale and subscale levels.

With confidence in the validity and reliability of these measures, they then published the results in a second study (Levenson & Macgowan, 2004). Like Frost, they began their study with the presumption that overcoming denial and disclosure of deviancy/offenses were central targets in treatment, which were necessary to promote meaningful engagement in group-based treatment. They found a strong positive relationship between treatment progress and engagement in outpatient sexual offender group therapy and a negative relationship to denial. Sexual offenders who were more actively engaged in their groups showed higher accountability, less cognitive distortions about sexual offending, and more progress toward treatment goals. Together, engagement and denial explained 60 percent of the variance in treatment progress, with engagement as a stronger predictor than denial (0.52 vs. −0.37).

In a third study of 338 outpatient sexual offenders in Florida and Minnesota, Levenson, Macgowan, Morin, and Cotter (2009) again used the GEM to assess engagement and surveyed the perceptions of sexual offenders about which features of group therapy were most helpful and satisfying. In addition to replicating the strong positive relationship between treatment progress and engagement in group therapy and the negative relationship to denial, they found a new and strong correlation between engagement and treatment satisfaction. Clearly those who were more actively engaged in group showed higher accountability, less cognitive distortions about offending, more progress toward treatment goals, and greater satisfaction with treatment.

Levenson and her colleagues repeated the measures used in this sexual offender survey in three subsequent studies as summarized below. In 2016, Jennings and Deming (2016) combined the satisfaction survey results from four Levenson studies and discovered striking similarities in the perceptions of sexual offenders regarding various aspects of treatment, and with group therapy in particular, across multiple programs and settings. The results of combining the four studies are presented in the following sequence of tables 2.1, 2.2, and 2.3. The following list identifies the size and type of sexual offender population contained in each of the four studies referenced in the tables:

- Levenson, Macgowan, Morin, & Cotter (2009)—338 sexual offenders in three outpatient treatment centers in Florida and Minnesota.
- Levenson & Prescott (2009)—44 sexually violent predators in a secure civil commitment facility in Wisconsin.
- Levenson, Prescott, & D'Amora (2010)—88 sexual offenders in three outpatient treatment centers in Connecticut.
- Levenson, Prescott, & Jumper (2014)—113 sexually violent predators in a secure civil commitment facility in Illinois.

By comparing the results of all four studies, Jennings and Deming (2016) found that the aspect rated as important by the highest percentage of sexual offenders across all settings was "I feel comfortable helping others in my group" (ranked first in three of the four populations), while "I feel comfortable participating in my group" had the second highest percentage overall (ranked first or second in three of the four populations).

TABLE 2.1 CLIENT PERCEPTIONS OF GROUP THERAPY AND RANKINGS ACROSS SEX OFFENDER TREATMENT PROGRAMS

Client Perceptions of Group Process	RANKING AND PERCENT ENDORSED AS IMPORTANT				
	All combined N = 539	IL SVP N = 113	FL & MN Outpatient N = 338	CT Outpatient N = 88	WI SVP N = 44
Getting help and support from others	1st 74%	1st 70%	1st 73%	1st 86%	NA
Hearing other perspectives and viewpoints	2nd 68%	2nd 54%	2nd 69%	2nd 81%	NA
Feeling as though I can relate to the other members of the group	3rd 56%	3rd 48%	3rd 54%	3rd 77%	NA
Sharing my experiences with other sex offenders	4th 50%	4th 42%	4th 50%	4th 63%	NA
Confrontation among the group members	5th 45%	5th 36%	5th 45%	5th 54%	NA
Client Perceptions of Group Therapy					
I feel comfortable helping others in my group.	1st 85%	1st 71%	1st 93%	3rd 79%	1st 62%
I feel comfortable participating in my group.	2nd 81%	2nd 66%	2nd 90%	1st 83%	3rd 45%
It is helpful to be able to talk with other people who have committed sex offenses.w	3rd 77%	3rd 65%	4th 87%	6th 68%	2nd 54%
My group usually feels comfortable.	4th 76%	4th 46%	3rd 89%	2nd 81%	4th 42%
My group members are pretty open and honest most of the time.	5th 68%	6th 43%	5th 81%	7th 64%	6th 39%
My group has enough structure.	6th 67%	5th 45%	7th 76%	4th 78%	7th 35%
My group members are pretty nonjudgmental most of the time.	7th 65%	7th 37%	6th 76%	5th 76%	5th 40%
I trust other members in my group.	8th 40%	8th 34%	NA	8th 55%	8th 23%

To the degree that "feeling comfortable in helping others" and "participating" in group are reflective of group cohesiveness and bonding, we believe that the high ranking of these elements would appear congruent with the other empirical studies showing the importance of cohesion and engagement. The fact that "helping others in the group" and "getting help and support from others" are ranked highest in importance in the two sets of items also supports the salience of cohesion as a therapeutic factor. It also suggests that Yalom's therapeutic factor of altruism is extremely important to sexual offenders. Certainly group therapists have observed altruism (expressions of caring) as a frequent and important phenomenon in sexual offender groups (Jennings & Sawyer, 2003), while altruism is a primary good in the Good Lives Model (Ward, Mann, & Gannon, 2007).

Clinical Advantages and Client Preference for Group Over Individual Therapy

Clinicians and researchers have asserted that group treatments for sexual offenders may be both more efficient and more effective than individual therapy (Marshall, Anderson, & Fernandez, 1999; Beech & Fordham, 1997; Reddon, Payne, & Starzyck, 1999; Marshall, Burton, & Marshall, 2013). But the available empirical evidence for such a differential effect is limited; only one study—by Di Fazio, Abracen, and Looman (2001)—has actually attempted a direct comparison of group versus individual treatment with sexual offenders. In their study, the 143 men in the "full treatment" condition received about five groups per week (on the topics of victim empathy, self-management, human sexuality, and social skills) and two individual sessions. The 62 in the "individual treatment" condition received four individual sessions per week and no groups. They found *no difference* in effectiveness between full-treatment-with-group and individual-only in reducing rates of recidivism. They did, however, conclude that individual treatment appeared better for individuals with psychiatric and cognitive impairments who might be more likely to misinterpret social cues in a complex group situation.

In their review article, Ware, Mann, and Wakeling (2009) summarized the main advantages and disadvantages of both group and individual treatment with sexual offenders. Group treatment appeared to be at least as effective as individual treatment, and there were several clinical advantages obtained through group processes, which are less easily obtained in individual therapy. In addition, the authors addressed the debate about the advantages of open-ended versus closed-group formats. Open-ended groups seem to offer more clinical advantages than closed groups, and in particular allow for treatment to be more responsive to individual needs, although there have been no direct comparisons of the two approaches with sexual offenders.

Despite the lack of direct comparative evidence, however, Marshall, Burton, and Marshall (2013) have stated explicitly that *group* cohesiveness and *group* expressiveness *are essential preconditions to positive change in sexual offenders.* If this is true, and the evidence does support this conclusion, it logically follows that group therapy must be a necessary component and modality in sexual offender treatment programs. In other words, group must offer something vital that *cannot* be obtained through individual therapy alone.

Many clinicians have asserted that there are properties of group therapy that make it especially well suited—often superior to individual therapy—for addressing particular problems and deficits of sexual offenders (Jennings & Sawyer, 2003; Jennings & Deming, 2013; Sawyer, 2000, 2002; Sawyer & Jennings, 2014; Ware & Frost, 2006; Ware, Frost, & Boer, 2015; Ware, Mann, & Wakeling, 2009). In the broadest sense, group work is uniquely capable of enhancing social awareness and relatedness, while simultaneously counteracting selfishness and isolation. For example, Marshall, Anderson, and Fernandez (1999) have argued that group therapy is especially useful with sexual offenders because they tend to be isolated and lonely, with pervasive deficits in interpersonal relations and intimacy skills. Group therapy is a rare opportunity to feel supported and encouraged, explore their interpersonal deficiencies, and give and receive feedback on behavior and social presentation. Similarly, Johnson and Lokey (2007) assert that group therapy is ideal for helping sexual offenders break out of their characteristically selfish, isolated, and self-absorbed style of life because they can develop a healthier sense of "social interest" (community feeling in which the offender feels he belongs) and "relationship" (feeling actively and meaningfully connected to others).

This is consistent with Hudson's (2005) extensive interviews with incarcerated sexual offenders, which showed that their primary concern was concealing their offenses to protect their public identity and avoid stigma. Consequently, they appreciated group therapy as a valuable opportunity to become more sociable, share differing perspectives, and develop empathy. As observed by Frost and Connolly (2004), the group experience may be the *only* place where child molesters can safely share their stigmatized status in society. In their review of the use of therapeutic communities (TCs) in secure settings with sexual offenders, Ware and Frost (2010) emphasize that TCs can maximize and intensify the benefits of group therapy by extending the group therapy process. The TC gives members added opportunities to discuss and apply what they are learning in the group to their broader lives in the TC, and they are more likely to get feedback from staff and other residents for behavior outside the group session, including both challenges to negative behavior and attitudes, and acceptance and support for prosocial changes. Of note, Ware and Frost (2010) frequently observed that men who made deep personal disclosures within the group sessions were pleasantly surprised to receive acceptance and praise from their peers, which encouraged them to invest in treatment in a more committed way.

Finally, in assessing the advantages of group therapy with sexual offenders, it is crucial to consider one more major source of empirical evidence: the opinions of the sexual offenders themselves. As summarized in table 2.2, four different studies by Levenson and her colleagues, as well as one by Garret, Oliver, Wilcox, and Middleton (2003), suggest that nearly half of all sexual offenders across multiple secure inpatient and community outpatient settings *prefer group over individual*, while one-third prefer individual, and one-fifth have no preference.

In their study of 12 intra-familial adolescent sexual offenders, Halse, Grant, Thornton, Indermaur, Stevens, and Chamarette (2012) found that every participant agreed that group therapy was *the most beneficial component of their community-based treatment*. To the degree that many or most sexual offenders prefer group to individual, it would be expected that they would be more motivated and engaged and able to benefit from treatment delivered in a group modality.

TABLE 2.2 CLIENT PREFERENCES FOR GROUP OR INDIVIDUAL THERAPY				
"I would rather attend individual therapy than group therapy."	Total N	Disagree or Strongly Disagree	I Don't Know	Agree or Strongly Agree
IL SVPs (Levenson et al., 2014)	113	44%	19%	38%
WI SVPs (Levenson & Prescott, 2009)	44	31%	23%	47%
FL & MN outpatient sex offenders (Levenson et al., 2009)	338	49%	20%	31%
CT outpatient sex offenders (Levenson et al., 2010)	88	44%	19%	36%
All Levenson sex offenders combined total	582	46%	20%	34%
All SVPs combined	157	41%	20%	39%
All outpatient sex offenders combined	426	48%	20%	32%
Prison and outpatient sex offenders (Garrett et al., 2003)	42	Prefer group 47%	No preference 34%	Prefer individual 13%
Garrett and Levenson groups combined	624	46%	21%	33%

Sexual Offender Perceptions of Therapeutic Factors

Reimer and Mathieu (2006) interviewed and surveyed adult sexual offenders regarding their perceptions of what was most helpful in their treatment from Yalom's (1995) list of 12 therapeutic factors. The factors of *catharsis* (relief from distress through emotional expression) and *self-understanding* were significantly rated most helpful, with *cohesion* (perception of belongingness and acceptance within the group) ranked third. *Imparting of information* (*guidance*) and *imitative behavior* (*identification*) were rated least helpful.

Reddon, Payne, and Starzyck (1999) obtained similar results when they utilized the Yalom Card Sort to ask 100 sexual offenders to rank order the importance of Yalom's therapeutic factors. They found that sexual offenders ranked the therapeutic factors in almost the same order as non-offending psychiatric outpatients with two notable differences: Sexual offenders ranked *family reenactment* three ranks higher and *interpersonal learning* ("input" subtype—receiving feedback from others) four ranks lower. Reddon et al. (1999) also observed some interesting correlations between the rankings and treatment length, offender age, and victim gender. First, the ranked importance of *instillation of hope* decreased as length of inpatient treatment increased (ranging from 6 to 18 months). Second, older sexual offenders tended to rank *instillation of hope* higher and *existential factors* (taking responsibility for one's decisions in life) lower than younger sexual offenders. Third, sexual offenders with male victims also tended to give higher ranking to the importance of *instillation of hope*.

Based on their analysis of the results from Levenson's surveys of 582 sexual offenders, Jennings and Deming (2013) found a high degree of consistency in how sexual offenders across multiple outpatient and civil commitment settings perceive the benefits and importance of different components of sexual offender-specific treatment. As shown in table 2.3, "accepting responsibility" was the component that was ranked as important by the highest percentage of sexual offenders in all programs and all settings. The component receiving the second highest percentage of endorsement was victim empathy, "understanding the impact of sexual abuse on victims and others in my life." The components endorsed by the smallest percentages of offenders are also very consistent across samples, with controlling compulsive sexual behavior, understanding family origins, basic life skills, and basic human sexuality, ranked 15th, 16th, 17th, and 18th, respectively.

TABLE 2.3 CLIENT RATINGS OF IMPORTANCE OF VARIOUS TREATMENT COMPONENTS					
Components of Treatment Program	All Combined N = 582	CT Outpatient N = 88	IL SVP N = 113	FL & MN Outpatient N = 336	WI SVP N = 44
Accepting responsibility for my sex offense(s). ACCOUNTABILITY	1st 94%	1st 99%	1st 91%	1st 94%	1st 95.2%
Understanding the impact of sex abuse on victims and others in my life. EMPATHY	2nd 88%	3rd 96%	4th 67%	2nd 92%	2nd 92%
Understanding my triggers and risk factors.	3rd 86%	2nd 98%	3rd 71%	3rd 87.8%	4th 89%
Understanding my offense chains, cycles, and patterns.	4th 83%	6th 89%	2nd 71%	5th 85.1%	5th 87.2%
Learning about what motivated me to offend.	5th 79%	8th 88%	8th 44%	5th 87.2%	3rd 89.2%
Understanding my own tendency to distort, deny, and make excuses. THINKING ERRORS	6th 78%	4th 96%	7th 50%	6th 78%	7th 84.8%
Developing a relapse prevention plan.	7th 77%	7th 88%	5th 55%	8th 80.6%	8th 83.8%
Learning to change or control my deviant arousal.	8th 76%	9th 88%	6th 52%	9th 80.1%	9th 83.8%
Learning how to create a more satisfying life for myself.	9th 75%	5th 90%	12th 31%	6th 84.2%	12th 83.2%
Understanding the needs I met through sexual abuse and learning how to meet my needs in healthier ways.	10th 73%	11th 86%	9th 41%	10th 79.3%	6th 86%
Learning about different forms of denial.	11th 69%	10th 87%	10th 87%	11th 75.9%	14th 74.8%

continued on next page

TABLE 2.3 CLIENT RATINGS OF IMPORTANCE OF VARIOUS TREATMENT COMPONENTS					
Components of Treatment Program	All Combined N = 582	CT Outpatient N = 88	IL SVP N = 113	FL & MN Outpatient N = 336	WI SVP N = 44
Learning about my grooming patterns or behaviors I used to gain access to victims.	12th 67%	16th 73%	10th 38%	12th 72.7%	11th 83.2%
Understanding the development of my sexual behavior problems.	13th 65%	13th 79%	14th 30%	13th 71.5%	13th 75.2%
Learning new relationship and communication skills.	14th 64%	12th 81%	15th 27%	14th 69.9%	10th 83.2%
Controlling compulsive sexual behavior (including masturbation and pornography).	15th 57%	14th 77%	11th 37%	NA	18th 68.4%
Understanding how early experiences and family life affected me.	16th 57%	15th 74%	17th 23%	15th 62.2%	17th 71.2%
Basic life skills.	17th 50%	17th 71%	16th 26%	NA	15th 71.6%
Basic human sexuality.	18th 44%	18th 68%	18th 14%	NA	16th 71.4%

It is interesting that sexual offenders themselves attribute so much importance to victim empathy, while the field has moved in the opposite direction in the recent years. Given the methodological problems of measuring general empathy and empathy for victims, and the inconsistent empirical results, empathy is less often a component of recidivism risk assessments and has been deemphasized as a primary treatment goal in many programs. Perhaps the perceived importance of empathy is a reflection of what happens in effective group therapy. The safety, acceptance, and caring of the group allows the members to break out of their self-absorbed isolation and be exposed to the personal experiences and perspectives of other people. This, in turn, helps them to awaken to the feelings of others and see how their sexually abusive behavior is seen and experienced by others, particularly those harmed by their abuses.

These findings may also reflect the philosophy of programs operating at the time the studies were conducted. For many years, clinicians in the field believed that empathy was a significant issue and that offenders' lack of empathy was a contributing factor to their offense behaviors. More recently the research suggests that, statistically, empathy is not significantly correlated to reoffense risk.

Finally, newly emerging research indicates that sexual offenders with different types of insecure attachment are differentially biased in their perceptions of the group therapeutic climate (Garbutt & Hocken, 2014; Garbutt & Palmer, 2015). For example, sexual offenders with avoidant-dismissive style are positively inclined to perceive therapist leader support, but those with preoccupied-anxious style are negatively disposed. This research is consistent with extensive research from the general therapy literature, which shows that secure attachment is strongly related to improved therapeutic alliances, while insecure attachment is related to poorer relationships in both group and individual therapy (Diener & Monroe, 2001). This research on group therapy and attachment is detailed in chapter 7.

Mixed Versus Specific Sexual Offender Types in Groups

The clinical practice literature includes articles about groups organized to treat specific types of sexual offenders. From the standpoint of RNR principles, one might expect that a homogeneous group (that is, one composed of one type of sexual offender) might be better able to be responsive to the criminogenic needs that may be shared by a given group of individuals. In practice, however, it is not that easy to separate sexual offenders by pure type. First, there are many variations of rapists and child molesters (including incest offenders), statutory rapists, child pornography users, voyeurs, exhibitionists, and more. Moreover, the frequency of cross-over crime by sexual offenders is high. Some rapists molest children, some child molesters rape adults, and some incest offenders offend outside the family (Heil, Ahlmeyer, & Simons, 2003). In view of these issues, the vast majority of groups are composed of mixed types of sexual offenders.

In their survey in the 1980s, Schwartz and Cellini (1988) observed that many treatment programs had tried to separate rapists, child molesters/pedophiles, and incest offenders into homogeneous groups, but discerned no particular advantage in doing so. On the contrary, they recommended mixing offenders because pedophiles tend to be passive and withdrawn, while rapists tend to be more assertive and talkative, and a mixed group can be more lively and share more diverse experiences.

Only one study, by Allam, Middleton, and Browne (1997), has shown a clear advantage for one type of specific group. They experimented with a specialized group for men with learning disabilities, a group for those who were child victims of sexual abuse, and a group exclusive to men who sexually abuse adult women. They reported that the adult-abusers-only group showed increased cohesiveness, more active participation, and more acceptance of personal responsibility than the typical mixed-offender group.

Studies by Tregaskis (2000) and Beech and Hamilton-Giachritsis (2005) found no significant differences in using mixed or homogeneous groups with sexual offenders. Harkins and Beech (2008) found the same results with one discernible difference. They compared the group environment and recidivism outcomes for two rapist-only groups, three child-molester-only groups, and 15 mixed-offender groups. The group environment was quite positive for all groups, but the mixed groups were significantly lower in *expressiveness*, which was defined as "how much freedom of action and expression of feelings are encouraged in the group." They suggested that mixing rapists and child molesters decreases the risk that offenders will collude with one another.

The clinical literature includes other examples of homogeneous groups for specific types of offenders. For example, Frey (1987), Fowler, Burns, and Roehl (1983), and Ganzarain and Buchele (1990) ran groups that were designed exclusively for incest offenders (but there was no comparison made to outcomes for incest offenders in a mixed group). Based on clinical impressions, Costell and Yalom (1972) reported that homogeneous groups work best with pedophiles, while heterogeneous groups were most successful with rapists, but provided no empirical support. Marshall, Bryce, Hudson, Ward, and Moth (1996) described a group treatment designed to increase intimacy skills for non-familial child molesters. In a 10-year study, Cook, Fox, Weaver, and Rooth (1991) separated a clinical subpopulation of 63 nonviolent sexual offenders on probation, but this included a mix of sexual offenses.

In conclusion, without clear empirical evidence of the superiority of homogeneous sexual offender groups, it remains more practical and a better use of resources to simply mix offender types. For example, in prison settings, mixing is typically more practical because of limited treatment resources (e.g., group rooms, clinicians, etc.).

SUMMARY AND CONCLUSIONS

In the field of sexual offender-specific treatment, most clinicians are expected to deliver much, if not most, of their treatment in the form of group therapy. Unfortunately, far too few receive any specific training in the complex practice of group therapy as its own modality, and few are aware of the extraordinarily rich empirical research regarding the many aspects of group therapy. Our first goal was to highlight some of the most crucial findings from the general group therapy that can and should inform and guide our group practice with sexual offenders. We discussed five key factors—formal change theory, group structure, small-group processes, the patient, and the group therapist—that are known to influence the quality and effectiveness of group work, as well as the enormous importance of cohesion. We then reviewed the empirical research on sexual offender-specific treatment group therapy. Here, too, group cohesion, with its healing powers of belongingness and acceptance, emerges as the preeminent therapeutic factor; if fostered properly, it naturally follows the same progressive course of development as other human groups. Sexual offender groups with strong cohesion are more effective. We also observed that the four therapist qualities of warmth, empathy, guidance, and encouragement—long recognized as crucial in the general therapy research—promote better outcomes. Just as important, confrontation is resoundingly ineffective and probably counter-therapeutic. There is also compelling evidence that sexual offenders prefer group over individual therapy. This is no surprise to the authors, for we have seen the remarkable potential of group acceptance and group belonging—the essence of a cohesive group—to motivate change for hundreds of self-loathing, isolated, lonely, and alienated sexual offenders.

CHAPTER 3

Ethical and Professional Challenges of Group Therapy with Sexual Abusers

Ethics is a skill.

—Marianne Jennings

Functioning effectively as a sexual offender-specific group therapist is challenging and complex because it requires three sets of knowledge and skills. First, it requires a specialized set of clinical knowledge and skills specific to the assessment and treatment of sexual abusers. Second, competency requires clinical knowledge and skills specific to conducting group therapy work with sexual abusers. And third, treating sexual abusers, particularly those who are court-ordered, requires the knowledge and skills to appropriately balance the role of therapist while also working closely with the courts. This chapter examines the professional practice of the group therapist and the importance of being competent to perform well in all three regards.

Sources of Professional Standards and Guidelines

We begin with the licensing boards and professional organizations whose standards and guidelines govern our practice.

Behavioral Health Licensing Boards

It is incumbent upon mental health care professionals in all behavioral health care disciplines to practice within the limits of their practice competence. This is true of social workers, psychologists, marriage and family therapists, professional counselors, psychiatric nurses, and other disciplines. While the specifics of what constitutes "competence" are not always clearly defined, there are professional licensing statutes and ethical codes that invoke standards of practice *indirectly* by stating that clinicians must practice within their scope of competence (Association of Social Work Boards, 2008; Minnesota Board of Social Work, 2009; American Psychological Association [APA], 2010).

The conduct of licensed mental health professionals with clients receiving services is addressed in both general and specific terms (Sawyer & Prescott, 2011) (see table 3.1). For example, as of 2008, twenty-five states mandate continuing education in ethics or professional–client boundaries as a requirement for annual or biannual social work license renewals (Association of Social Work Boards, 2008). This means that, when necessary, practitioners are expected to seek guidance, supervision, or training specific to their area of practice to assure a minimum level of knowledge or competence. In our case, this means that you must have knowledge and competence in the general topics of sexual abuse and offending and the established methods of sexual offender-specific treatment, which typically includes group therapy.

TABLE 3.1 EXAMPLES OF ETHICS AND STANDARDS IN PROFESSIONAL ASSOCIATIONS AND STATE LAW						
Issues	NASW[1]	APA[2]	AGPA[3]	ATSA[4]	Social Work Licensing Board[5]	MDH Patient Rights[6]
Dignity of the person No discrimination	X	X	X	X	X	X
Avoid Harm	X	X			X	X
Informed Consent	X	X	X	X	X	X
Conflict of Interest	X	X	X	X	X	
Multiple or dual relationships	X	X	X	X	X	
Sexual relationships or intimacies	X	X	X	X	X	X
Sexual harassment	X	X		X	X	X
Physical contact	X					
Protection of privacy	X	X	X	X	X	X

1. NASW: National Association of Social Workers. 2. APA: American Psychological Association. 3. AGPA: American Group Psychotherapy Association. 4. ATSA: Association for the Treatment of Sexual Abusers. 5. Minnesota Board of Social Work. 6. Minnesota Department of Health, Patient Rights.

This professional obligation invokes an ethical question: If you are treating a specific population (e.g., sexual offenders) and using a particular treatment method (e.g., group-based treatment or group therapy) then is it not incumbent upon you to be minimally competent regarding *both* the clinical population and the treatment modality? For clinicians early in their careers, gaining such competence in a specialty area is daunting, and the reality in most settings is that learning happens on the job. Many of us have experienced situations where we were thrown in the trenches and forced to learn as we went.

Unfortunately, many new therapists in this field are thrown into group leadership without adequate training or supervision in group therapy. We learn what we need to know in the moment or what is specific to a particular situation. But without some kind of supervision or guidance, this kind of on-the-job training can rob a novice clinician of the opportunity to learn in a structured, sequential style that integrates the complex clinical specialty of sexual offender-specific treatment with the complex group skills needed to facilitate effective groups. When this happens, we have a professional obligation to supplement learning and build competency by seeking additional training, reading, consultation, supervision, or other self-learning activities.

The limits within which professionals must operate are defined in all health-related professional practices, and group therapists have the same obligations and demands on their practices. Just as not every psychologist can interpret psychological test results, not every mental health practitioner is a competent group therapist. All those providing group therapy have the obligation to attain a level of competence adequate for the setting and clients they serve. Likewise, the agency, organization, or university practicum has an obligation to support competent group therapy practice and provide adequate supervision for the group therapists it employs (Cox, Ilfeld, Ilfeld, & Brennan, 2000).

Professional Association Standards

Similar to licensing boards, the conduct of mental health professionals is also governed by professional standards and ethics policies and documents that are formulated and espoused by professional organizations (APA, 2010; National Association of Social Workers [NASW], 2008; American Group Psychotherapy Association [AGPA], 2002; Association for the Treatment of Sexual Abusers [ATSA], 2014; American Counseling Association, 2014). These standards provide guidance for member professionals and make a statement to the public and to the consumers of those professional services about the integrity, philosophy, and general practice of association members. Collectively, these organizations provide, in different levels of detail, standards that protect the client and support the integrity of clinical practice. Being a member of any of these organizations encumbers the member to abide by the standards set by the organization.

For example, the Association for the Treatment of Sexual Abusers has formulated a *Professional Code of Ethics* (ATSA, 2001), which addresses ethical standards that encompass professional conduct, client relationships, confidentiality, professional relationships, research and publications, public information, advertising, and compliance procedures. ATSA has also created *The Practice Guidelines for the Assessment, Treatment, and Management of Male Adult Sexual Abusers* (ATSA, 2014), which covers practice in the areas of assessment, treatment, risk reduction, and risk management of sexual offenders in the community.

The International Association for the Treatment of Sexual Offenders (IATSO, 2016) has also adopted standards of care that address client protection and professional standards. These standards, *Treatment of Adult Sex Offenders: Standards of Care*, originally published in 1995, outline types of treatment, professional competence, antecedents to sexual offender treatment, and 14 Principles of Standards of Care. While these standards do not specify competency in group therapy, IATSO members are professionally obligated to attain the minimal level of competence in the treatment modality that they use—and group therapy is suggested as a likely treatment modality to be used in this specialty field.

Another example of professional guidelines for the practice of group psychotherapy is *The Clinical Practice Guidelines for the Practice of Group Psychotherapy* (AGPA, 2007), which is a product of the Science to Service Task Force of the American Group Psychotherapy Association. These comprehensive practice guidelines address practitioners who practice dynamic, interactional, and relationally based group psychotherapy. This model of group psychotherapy utilizes the group itself as a therapeutic agent for change and pays careful attention to the three primary forces operating at all times in a therapy group: individual dynamics, interpersonal dynamics, and group-as-a-whole dynamics. The AGPA guidelines provide a wealth of information and guidelines for practice in nearly every area of group practice, including starting a group, selecting and preparing group members, therapeutic factors and mechanisms, group development, group process, ethical practice, types of interventions, termination, reducing adverse outcomes, and more.

The American Group Psychotherapy Association and the International Board for Certification of Group Psychotherapists (IBCGP) produced the *Guidelines for Ethics* (AGPA, 2002) to help group therapists manage two fundamental areas of group practice. The first, "responsibilities to the client," emphasizes three basic tenets: respect for each client and client rights, privacy/confidentiality, and public protection/professional incompetence. The second, "professional standards," focuses on the integrity of the practice of group psychotherapy. Specifically, group therapists are expected to maintain competence, contribute to professional knowledge, and report professionals whose behavior appears unethical, illegal, or potentially incompetent.

The Association for the Advancement of Social Work with Groups, Inc., An International Professional Organization (AASWG, Inc.), has also developed standards for working with groups in social services. Their *Standards for Social Work Practice with Groups* (2006) are applicable to all service settings and all types of groups used by social workers, including treatment, support, psychoeducational, task, and community-action groups. The AASWG *Standards* draw heavily from the *NASW Code of Ethics*, as well as group theory, social work group practice, and empirical research. The AASWG *Standards* explicitly state that "the role of the social worker, as articulated in the standards, reflects the values of the social work profession generally, *as well as the unique features associated with social work with groups*" (AASWG, 2006, p. 1, italics added).

Of note, the AASWG standards are uniquely organized by the developmental stages of all therapy groups—pre-group, beginning, middle, and ending phases—and delineate the core knowledge, values, and tasks of the group leader for leading any group as it moves through its developmental stages.

The American Counseling Association (2014) also provides guidance specifically about working with groups. This includes screening to ensure that a client is appropriate for the group and that a client will not impede the group. In addition, the ethics guidance advises taking reasonable precautions to prevent any harm to a client in the group.

By joining a professional organization, members are obliged to know and apply certain ethical and professional standards, such as those above. In addition to gaining guidance for ethical and competent practice from the standards, professional organizations like AGPA typically support members with practice resources, such as journal publications, training opportunities, and access to similar professionals. For example, the American Group Psychotherapy Association offers *The Principles of Group Psychotherapy* course curriculum as a valuable resource for training in group therapy (Weber, 2003). This structured, module-based training curriculum includes topics such as foundations of group therapy, group dynamics, change process, and the role of group leader.

Being a member of most professional associations means you agree to adhere to the standards of the association. This agreement also provides an implicit statement to clients and the public that the member, as a professional and specialist, subscribes to professional standards that are designed to ensure competent practice and maintain current knowledge in the field.

PROFESSIONAL CHALLENGES CREATED BY CRIMINAL JUSTICE INVOLVEMENT

Most sexual abuser clients are involved in the criminal justice system. Clinicians working with court-ordered clients have responsibilities for the welfare of the client but, unlike traditional therapy relationships, they have an added accountability to the court *and* community safety. This situation can sometimes conflict with the ethical and professional principles governing clinical practice. In particular, the sexual abuse clinician is challenged to adhere to certain basic principles, such as confidentiality, avoidance of multiple relationships, and maintenance of professional boundaries. In the next section, we discuss how these challenges impact our group work with sexual abusers.

Limits to Confidentiality May Impact Upon Openness

In a traditional therapy situation, the client is free to reveal personal and embarrassing information with the assurance of confidentiality. But a court-mandated client has a legitimate fear and concern that revelations of prior criminal sexual behavior, as well as disclosure of current thoughts and urges to commit deviant sexual acts, could result in additional charges, negative consequences, or heightened restrictions from criminal justice authorities. In many cases, the therapist is expected to share information with county/state corrections and/or parole/probation as required by law or by contractual obligations, or as needed to protect the community. To the degree that the therapist is perceived as an agent of the courts or corrections, the involuntary client may withhold certain information and is reluctant to freely express his needs or disagree with the therapist's feedback or recommendations. The client might appear to agree with the therapist simply because he fears the adverse consequences of expressing disagreement or revealing incriminating information.

The therapist may have great power over the fate and freedoms of an involuntary client. In his or her relationship with the courts/corrections/parole, the therapist is typically expected to provide an assessment of the client's level of participation and cooperation with mandated treatment and/or the client's current potential for risk. A negative status report from the therapist can be the critical factor in decisions by criminal justice authorities to apply sanctions, such as denial or revocation of parole and re-incarceration or loss of privileges. In effect, by serving both the client and mandating authorities, the therapist is faced with the potential problem of multiple relationships.

Avoiding Multiple Relationships

As defined by the American Psychological Association (2010), a therapist enters into a *multiple relationship* if he or she also has a personal or business relationship with the client that goes beyond therapy, or has an actual or potential relationship with another person who is close to the client. The APA and other mental health professional organizations typically prohibit multiple relationships because of the inherent loss of clinical objectivity and the potential for exploitation and harm to the client. For example, the Association for the Treatment of Sexual Abusers *Professional Code of Ethics* (ATSA, 2001, p. 9) states in part that "*multiple relationships may impair professional judgment and pose a significant risk for client exploitation.*" Similarly, the American Group Psychotherapy Association code of ethics (2002, sec. 3.2, p. 2) states in part that "*the group psychotherapist shall not use her/his professional relationship to advance personal or business interests.*"

Engaging in multiple relationships with a client receiving mental health services is widely accepted as having a potentially harmful impact on the client or the neutrality of the mental health professional. When professionals have multiple roles with clients, such as the dual roles of therapist and agent of criminal justice/community safety, the primacy of the therapeutic relationship is compromised. This type of dual role impairs the ability of the practitioner to place the client's needs above professional demands during the therapeutic encounter, and if problems occur in either role, judgment can be compromised.

Some multiple relationships are unavoidable while others occur and must be addressed or navigated. For example, clinicians who live in small towns or rural areas are much more likely to encounter clients outside of the therapy room and/or to know people in common with the client (Campbell & Gordon, 2003). In all cases, the burden of responsibility is on the professional to identify the situation and prevent multiple relationships from occurring. If a multiple relationship does evolve, then it is incumbent on the professional to work to resolve the boundary issue and operate in the best interest of the client.

In the field of sexual abuser assessment and treatment, most clients are involuntary because they are court-ordered to treatment as a condition of probation or parole. Others are mandated or obliged to participate in treatment as a way of avoiding prison, to gain release from civil commitment, or to earn privileges or early release from prison. As such, involuntary clients are distinctly vulnerable to therapist influence and boundary violations because of the power the therapist has to influence decisions about court-ordered rules and restrictions, and ultimately a client's potential loss of freedom imposed by the criminal justice system and the requirements of the court.

Maintaining Professional Boundaries

The challenge of balancing therapeutic and accountability roles can also take the form of boundary issues. Maintaining appropriate professional boundaries is a fundamental responsibility. Smith and Fitzpatrick (1995, p. 500) differentiate between boundary crossing and boundary violations. *Boundary crossing* is a non-pejorative term that describes departures from commonly accepted clinical practice that may or may not benefit the client. But a *boundary violation* is a departure from accepted practice that places the client or the therapeutic process at serious risk. Gutheil and Gabbard (1993) defined professional boundaries in terms of the mental health professional's role, time, place, and space (of the session), money (paid or received), gifts, clothing, language, self-disclosure by the professional, and physical contact with the client. Using these dimensions, they explored the various ways, both blatant and subtle, in which therapists may cross or violate boundaries in professional practice. For example, *time boundaries* refer to the importance of both starting and finishing each therapy session at a consistent time. Therapists should not allow sessions to go beyond the set ending time regardless of what may occurring in the session as it comes to a close, unless crisis intervention is required.

Boundary issues typically involve a violation of agreed-upon interpersonal or relationship structure, or some form of a dual relationship. Structural boundaries include clarity and consistency regarding the time and place of the service, fees, and agreements regarding the service provided to the client. Such boundary issues can become challenging in any setting. For example, if the group facilitator pays special attention to one client and/or ignores another client, it may appear as special treatment. The same would be true if the clinician gives extra time to a client, such as an extra session or personal time outside of the group. The clinician may have good intentions, such as trying to give added support to a client during a crisis, but significant departures from established routines and the norms of commonly accepted professional practice always present the risk of violating boundaries. The decision to depart from established practice must be carefully considered and based purely upon the needs of the individual client. If needed, the clinician is wise to consult with a peer or clinical supervisor.

Boundary Issues with Sexual Offenders

How are ethical questions relevant to treatment of sexual offenders? Sawyer and Prescott (2010) observed that one of the most significant issues is the fact that most sexual offenders are involuntary clients in structured treatment programs, under a court order, and supervised by a probation or parole agent. Given these mandates and external controls on the client, mental health professionals can be drawn away from considering an offender as a client with the same rights and vulnerabilities as a traditional mental health client. The clinician might slip into thinking, incorrectly, that *this guy is a sexual offender, he doesn't want to be here, he has lost his rights*. This bias and the inherent power differential put the therapist at risk of treating an involuntary client differently from a traditional client. Even though a client may have committed a sexual crime and been mandated to participate in treatment, he can be just as distressed and vulnerable as a traditional client who is voluntarily seeking relief from anxiety or depression. The involuntary client should be treated with the same clinical objectivity and with the same regard for rights, privacy, and dignity as any client seeking mental health services.

When clients first present for therapy after a criminal justice intervention, they experience fear, shame, loss of family and friends, loss of livelihood, and damaged or diminished self-esteem. Given so much loss, grief, and depression are added to the misery. Under this type of intense stress, sexual abusers naturally resort to psychological defenses, such as denial, minimization, and rationalization to protect themselves and salvage what dignity they have left. These defensive tendencies are further exacerbated by the intense scrutiny of criminal justice authorities, which force the offender to face ugly truths about himself that he had previously denied and rationalized. For example, a man who is arrested for child pornography or child molestation may have to come to terms with a lifetime of accepting his sexual attraction to children (e.g., pedophilia).

The case example below explores the use of authority to further therapeutic goals.

Therapeutic Use of Power

The group began as usual with a brief check-in. On this occasion, however, the members were lethargic and no one offered anything of substance, and the group quickly fell silent. Hoping to activate the group, the therapist asked, "Who wants to start with goal work?" No one volunteered. The group sat silent, avoiding eye contact with the leader. After more silence, the therapist began asking each member if he was prepared for today's group and, if not, why not. The members offered a variety of excuses as to why they were not prepared or did not have their treatment materials with them. This lack of participation and limited engagement had been present at various times in prior group sessions, but this time the group therapist lost his patience. With clear irritation in his voice, the therapist gave a sharp reminder that each member had signed a treatment agreement, as well as a group therapy agreement, in which each had agreed to attend sessions, participate meaningfully, and come prepared to work on treatment goals, homework, and other relevant issues. The group therapist went on to "remind" them that failure to participate in group could result in termination or serious negative consequences.

This was a frustrating moment for the therapist, who probably felt disrespected and maybe doubted his competency. But threatening an adverse discharge from treatment is, of course, unlikely to be effective. It is most often counter-therapeutic because it reinforces the power differential between the therapist and clients, increasing distrust and guardedness and doing little to empower clients to move beyond their passive/resistant stage of change to a more productive personal investment in their treatment.

Instead, the group leader could have used a group-centered intervention that turned the issue of responsibility back to the group. He could have fostered an open discussion of how the group felt about the agreement and lack of engagement. He could encourage the group to express why the agreement is important or discuss the impact on the group when members do not participate or come prepared, or what the members can do differently to make the group experience as beneficial and meaningful as possible. Optimally, in the longer run, the group members (not the therapist) will take the initiative in challenging and supporting members who are failing or struggling to engage in treatment.

Balancing the Dual Roles of Therapist and Authority

As shown in the example above, the group therapist had a hard time balancing being therapeutic with the issue of holding clients accountable. When he opted to use his authority to enforce compliance with treatment, he lost his credibility as a therapist. This is a common and fundamental dilemma for group therapists working with sexual abusers. The research tells us to be engaged with our clients, show support, and to encourage them by using positive messages. That is how we are trained as therapists. For many clinicians, however, this stance is difficult because sexual offenders can sometimes be demeaning, negative, self-centered, antisocial, or even aggressive. Given their behavior and personalities, our clients can often evoke a variety of emotional reactions inside us, both direct and subtle, that influence how we respond. Their sexually abusive behavior is unacceptable, if not reprehensible, yet we must form a therapeutic relationship with them and do what we are able to help them change. This requires us to believe that they really can change. Do you believe that your clients can change? Do you believe that they won't change without the external threat of sanctions? Your attitude and beliefs may be revealed in your verbal and nonverbal communication in the group, and in how you offer feedback, direction, or other therapeutic interventions.

The differing roles of therapist and authority raises the issue of personal style. How would you describe your style of group work with sexual offenders? Authoritative? Casual and easygoing? Staunch? Warm and compassionate? Detached and objective? Is it your nature to show care and concern? Most clinicians choose the health profession because they want to help others and improve the lives of those in need.

How do you feel about having power or control over your clients' lives? For many therapists, wielding this power is not comfortable. Some clinicians shy away from the inevitable exercise of authority, which often results in power struggles with clients. We have significant power by virtue of the fact that our clients have been court-ordered into treatment. Even though they must consent to participate in treatment, clients are subject to potential legal consequences if they are not compliant or do not complete treatment. As a result, our determination of a client's progress or failure to make progress may result in adverse legal consequences. How we wield that power, or shy away from it, or use it therapeutically is one of the most significant professional responsibilities we face in our work.

Outside Influences That May Impact Upon Group Therapy

In this final section, we look at the ethical and professional challenges that are created when the sexual offender group therapist may be influenced by outside authorities. In particular, we will look at the challenges created when criminal justice authorities become directly involved in group treatment and when administrative authorities exert control over how group therapy is conducted.

The Problem of Probation Officer Co-Facilitation of Groups

It is not uncommon to find sexual abuser-specific treatment programs in which a licensed mental health professional co-facilitates a therapy group with a probation (or parole) officer and the probation officer is also responsible for court-ordered supervision of the clients in the group. When a probation officer participates in a therapy group for sexual offenders, it creates multiple ethical dilemmas related to conflict of interest, dual relationships, and therapeutic boundaries (Sawyer & Prescott, 2011):

1. The treating clinician and the probation officer may be viewed as co-equal because group leadership is shared, information is shared equally, and both are seen as authorities or power figures. But they may not be equal because, in many jurisdictions, the treatment provider is often contracted by the same corrections

department that employs the probation officer. This creates a potential conflict of interest for the therapist, who has a financial interest in keeping the contract. To the degree that the probation officer has influence over the therapist's contract, the officer is in a position to influence how the therapist conducts the group.

2. When viewed from the client's perspective, these two separate group leaders are viewed as having equal responsibility for the client's psychological and emotional welfare when, in fact, the probation officer's first responsibility is to the court and public safety.
3. The therapeutic alliance with the therapist is compromised if the client sees the therapist as a collaborator with the court (i.e., in a dual relationship).
4. The presence of the probation officer can directly influence the therapist's choice of interventions. The group therapist may be hesitant to use certain interventions or pursue a certain line of inquiry because the client may disclose information that, while therapeutic, may be incriminating in the eyes of the probation officer and subject to sanctions.
5. The presence of a probation officer eliminates the traditional therapeutic protections of privacy and confidentiality of information. Anything that a client reveals in the group could potentially be used against him by the criminal justice authority. It sacrifices the privacy of the client and the therapeutic relationship—which, research has shown, is of vital importance to successful therapy (Lambert & Okishi, 1997).

Compare this situation with being pulled over on the highway by an officer of the state highway patrol. If you were speeding and using alcohol, would you roll down your window and confess your actions to the officer before you were asked? Most drivers would avoid this kind of self-incrimination. Would you admit this to a therapist in a treatment program? Hopefully you would. Why? You know the therapist has your best interest as a priority and you trust the therapist and the confidentiality of the relationship. The police officer has a duty to observe your behavior and arrest you if a crime is committed, but not to prosecute you, find you guilty, or treat you. Prosecution, determining guilt, and rehabilitation are the roles of other professionals. That fundamental separation of roles underpins the system of rights in the United States and many other countries.

Informed Consent

For any and all of the five reasons listed above, a sexual abuser may not be willing to participate in a therapeutic group process in which his probation officer serves as a co-facilitator. Even though such refusal may be valid, the involuntary client may not believe he has a legitimate freedom to decline participation because he fears the judicial consequences, or he may not be given an alternative. In other words, informed consent cannot occur if the client has no choice to refuse the treatment. In this case, it would be necessary to offer the client reasonable alternatives that meet his therapeutic needs, at the same time meeting minimum acceptable standards of treatment. As an officer whose first responsibility is allegiance to the court, the probation officer cannot have the client's well-being as his or her *first* priority. On the other hand, as mental health professionals, sexual offender therapists are ethically bound to standards requiring that the welfare of the client is their primary responsibility. That responsibility is tempered only by the legally required exceptions related to the safety of others and child abuse reporting.

ATSA practice standards and guidelines assert that community safety is a primary concern when assessing or treating sexual offenders. The licensed therapist treating sexual abusers has an *ethical* responsibility to the client, a *legal* responsibility to the court, and an ethical/moral responsibility to the community. The therapist's primary responsibility to the client's welfare is influenced in part by the standard of practice to share information with county/state corrections and/or the community as required by law or by contractual obligations, or as needed to protect the community. This is accomplished through informed consent from the client, or as needed by law. Within these limits of confidentiality, however, the therapist's focus is on the sexual offender client and his clinical needs. The client is best served—and the public is best served—when the therapist and the client develop a therapist–client relationship that is separate from the sexual offender's relationship with the probation officer and the court. Thus, any therapeutic model that allows the probation officer to be a co-facilitator may not be in the best interest of the client simply by the fact that the client is not the probation officer's first client. In our view, this has the potential not to be in the best interest of the public as there are inherent treatment biases that could limit the effectiveness of the treatment service.

Balancing Curricular Demands with Dynamic Group Process

There is another way that the therapeutic freedom of group therapists may be challenged by external or potentially competing interests. In the field of sexual offender-specific treatment, many treatment programs require group therapists to use cognitive-behavioral principles and adhere to a group session agenda that is driven by a preset standardized curriculum. This is especially true for so-called psychoeducational and educational groups in which the group therapist may be obliged to cover a particular lesson topic or teach a particular skill within the time allotted for that group session. One could argue that such manualized treatment is more accurately seen as group-based classroom education rather than true group psychotherapy. We argue that any group has the potential for valuable group interaction.

We recognize that fostering interaction among members in a sexual offender-specific psychoeducational group is typically not a primary focus. It may even be discouraged to the degree that it may detract from the primary objective of imparting information to the group. Nevertheless, despite the common pressure to stick to the script in a structured psychoeducational group, we believe that you can still take advantage of group dynamics. In fact, group interaction can improve learning because the participants will be more active, engaged, and able to make the educational material more personally meaningful.

Remember that there are always some observable group processes and group dynamics occurring in every type of group—even in an explicitly educational group—whether it be psychodynamic, cognitive-behavioral, or some other theoretical model. Even when our sexual offender clients are quietly sitting in a classroom, it is possible to identify group dynamics and gather valuable clinical information about the members and their relatedness. We can note their level of attentiveness and engagement in learning the material, as well as their demeanor with their peers while doing so. The group leader can observe who responds to questions about particular content, the tone and quality of interaction among the group members, and the patterns of how individuals engage or withdraw from the discussion.

Even in an explicitly educational session, member-to-member discussion should be facilitated because active participation enhances learning and improves internalization of the concepts through personal engagement. Simple member-to-member interaction can also activate group therapeutic factors, such as universality, instillation of hope, and cohesion, because members see how much they share in common as they learn the material and that they struggle with the same problems and emotions.

The next case example explores how to use group interaction to energize an educational group.

Using Group Interaction to Enhance a Psychoeducational Group

Rebecca was having a difficult time with her group. Since the concept of thinking errors was an important part of the treatment curriculum, she made sure that every member completed his homework assignments and took his turn to present his homework sheet during the group session. One at a time, each member would list three cogni-

tive distortions, identify the type of thinking error (e.g., rationalization, minimization, blaming, etc.), and note the appropriate correction. Rebecca succeeded in having every member present his homework every week, but there was no energy in the room. The members sat in silence, yawning and dozing off in boredom until it was their turn to present. Rebecca felt like she did all the work and began to dread the next meeting of the boring group.

Fortunately, with the help of her clinical supervisor, Rebecca was encouraged to focus less on covering the lesson content and more on the here-and-now group interaction. Instead of making sure everyone presented every week, Rebecca focused on encouraging the members to respond to the presenter. She praised members for their feedback and participation. She pointed out the positive emotions that ensued for both the giver and the receiver of feedback. She drew attention to the similarities among the members in their thinking, feelings, experiences, and struggles—and pointed out moments of acceptance and belonging. Within a few weeks, Rebecca no longer needed to elicit responses, because the men were actively participating. There was enthusiasm, spontaneous feedback, and free expression of ideas and emotions. In fact, there was so much participation that only two or three men ever had the chance to present their homework during a session. But now every member was engaged in every session.

Summary and Conclusions

This chapter looked at the many ethical and professional challenges that confront clinicians who conduct group therapy with sexual abusers. In addition to compliance with state licensing standards specific to one's clinical discipline, sexual offender-specific therapists may also be obligated to follow the ethical and practice standards of their professional associations—both discipline-specific associations, such as APA (psychologists) and NASW (social workers), and specialty practice organizations, such as ATSA (sexual abusers) and AGPA (group therapy). Such organizations also provide valuable resources to members, including practice guidelines and training opportunities to improve one's knowledge and skills.

All licensing boards and professional organizations require mental health professionals to practice within the limits of their practice competence and to obtain additional training and guidance specific to their area of practice to assure competence. Given the fact that the great majority of sexual offender-specific treatment is delivered in group formats, we believe that the competency principle requires clinicians in our field to have knowledge and competence in the established methods of sexual offender-specific treatment *and* group therapy. Unfortunately, many new therapists in our field are thrown into group leadership without adequate training or supervision in the complex skills needed to facilitate effective groups. We believe that both the clinician and the program/agency that requires him or her to conduct groups have an ethical obligation to obtain and maintain competency in group therapy as well as sexual offender-specific competency.

Sexual offense-specific group therapists also face unique ethical challenges because our clients are typically involved in the criminal justice system and are court-ordered or involuntary. As mental health professionals, we all have a primary responsibility for the well-being of the client. But with sexual offending clients, we also have an ethical responsibility to protect public safety and hold our clients accountable for their behavior. The strain of serving dual responsibilities is heightened when therapists are employed or paid by criminal justice authorities, such as probation, parole, corrections, and forensic and civil commitment programs, or, in the most extreme case, when probation agents serve as co-facilitators of sexual offender groups. Many sexual offender-specific group therapists are uncomfortable with the power they possess over involuntary clients. This is especially difficult when clients behave in negative ways and the therapist might need to report high-risk behavior or noncompliance with treatment. It takes skill and experience to integrate the therapeutic stance of warmth, directness, and support—while also holding clients accountable.

Finally, we considered the challenges that group therapists may face in treatment programs with highly structured curricula that expect the therapist to "teach" particular concepts and principles in their groups. We believe that, even in the most explicitly educational or psychoeducational group, interaction and group dynamics are important and should be used because learning is always more effective when the group members are actively engaged.

CHAPTER 4

Composition and the Essentials of Group Structure

I am looking forward to learning about why I did what I did that got me into this group.

—Comment from a new client during the second session of a new group

I can change. I don't have to be caught in the prison of the past.

—Client comment on the night he finished treatment

Planning and preparation are important to the successful creation of a new group. There are many questions to consider: Who will be the group facilitators? Are they fully trained? Is there a long-term plan for group leader stability? If the group is co-facilitated, have the group leaders discussed their leadership styles and resolved significant differences? Is clinical and administrative supervision available? Is the group open-ended or time-limited (i.e., will membership be "rolling" over time so that members complete and new members enter)? Are there criteria for admission to the group? Have the group rules and the content of the group agreement been determined? Have all necessary handouts been prepared?

After answering these initial planning questions, the group therapist(s) can turn to the important task of selecting group members: group composition. The principles for group composition are the subject of the first half of this chapter. The second half is dedicated to the principles of group structure, which are essential for maintaining an effective group.

Principles of Group Composition

In the general field of group therapy, selection of new group members is a critical factor in forming a group and ultimately in how the group functions. However, in the field of sexual abuser-specific treatment, group therapists typically have little control over the selection of who is placed in their groups. In this section, we will discuss member selection criteria and ways to manage the challenges of less-than-optimal composition.

The Challenges of Group Composition with Sexual Abusers

In the general field of group therapy, significant attention is given to the thoughtful selection of group members. But in our field of sexual offender-specific treatment, we are often limited in our ability to select group members for two reasons. First, sexual abusers are most often mandated or otherwise obliged to enter treatment by criminal justice authorities, and we rarely have any control over who gets referred by those authorities. Second, resources may be quite limited. All too often, there are only a few groups available, thus limiting placement options, or the program structure may require placement in certain groups at certain stages of treatment. In some settings, clients are placed based on their schedules (e.g., the client works at a second-shift job and needs a morning group). These real-world constraints often result in less-than-ideal group composition, which hampers the development of optimal group processes. Nevertheless, we can increase the potential for the group to be beneficial by paying careful attention to individual member traits, skills, personalities and psychopathology, capacity for insight, and interpersonal characteristics. As presented in table 4.1, the general group literature (Burlingame et al., 2002) advises us to compose a group as fully as possible with members who possess six particular capabilities and characteristics. But what do we do if our clients are lacking in these areas? When it comes to sexual abusers, they are typically deficit in every one of these six criteria.

At first glance, the characteristic deficits of sexual abusers would suggest that they are less-than-optimal candidates for group therapy. The paradox is that group therapy is just the right modality for addressing these same deficits. Therefore, even though you may have limited choices about who is placed in your particular group, there are two ways that you can still apply these six recommended criteria: (1) Prepare candidates with deficits for participation in your group; and/or (2) create multiple groups to accommodate members with differing levels of functioning (i.e., a higher-functioning group and a lower-functioning group).

TABLE 4.1 THE CHALLENGES OF SELECTING MEMBERS FOR SEXUAL ABUSER GROUPS

Recommended Criteria for Selecting Group Members	Challenges Specific to Sexual Abusers
1. Motivation to change and improve.	May be absent or lacking due to external pressure from court, legal, probation, or corrections authorities.
2. Skills and capabilities to participate in reciprocal group interactions.	Often limited by characteristic deficits in intimacy skills and social skills.
3. Ability to express emotions effectively.	May be seriously lacking in many sex offenders, especially dismissive/avoidant types who suppress emotions and present as stoic.
4. Recognition of the interpersonal nature of their problems.	May be compromised by characteristic isolation, loneliness, and poor interpersonal relationships.
5. Capacity for empathy.	May be seriously lacking in many sexual abusers, particularly victim empathy.
6. Capacity to give and receive feedback.	May be resistant to feedback because of denial or minimization of offending behavior.

With regard to the first, *preparation for group*, if possible, postpone an individual's entry into the group until you have had time to further assess his capacity to function there, and use individual sessions to prepare him for eventual entry. Or you may develop a pre-treatment group to work on motivation and capacity for more effective participation in a treatment group, such as the program created for treatment-resistant sexually violent predators (Prescott, 2008).

With regard to *functioning levels*, you should strive for as much homogeneity as possible in terms of level of intellectual, cognitive, and social functioning. This would encompass factors such as age, intelligence, ability to provide and accept feedback, psychological organization, ability to tolerate anxiety, verbal articulation, degree of emotional disclosure, risk taking, and types and degree of pathology. If you are able to offer lower-functioning and higher-functioning groups, you can increase the homogeneity of functioning level within each group.

Finally, in chapter 6, some facilitation techniques are discussed that can help mitigate the negative impact of individual deficits in each of these six recommended criteria for group composition. The next case example illustrates the problem of homogeneity of certain member traits.

Too Much Similarity in Group Composition

After meeting for six months, the Tuesday-night group continued to lack energy or engagement. It still felt like a circle of strangers. Emotions were constricted. The members frequently sat in silence, rarely sharing anything personal. The group therapist would often prompt the men to respond to one another, but they never seemed to connect in a meaningful way. One night, the group therapist prompted Charlie to redirect his feedback to Jim. "Can you say more to Jim about that?" Charlie shook his head and grunted, "That ain't my style." Jim joined in, saying with an angry tone, "It ain't mine, either."

In that moment, the group therapist realized that Charlie and Jim weren't the only members who shared the same personality "style." He had a room full of avoidant men. The group therapist realized that he had erred in the composition of the group. He had selected men who had similar traits of social avoidance, isolation, introversion, impaired self-esteem, and emotional constriction. It was no wonder that the members were not relating to one another. He had inadvertently stacked the deck against social interaction.

The group therapist had applied the composition principle of assembling a group of men who were homogeneous in their level of functioning and who shared the same primary problem of social isolation. But the group was *too* homogeneous. With this recognition, the group therapist made a conscious decision to bring in new members who were more extroverted, emotional, and desirous of connection. A second composition change was made by moving Charlie and Jim to a different group with men who were more animated and interactive.

In situations like this in which the group composition is already established, the group therapist has two options. First, it may be possible to change the membership by assigning members to different groups to create a better mix of member traits. This might be done to increase heterogeneity or to increase homogeneity, depending on the problematic composition of the group. If it is not possible to change groups, the second strategy is to actively engage the group using techniques that facilitate more meaningful interaction and member-to-member connections (as we describe in more detail in chapter 6).

FOUR GUIDELINES FOR MEMBER SELECTION AND GROUP COMPOSITION

As we discussed, few programs have the freedom or flexibility to include or exclude members; nor do programs typically examine group placement in terms of "fit" in the group. Hence, groups are often composed of members who have personality traits, cognitive or intellectual deficits, psychiatric symptoms, or other issues that impede appropriate and meaningful group participation. Despite these real-world constraints, we can use the group therapy research to inform us about what to look for, how suboptimal group placements might impact group functioning, and what we can do to accommodate clients whose participation is a challenge for the group. In this regard, Burlingame, Fuhriman, and Johnson (2002) offer four empirically investigated principles for selecting group members, as shown in table 4.2.

TABLE 4.2 PRINCIPLES FOR SELECTING GROUP MEMBERS

Include Clients Who:	Exclude Clients Who:	Seek Diversity in These Traits:	Seek Consistency in These Traits:
• define their problems as interpersonal • are able to give and receive feedback • have some capacity for empathy • are highly motivated	• are psychotic • are difficult to establish rapport with • are severely limited in interpersonal skills	• verbal passivity vs. activity • intellectualizing vs. emotional disclosure • risk taking and providing of support • types of pathology	• ability to provide and accept feedback • intellect and age • psychological organization • ability to tolerate anxiety • ability to give and receive help

The four principles of group composition tell us to seek a mixture of personality traits for group members who share a similar level of intellectual and psychological functioning. Thus the group therapist should seek variation or diversity in the clients' verbal passivity versus verbal activity, intellectualizing versus emotional disclosure, risk taking versus supporting styles, and types of problems, while seeking homogeneity in their ability to tolerate anxiety and provide and accept help and feedback.

As shown in the example above, the Tuesday-night group achieved a common level of functioning, but lacked the desired variation of personality traits. The group had too many socially avoidant clients with limited interpersonal skills and limited capacity for empathy, and too few clients who defined their problems as interpersonal and were able to engage in emotional expression. The poor group composition required an excessive, and perhaps insurmountable, effort by the group therapist to draw out members who were all characterologically withdrawn and withholding. The presence of a few members who were more extroverted and desirous of connection would have provided more energy and living examples of alternative ways of relating.

The next case example explores a diferent problem with composition.

Too Much Disparity in Group Composition

An ongoing, open-ended outpatient group had been meeting for several years with some probationers and parolees finishing treatment and others just beginning. At one point, four of the long-standing members were well-educated professionals or businessmen who had never been incarcerated, while three of the newer members came directly from prison, had never finished high school, and had no careers. The established members were accustomed to lively group discussions that often applied the treatment terminology of cognitive distortions and offense patterns. But the newer members struggled to understand the vocabulary and treatment concepts being discussed. The differences in education and socioeconomic status sometimes caused the group to break into two factions. The educated and experienced members were frustrated by the need to stop and simplify the discussion for the less educated beginners, who resented the obvious attitude of superiority.

During one particularly intense session, the educated members were discussing the moral principles of consent regarding the rape of a teenage girl who passed out after drinking too much alcohol at a party. Joe could not comprehend the intellectual discussion of "moral principles" and grew angry when the others ignored his attempt to ask a question. "Sounds like a bunch of bullshit to me."

This is an example of poor group composition. The sharp differences in education, intellectual sophistication, and socioeconomic status caused the group to break into two conflicting subgroups. This presented a continuing challenge to the group therapist, who tried to overcome the differences by facilitating clarification feedback, such as, "Joe, do you understand what Tom meant?" or "Tom, would you talk to Joe and explain more about what you are saying?" The group therapist also tried to reframe their differences as opportunities for learning tolerance, compassion, and cooperation. He pointed out instances in which the members shared very similar feelings, fears, and beliefs, and instances in which they supported and helped one another regardless of their subgroup differences: "Like Tom said, having a college education and a good job doesn't mean you don't make bad decisions." "It seemed like the whole group felt good just now when Tom apologized for talking down to Joe. Why are you guys nodding?"

Composition and the Question of Mixing Offense Types

Given what we know about composition, is it better to treat different types of sexual offenders together or separately? As shown in chapter 2, there is no definitive research that homogeneous or heterogeneous groups based on offense type are more or less effective. As clinicians we, the authors, have had the opportunity to see men in mostly mixed-offense-type groups, and generally most programs have groups of mixed offense types. In our opinion, it is more important to maintain homogeneity in level of functioning and heterogeneity in personality styles than homogeneity of offense types.

There is, however, an issue that frequently arises in mixed-offender groups that is worth addressing. It is not uncommon to observe one type of sexual abuser saying that his offense was not as bad as another type. For example, an exhibitionist or voyeur may say his offense was not as bad as a contact offense; or a rapist may say his crime was not as bad as molesting a child; or a child pornography user may insist he never touched a child. This tactic of comparing crimes essentially serves as a way of bolstering one's self-esteem and/or minimizing the severity of one's problems and the need for treatment. Left unaddressed, this behavior can create a negative hierarchy that can detract from, or completely inhibit, effective group interactions, and eventually preclude critical self-exploration. When members attempt to set themselves apart from the group in this way, they disengage from their connection to the group and devalue other members, which impairs cohesiveness. Such attitudes are distancing, judgmental, and impersonal, and ultimately degrade the interpersonal risk-taking milieu of effective groups.

An effective way to handle this problem is to consistently emphasize the many commonalities among group members in their attitudes, feelings, experiences, and negative self-image, such as their shared feelings of loneliness, shame, hopelessness, and social rejection This is done by maintaining a consistent focus on group process, group interaction, and member-to-member interaction while protecting the group from acts of shaming or attack.

Principles of Group Structure

Group structure is absolutely crucial to starting a new group and it continues to be important throughout the life of the group. This section presents nine key elements of group structure that establish the foundation for an effective therapy group.

The Group Agreement

The agreement to participate in group therapy is a cornerstone of the essential structure of successful groups (Rutan & Stone, 1993). The agreement spells out expectations between the therapist and the client in both prescriptive and engaging language. Agreements typically cover topics such as attendance, participation, confidentiality, financial responsibility, and contact between members outside the group; they may even include expectations about doing homework assignments that are discussed in the group. The group agreement is a working contract between the therapist, the client, and the group. It is most effective when reviewed in detail with the client to ensure that he has a clear understanding of what the group experience will be like and what is expected of him as a group member. Most important, the agreement helps the client to become engaged in his own treatment because it affirms that he has a valuable contribution to make to the group and is making a commitment to his fellow group members. In other words, it lays the groundwork for commitment to treatment and interpersonal caring, both of which are fundamental dimensions of group cohesion.

In creating a group agreement, Rutan and Stone (1993) recommend the following seven rules or expectations:

1. To be present each week, to be on time, and to remain throughout the meeting.
2. To work actively on the problems that brought you to the group.
3. To put feelings into words, not actions.
4. To use the relationships made in the group therapeutically, not socially.
5. To remain in the group until the problems that brought you to the group have been resolved.
6. To be responsible for your bill.
7. To protect the names and identities of fellow group members.

In addition, we recommend an eighth rule about protecting confidentiality, which is an essential condition for a safe and trusting group environment. The rule could be stated: "Group members agree to respect the confidentiality of the group and agree to not disclose personal information about group members to anyone outside of the group."

Preparing Members for Group

Preparing members for group participation is important, but often overlooked. Few men, and even fewer men convicted of a sexual offense, have ever had the experience of an intense, personal, and extended group interaction of this kind. They may have been to parties, work gatherings, or family events where the nature of the group conversation was casual, rambling, or impersonal. A few may have been part of a spontaneous group or family encounter that became emotional or in some way unexpectedly personal. But group therapy is an intimate and anxiety-provoking experience that can become emotionally intense. In the words of one client, "It is hard being in a room with everyone looking at me, and expecting me to share something really personal." This anxiety is normal and can be a positive activating force that intensifies the emotional energy in the group and animates group relationships and treatment tasks.

Preparing members for group is more than a review of the group agreement and the basic rules and expectations for participation as described above. Clients need to be educated about the anxiety they are likely to experience in the initial phases of their participation, and reassured that this is a normal reaction. They need to be aware that the group treatment experience may be difficult and uncomfortable at times. It can be helpful to invite the individual to share his fears or concerns about entering group. In most cases, it is an easy matter to allay such fears, and the client feels understood and safer.

Preparation should explain that the focus of group is learning how to share experiences and relate to others in an open and respectful way that will feel positive and supportive. Preparing clients for this style of interpersonal interaction is consistent with the research findings that clients who define their problems as interpersonal (relational) are more able to contribute to cohesion in the group. In addition, it is helpful to clarify the roles and responsibilities of the leader and the members and to explicate the professional and personal boundaries among members and between the leader(s) and the group. Ultimately the goal of pre-group preparation is to establish positive expectations and motivate members to participate fully and contribute to an effective group process.

Setting Norms in Early Sessions

If you are starting an entirely new group, or just introducing a new member to the group for the first time, the first few sessions can go a long way toward establishing the norms for behavior and a positive therapeutic culture. It is helpful to begin with a welcoming statement that conveys confidence that this will be a positive and rewarding experience for all, including yourself. You can acknowledge the common experience of anxiety, but also excitement about coming to know one another well and forming meaningful working relationships. The opening statement affirms that all members are in treatment for different reasons, but that everyone is equal and shares similar goals to improve their lives, behavior, and relationships. The group leader should review the group agreement that everyone signed so all members hear and understand the same expectations. The structure of the group and the nature of process are explained clearly before treatment, and repeating those agreements is helpful in early sessions. Any other unique program expectations are also explained and repeated as necessary. After the essential information is given, time should be spent in allowing the members to introduce themselves. This exercise is repeated every time a new member joins the group.

It is vitally important to adhere to the structural rules and expectations during the early sessions (and for any group session, for that matter) because structure is absolutely essential to effective group therapy. It is the foundation for the group norms that will govern respectful behavior and engagement.

Establishing Group Structure

Structure serves as the safety and security net for the group. It creates a predictable environment that is experienced as socially, physically, emotionally, and psychologically safe. If the group therapist does nothing else, establishing and maintaining stable and predictable structure is essential to positive group functioning. We have already discussed three important foundations for group structure: selection of members for optimal composition, processing the initial group agreement, and preparing the new member for group. Once the group is operating, structure is maintained by adhering to time boundaries, protecting members from attack or shaming, and reinforcing the core expectation that all members will abide by the agreement to participate. Structure includes time, physical space, facilitator and member roles, absences, tardiness, privacy, extra-group relationships, and clarity regarding how the group operates. Structure also includes a designated setting—a space that is private, will not be interrupted, and allows the group to sit in a circle.

Maintaining an Equidistant Circle

Sitting in a circle conveys that all group members are equal in value and enables all members to see one another. But it must be an equidistant circle. Jennings and Deming (2013) make a strong point of avoiding rooms and seating arrangements that can allow for "seats of power" within the group. They urge group therapists to use similar chairs for everyone so that members do not lay claim to the most comfortable chair as a symbol of seniority or status. It is also essential to maintain the integrity of the circle. Many members will attempt to move their chairs outside the circle. For some it may simply be a way of decreasing their anxiety by hiding from the eyes of the group. For others it can be a literal expression of pulling out of the group, showing their hostility to the group or an intention to avoid participation, or even a fear of trust and bonding. For still others, moving outside the circle is a way to establish superiority by gaining a vantage point of observing, but not being observed. The equidistant circle enables everyone to see and be seen by everyone else. For this reason, there should be no tables or obstructions inside the circle, and no potential distractions like coffee cups, water bottles, and fiddling objects. In fact, smoothing out the circle can be one of the first routine things that the group does—together—to set the stage for interaction.

Start on Time

Starting on time demonstrates that the group structure is stable, safe, and predictable. It reinforces the shared commitment of everyone to arrive on time (and also prevents disruptions or the appearance that any member has special or privileged status by arriving late). Starting on time—every time—puts a boundary around the group that enhances psychological safety and facilitates trust. Consistency and clear boundaries are especially important for sexual offenders who very often have problems with poor boundaries, attachment issues, and basic trust.

Starting on time is an expectation that can be highlighted when a member is late or resists beginning on time. When all group members understand and commit to the importance of being on time, then violations of that norm become very significant. It should be addressed whenever it occurs to reinforce the norm, prevent future boundary violations, and illuminate its meaning—for both the individual and the group as a whole. Group members who are late for a session learn the impact of their behavior on others, and have the opportunity to practice appropriate social skills, such as making an apology or offering a reasonable explanation if being late was truly out of their control.

Close the Door

While seemingly simple, this action demonstrates the importance and respect of privacy and boundaries with men who have often come from family environments that lacked, or routinely violated, interpersonal boundaries. Many have been victims of abuse and have abused victims behind closed doors. Closing the door—to create safety and trust –is the therapeutic opposite of their prior experiences of fear, secrecy, distrust, and victimization. Closing the door for safety and privacy is the physical representation of safety in the group and fosters trust in the group leader, who is a positive role model of authority and parenting.

Everyone Stays Until the Session Is Finished

Trust is an essential building block for cohesion and one of the foremost issues in the early developmental stage of group. The agreement to stay focused on the therapeutic work and make use of every minute of group time reinforces commitment to the group and builds trust in the facilitators and group members. Making this commitment helps men who are in the preliminary stages of change (e.g., denying responsibility, blaming others, lacking in motivation to change) to move forward to the stages of action that invokes engagement in the group and treatment.

End on Time

Group participation can be a threatening, anxiety-provoking, and even tiring experience. Adhering to clear time boundaries is another important part of the consistency, stability, and predictability that defines the therapeutic environment of group. It conveys safety and respect. It signifies the value of the limited time available to do therapeutic work and honors the need to address therapy issues during the group time. It also limits last-minute demands for special attention.

SUMMARY AND CONCLUSIONS

This chapter presented two key foundations for creating and maintaining effective groups: group composition and group structure. Even though therapists in the field of sexual offender treatment rarely have the option to select (or exclude) members to create the ideal group, we can apply the principles of composition to recognize and facilitate in ways that can counteract the impact of negative traits and less-than-ideal composition. With regard to composition, group therapists should strive for homogeneity in the levels of intelligence, psychological functioning, commitment to treatment, interpersonal skills, and emotional awareness—and heterogeneity in interactive styles.

As a group, sexual offenders tend to display traits such as emotional constriction, interpersonal avoidance, acute absence of motivation, lack of empathy, and direct resistance to treatment, all of which can be barriers to participating in the interpersonal interactions that are essential for group therapy. Nevertheless, group therapy is the ideal modality for helping men to develop the interpersonal trust, skills, and bonds they need. In this regard, principles of group structure, the second half of this chapter, are absolutely crucial to establishing and maintaining the predictable, accepting, and safe environment that enables men to grow in these areas.

CHAPTER 5

Understanding Group Dynamics and Developmental Stages

*Group is easy. We are all the same. This is the only place
I can talk about what I did where there is no judgment.*

—Newer client in an ongoing group

The group therapist has unlimited opportunities to witness complex and ever-changing group dynamics when facilitating group therapy sessions. Group dynamics evolve over time as the group moves through the stages of group development. Knowledge of group dynamics, the skills to recognize and use those dynamics, and a healthy curiosity about what makes a group tick combine to make group therapy into a fascinating and fulfilling professional endeavor.

PROCESS, CONTENT, AND STRUCTURE

Three terms are used in the general group therapy field to describe group dynamics: process, content, and structure. *Process* is the here-and-now experience and responses of the group as they interact with one another and the leader. *Content* is the subject or topic being discussed in the group. It includes spoken words—who said what to whom; nonverbal communications such as body language; and any materials used in the group, such as homework or handouts. *Structure* is the frame within which the content and process occur—the time, place, rules, and expectations that all group members have agreed to follow. Here's an example to illustrate these three concepts.

Group Dynamics at Work: Structure, Content, and Process

Aaron had been a member of the outpatient group for over a year. He was a 69-year-old married man who was a self-defined loner, often saying "I don't need anyone." He had sexually abused his granddaughter. During this session, Aaron asked to take time to talk about one of his treatment goals, which was to compose an (unsent) letter of apology to his daughter, who had virtually shut off any contact with their family. Aaron began talking about the impact of his offense and the harm he had done to his family. But as he continued talking, he began rambling and diverged into a philosophical tangent about God and forgiveness. Group members began looking at one another in confusion. Mike interrupted to say that Aaron had drifted off topic. Aaron became defensive and angry, insisting, "I know exactly what I'm saying." He crossed his arms and sat frowning. A long, tense silence ensued. The therapist intervened to ask the group, "What just happened between Aaron and Mike?" A third member replied, "I think Mike was trying to help, but Aaron didn't see it as help." Charlie added, "It's just like with his daughter, or me and my stepdaughter. She doesn't want an apology from me." Several other group members commented about forgiveness. These comments led to a fruitful discussion of victim empathy and members were able to recognize—using the exchange between Aaron and Mike—that seeking forgiveness can be selfish if you don't see the perspective of the person who was wronged.

In this example, the group was following their established *structure* in which members could request time in the group to work on a treatment goal. The *content* included what Aaron said about the harm he had caused and his off-topic ramble, Mike's interruption, Aaron's negative reaction, and the group's comments about the exchange and forgiveness. The *process* was how the group listened to Aaron as he explained his goal, then became frustrated with his rambling, and how Mike's attempt to help get Aaron back on topic caused discord, which led the group to realize that pushing for forgiveness can be insensitive to the victim who is not ready to forgive. All three elements are present in every session and all three can be the subject of the facilitator's observation or intervention as needed.

Using Structure as an Intervention

As discussed in chapter 4, the group agreement and group rules are the cornerstone of structure. The agreement establishes an informal contract among members and between members and the leader. When those rules are not followed, the group can experience a breakdown. It disrupts the predictability and security of a shared commitment, threatens trust in the group and the leader, and undermines the presumption of cooperation—all of which threaten group cohesion. Failure to follow the group agreement is usually an expression of resistance. It can occur in many forms, such as arriving late for group, not completing treatment work to present to the group, or not participating in the work of other group members. What might appear to be a minor matter of forgetfulness can, in the context of the agreement, assume major importance to the group as an act of disrespect, devaluation, or demonstration of superior status ("I'm above the rules"). Group facilitators and group members can get very angry and lash out at members who break the rules. Serious and/or repeated violations of group rules—as expressions of resistance to treatment—can become grounds for an adverse discharge from the group.

At the same time, structure itself can be used as a tool for addressing and managing resistance. Let's look at an example.

Using Structure to Address Tardiness as Resistance

Roy was often the last to arrive, and the group made a joke out of his being "fashionably late." Even though the group did not seem to mind, the group facilitator wanted to address this recurring violation of group structure. He invited the group to talk about Roy's pattern of tardiness, which violated the group's agreement to arrive on time. Roy responded by saying, "I'm sorry. I really didn't realize I was late that often." He denied any negative attitudes toward the group and insisted that he had a good reason for each time he was late. One week it was a work-related delay; another week it was a problem with one of his children; another time his car broke down. The other group members helped him to appreciate how his behavior was disruptive and disrespectful and made him different from the rest of the group. Roy apologized and consistently arrived on time for all subsequent meetings. A few months later in treatment, Roy was able to identify the selfishness in his habitual pattern of seemingly minor disregard for the expectations of others, and how it was rooted in his childhood history of abuse.

Other forms of resistance can also be addressed using the agreed-upon group structure. Payment of fees is common in community-based programs and should be clearly discussed prior to beginning treatment. When a client does not pay the required fees as agreed (at each session, every week, or monthly), it is a violation of the agreement. The failure to make payments should be explored to understand why the client is not following what he agreed to do when he started the group. Sometimes there is a financial problem, other times there is anger at having to pay the fees, or it may be a symptom of a passive-aggressive attitude. The underlying cause can be explored as a step toward greater self-understanding and possible solutions.

In an earlier example, we saw a therapist who became angry at his group because they were not doing their homework or participating as expected. He chastised the group for not following the group agreement and threatened to discharge noncompliant members. In this instance, the group therapist clearly used structure—but in a punitive and ineffective way. The agreed-upon structure was that all group members would come to each group prepared to work on their treatment assignments. He could have used structure positively by asking if there was something that was making it hard for group members to prepare their treatment assignments—and then waiting for them to respond.

Integrating and Interweaving Structure, Process, and Content

Most sexual abuser treatment programs use a curriculum of some kind and expect clients to present and work on their treatment goals during group sessions. Even though the program design imposes behavioral expectations and predetermines some of the content of any given group session, there are ongoing opportunities to engage the group in spontaneous, intimate, and potentially deeply personal encounters that extend the more structured goal-based "presentations" into a process of exchange and personal interaction. In short, group leaders manage and maintain *structure*, attend carefully to patterns of *content*, and facilitate *process*—as shown in this example:

"A Stupid Thing to Say" Is Reframed as an Expression of Caring

After sitting in silence with a sullen expression, Mike shared a painful week. "I feel horrible. I started feeling bad on Friday. I went to work Monday, but left early because it felt like torture to me. When I got home, I called and told the boss that I wasn't coming back. I feel very afraid. I've stayed in bed for two days because sleep is the only time I can escape these feelings. But I managed to get myself here tonight." The group was stunned by this unexpected and unusual expression of gloom. Most of the time, Mike was an upbeat and frequent contributor even though the legal disposition of his felony case had been hanging over his head for months.

Henry offered support. *"I've felt like you're feeling now. I remember how bad I felt on the day I was investigated. I was depressed and terrified at the same time. I needed support from my friends and family."* Charles offered, *"Have you thought about what you can do?"* Mike looked at Charles with irritation, saying *"Don't you think I've done that a thousand times already?"* Charles quickly apologized. *"I'm sorry, Mike. That was a stupid thing to say."* The group therapist asked Charles to try a second time to say what he wanted to say. *"Well,"* Charles replied, *"I guess I just wanted Mike to know that I feel bad for him and I want to help."* This response led to an outpouring of shared fears and open expression of mutual caring.

Mike followed the *structure* by asking to talk about a personal experience, and the group followed the *structure* by listening intently until he was finished. Mike's disclosure was *processed* as a moment of intense and transparent pain that pulled on the heartstrings of all of the members. The group then followed the *structure* of giving support and feedback after a member shares something personal. The group therapist used the same *structure* by encouraging Charles to try a second time to give his feedback. As the group members struggled to articulate meaningful replies *(content)*, they were learning how to identify and communicate their own inner emotions and *processing* how to work together in a moment of emotional crisis. They were able to connect this experience to their own treatment goals related to communication and emotional expression *(content)*. Several reflected on how their constricted emotions and fear of expressing caring had diminished the emotional intimacy in their relationships, which led to sexual abuse behavior, such as callousness, exploitation, and the use of dehumanizing pornography. The *process* of open sharing further strengthened the trust and intimacy of the group.

The next example illustrates how structure is essential to emotional safety in the group.

Using Structure to Safely Contain Emotional Disclosures

Randy followed the group structure by asking for time to work on a specific treatment goal. He followed the agreed-upon procedure and spoke at length about his history. The group listened closely as Randy disclosed the abuse he had experienced as a boy and struggled to express the shame that still affected him. After he finished, others felt safe enough to reveal new details of their own abusive family relationships and lasting feelings of shame. The content shifted from an individual focus on Randy's treatment goal to an unplanned, spontaneous process of empathic sharing. As each member told the painful story of his own childhood to the group, there were opportunities for new emotional and relational intimacy among members. Remarkably, the group was able to hold all of the seemingly disparate elements of their collective family histories as one safe unity of mutual compassion. They were able to see patterns in their own lives that illustrated how they avoid painful past experiences.

In this example, the *structure* of taking group time to work on a goal was the container that held the spontaneous *process* of trusting the group to make intimate emotional disclosures. The *content* was what the group members disclosed and said to one another. Once again, the group therapist blends the structure, process, and content of group dynamics to achieve a powerful therapeutic result.

UNDERSTANDING DEVELOPMENTAL STAGES IN GROUPS

One of the most important elements of group dynamics is the evolution of group relationships that occurs over time. In fact, there is a wealth of research and theory about how group relationships progress through a sequence of somewhat predictable, though not necessarily linear, stages of development. Cohesion may be the most important dimension of how groups change over time. Generally, most groups develop in a predictable pattern of increasing cohesion. This pattern is true for all types of groups, even work groups in business settings, or study groups in college. It is also true of sexual offender-specific groups, both psychoeducational and therapy process groups. As noted in chapter 2, empirical studies have shown that cohesiveness increases in strength over the course of sexual offender-specific group therapy (Aylwin, 2010; Houston, Wrench, & Hosking, 1995), even for groups composed of the most treatment-resistant psychopathic sexual offenders (Harkins, Beech, & Thornton, 2013).

Models of Group Developmental Stages

Many theorists and researchers have proposed theories or models of group development. Table 5.1 summarizes six models of the stages of group change, three of which we will discuss in more detail. Notice the many corresponding themes across the models, suggesting that there is a discernible course of development for all groups from the early to middle to mature stages.

One of the earliest to study group development was Kurt Lewin, who introduced the term *group dynamics* (Arrow et al., 2005). His ideas about mutual, multi-level influence, although uncommon in the traditional empirical research on group development, have resurged recently. He described group development as a three-stage process: unfreezing, change, and freezing. *Unfreezing* reflects the initial reticence of a new group as the members begin to open up and challenge the long-standing beliefs and behaviors with which they are currently comfortable. *Change* is the stage where the members are increasingly uncomfortable with their current mind-set and modes of behavior, but they are still exploring the possibilities and testing new ways of thinking and relating. *Freezing* is the stage in which members gain a clear understanding of how they want to be—and become comfortable with the new, more fulfilling, and more authentic way of living.

In another model of group developmental stages, Tuckman and Jensen (1977) offer a five-stage schema of five rhyming phases: Forming, Storming, Norming, Performing, and Adjourning.

Stage 1. Forming The *forming* stage is characterized by dependence and the need for safety provided by the group leader. Group members have a need for acceptance by the group. Therefore implicit rules of behavior tend to be simple to avoid controversy, and serious topics and feelings are often avoided. For the group to move from this stage to the next, each member must relinquish the safety of nonthreatening topics and risk the possibility of conflict.

Stage 2. Storming *Storming* is characterized by competition and conflict. Conflicts may or may not surface as overt issues for the group, but they do exist. Common conflicts include leadership, structure, power, and authority. There may be wide swings in members' behavior based on emerging issues of competition and hostilities. Because of the anxiety generated during this stage, some members may remain completely silent while others dominate to reduce their discomfort. In order to progress to the next stage, group members must move from a stay-safe mentality to one of risk taking. The most important individual member trait in helping groups to move on to the next stage seems to be the ability to listen and tolerate interpersonal tension. Leaders among the group members, such as the task leader or the emotional leader, sometimes emerge during this stage. Emerging leadership by group members is beneficial as the group moves beyond dependency on the therapist and the safety of formal structure. This evolving leadership should be monitored to ensure that the members are responsive and that destructive power imbalances do not emerge.

Stage 3. Norming In the *norming* stage, interpersonal relations are characterized by cohesion. Group members are engaged in active acknowledgment of all members' contributions, community building and maintenance, and solving of group issues. Members are willing to change their ideas or opinions on the basis of feedback and disclosures from others and they actively ask questions of one another. Leadership is shared and cliques dissolve. As members begin to know and identify with one another, the level of trust in their personal relations contributes to the development of group cohesion. It is during this stage of development (assuming the group gets this far) that members begin to experience a sense of group belonging and a feeling of relief as a result of resolving interpersonal conflicts. During this stage, members share feelings and ideas and solicit and give feedback to one another. Creativity is high. The members feel good about being part of an effective group. The major challenge of the norming stage is that members may begin to fear the inevitable future breakup of the group and they may resist change of any sort.

Stage 4. Performing The *performing* stage is not reached by all groups. Groups are most productive at this stage. Their capacity, range, and depth of personal relations expand to true interdependence. Individual members are much more self-assured and minimally concerned with group approval. Members are both highly task-oriented and highly people-oriented. There is unity: Group identity is evident, group morale is high, and group loyalty is intense. There is support for risk taking in solving problems and an emphasis on achievement.

Stage 5. Adjourning This stage involves the termination of accustomed treatment task behaviors and disengagement from the relationships formed in the group. Concluding a group can, however, create some serious apprehension—in effect, a minor crisis. The termination of the group is a paradoxical regression from independence (as members prepare to leave the group) to dependence (needing the group therapist to resume a more directive role to facilitate the emotional impact of the departure). Structure can be used as a technique to facilitate the termination and disengagement process. A planned conclusion usually includes recognition for participation and achievement, an acknowledgment of the ending of the relationships, and an opportunity for members to say personal good-byes. Examples could be a ritual of "graduation," saying good-byes, and/or sharing of poignant moments together—and can take the form of symbolic gestures or physical tokens of the group experience, such as a certificate of completion.

TABLE 5.1 SIX THEORIES OF THE STAGES OF GROUP DEVELOPMENT

	Early Stage		Middle Stage			Late Stage		
Lewin (Arrow et al., 2005)	Unfreezing		Change			Freezing		
Yalom (1995)	1. Initial stage: Orientation, hesitant participation, search for meaning, dependency		2. Second stage: Conflict, dominance, rebellion			3. Third stage: Development of cohesion		
MacKenzie & Livesley (1984)	1. Engagement	2. Differentiation	3. Individuation	4. Intimacy	5. Mutuality		6. Termination	
Tuckman (1965); Tuckman & Jensen (1977)	1. Forming	2. Storming	3. Norming		4. Performing		5. Adjourning" (mourning)	
Wheelin (1990; 1994)	Stage I: Dependency and inclusion	Stage II: Counter-dependency and fight	Stage III: Trust/structure		Stage IV: Work productivity		Stage V: Final	
Beck (1981)	1. Making a contract	2. Establishment of a group identity	3. Exploration of a group identity and direction	4. Establishment of intimacy	5. Exploration of mutuality	6. Achievement of autonomy through reorganization of the group's structure	7. Self-confrontation and achievement of interdependence	8. Independence and the transfer of learning	9. Termination

Building on Tuckman's model and her own empirical research, Susan Wheelan proposed an "integrated" model of group development (Wheelan, 1990; 1994). In her model, the early stages of group development are associated with specific issues and patterns related to dependency, counter-dependency, and trust, which must precede the deeper work conducted during the more mature stages of group development.

Stage I. Dependency and inclusion The first stage of group development is characterized by significant member dependency on the designated leader, concerns about safety, and anxiety about inclusion. In this stage, members rely on the leader and the more dominant group members to provide direction. Members may test the waters by engaging in pseudo-work, such as exchanging stories about outside activities or topics that are not relevant to group goals.

Stage II. Counter-dependency and fight In the second stage, members disagree among themselves about group goals and procedures. The group's task at this stage is to develop a unified set of goals, values, and operational procedures, which inevitably generates conflict. But conflict is actually necessary for the development of trust and a climate in which members feel free to disagree with one another.

Stage III. Trust and structure As the group manages to work through the inevitable conflicts of stage II, members develop more trust, commitment to the group, and willingness to cooperate. Communication becomes more open and task-oriented. The third stage is characterized by more mature negotiations about roles, organization, and procedures. It is also a time in which members work to solidify positive working relationships with one another.

Stage IV. Work productivity As its name implies, the fourth stage of group development is a time of intense team productivity and effectiveness. Having resolved many of the issues of the previous stages, the group can focus most of its energy on goal achievement and task accomplishment.

Stage V. Final Groups that have a distinct ending point experience a fifth stage. Impending termination may cause disruption and conflict in some groups. Separation issues need to be addressed, and members need to express their appreciation of one another and the group experience.

All of these models suggest that progression in a group's relationships begins with initial relationship formation, moves through resolving questions of trust to more complex issues, such as conflict and intimacy, and concludes with a deeper level of interpersonal interaction. Group developmental theory holds that each group moves through these stages at a unique pace and that the group must, to some degree, regress to early-stage issues whenever new members are added. The potential therapeutic benefits of the group are tied to the group's ability to successfully navigate these stages. Ultimately, as observed by MacKenzie (1983), future success is correlated with relatedness, which is a function of developmental progress. Consequently, the group therapist needs to attend to stages of developmental growth and assist the group to move beyond initial reticence to trust and cohesion.

Regardless of which developmental model you may prefer, there is an evolving kaleidoscope of dynamic interchange within every group as members work more closely together, resolve conflicts, and gradually settle into more deeply rooted and safe working relationships.

Applying Knowledge of Group Developmental Stages

As an overarching principle guiding group practice, group therapists should endeavor to facilitate member-to-member interactions so that the group can progress from the early stage issues of distrust, anxiety, and dependence on the therapist to the middle and mature stages where members engage in the types of constructive conflict and risk-taking openness needed to evolve toward increasing intimacy and cohesion. To do so, the group therapist should be attentive to the current developmental stage of the group so that the choice of interventions and facilitation are appropriately matched to the current level of functioning. Accordingly, we recommend the broad guidelines shown in table 5.2 for facilitating the early and later developmental stages of a group.

Remember also that, for open-ended groups, *the earlier group developmental stages are revisited each time a new member joins the group.* In particular, when a new member joins a group, the initial stage of trust is automatically experienced by all members. The group therapist needs to be attentive to both the experience of new members, and how the new member is affecting established members, and adjust his or her facilitation accordingly. Attention should be paid to how members welcome the new member and how the new member is invited to participate so that he is not left to sit in silence for weeks on end.

TABLE 5.2 FACILITATING EARLY AND LATER DEVELOPMENTAL STAGES OF A GROUP

Early Stage of Group:	Middle and Mature Stages of Group:
• Do not expect (or push for) too much sharing or open risk-taking in group until some initial trust has been established.	• Expect and facilitate openness, emotional expression, and intimacy.
• Make frequent reference to the structural integrity (group agreement) of the new group. Adherence to clear predictable rules and boundaries provides a sense of safety and security for anxious and inexperienced members.	• Structure has been incorporated into the norms and values of the group and does not need to be explicitly invoked unless there is testing of the roles or boundaries.
• Expect a higher level of reticence and greater dependence on the group therapist to actively guide and support the members.	• Facilitate increasing self-directed participation from the group and allow the group to try to manage its own struggles/conflicts.
• Be prepared to be more active, educative, and directive with a new group, providing clear encouragement and strong explicit reinforcement of member participation.	• Expect the group to self-initiate participation, while facilitating deeper expression of emotions.
• Be very careful about allowing too much anger too soon. Act quickly and decisively to stem harsh communications that can be attacking, shaming, threatening, or intimidating. Members are already fearful and need the reassurance that they are safe from attack.	• A group with well-established trust and cohesion can tolerate and manage very intense emotions like anger. Intervene if necessary, but allow the group to process and manage the situation themselves so they can learn how to manage intense emotions constructively.
• Draw attention to instances in which members help other members. Reframe ineffective attempts as well-intended help, and suggest a better way to give constructive feedback.	• Draw attention to the deeper emotional value and bonding that results when members help other members.
• Be careful in managing silence. An extended period of silence can be especially frightening for new members. Acknowledge silence as a normal and potentially positive event. Give the group reassurance during silence to "take your time." Reframe silence as an opportunity for members to introspect and feel more deeply and to simply be together.	• Use silence as an opportunity for members to feel more deeply in the here-and-now and/or to process profound moments in the group – together as a bonded and caring group.

In the next example, a group in the early developmental stage needs leader intervention and structure.

A New Group Needs More Direction and Structure

Dave was talking about his family of origin and how women were treated differently in his patriarchal family. When Dave described an incident at home with his wife, Mike responded with the dismissive comment, "Well, you know, shit happens." Dave erupted with anger, pointed his finger and exclaimed, "You're racist. Don't treat me that way." Mike countered by saying, "Well, you're always preaching to us." This sort of spontaneous emotional attack had never happened in this group, which had been meeting weekly for about three months. The two group leaders intervened to stop the angry exchange from escalating further. They summoned the group's rules of respectful listening and feedback and took a more directive role for the remainder of the session.

In the next session, the leaders asked the group how they felt about the eruption, and what members needed in order for the group to feel safe and respectful again. The members complained of inequality between members who prepared their assignments and those who did not, as well as difficulties with keeping focused on the treatment goals, and often losing valuable time with chitchat and digressions. The group wanted more active involvement and direction from the leaders to maintain focus on goals. Members also asked for more educational handouts, a stronger rule against interruptions, and help from the leaders to enforce homework preparedness. Clearly, the desire for a more active group leader role was a reflection of early-stage dependency and limited trust among members.

Although the angry outburst this group experienced was atypical and upsetting, it can also be seen (positively) as a somewhat normal characteristic of a group moving from the early to middle stages of development. Depending on which model you prefer, this could be viewed as a group moving from the Forming stage to the Storming stage (Tuckman, 1965) or, alternatively, as a group entering the middle stage of conflict, dominance, and rebellion (Yalom, 1995) or stage II counter-dependency and fight (Wheelan, 1994).

In this case, the two group therapists conferred with each other and recognized that the outburst may indeed have been reflective of the group's stage of development. They concurred that this early-stage group was not mature and cohesive enough to manage this level of emotional conflict yet. They decided to slow down and reaffirm the protective structure and rules of the group to restore safety and stability, and to take a more directive role in steering communications within the group.

Remarkably, the very process of working together to discuss and identify what they wanted for "our group" served to strengthen trust and commitment and became an important turning point for the cohesion of this group.

Compared to the prior example, a mature group is able to work with each other in an intense emotional moment.

A Mature Group in the Working Stage

Bill had a history of drug and alcohol use and had sexually abused the five-year-old daughter of his girlfriend. He asked for time to work on his own abuse experiences and to read an unsent letter he had written to his biological father, who had been murdered more than 20 years before. As Bill read the letter, his verbal tone was stiff, monotone, and constrained. Given his lack of emotion, the group leader asked how he was feeling. "It's hard to say. I'm angry and sad both." The group knew that one of Bill's treatment goals was allowing himself to experience his emotions in the moment without engaging in suppression defenses. One member gently challenged Bill, saying, "You read the letter but you didn't feel what you were feeling." Bill nodded. "I know. It's hard for me. When I was little, I was scared to show my feelings because it meant I was weak." The group members shared similar feelings of anger at their own fathers and similar stories of trying to act tough to hide their fear and weakness. Roy said, "You read your letter without any feelings. I did the same darn thing." The group broke into laughter at their similarities—with tears in their eyes.

The therapist said very little during this exchange, allowing the group to work together to support Bill by sharing their own similar experiences, and allowing them to challenge Bill in how he was continuing to suppress very strong and conflicted feelings about his father. Clearly, this is a more mature group that has the strong trust and cohesion that enables them to confront each other and risk openness in expressing vulnerable emotions.

Depending on the particular model you prefer, this group could be characterized as stage 4, intimacy (Mackenzie & Liveley, 1984); stage 3, cohesion (Yalom, 1995); or stage 7, self-confrontation and achievement of interdependence (Beck, 1981). Whatever the term, this group was in a *working stage* of late-middle group development. The members were highly engaged, communicating directly and honestly to one another, and showing a balanced expression of both support and challenge. The group experienced universality from its deeply shared sense of common experience, altruism from members freely helping one another, and cohesion from their feelings of belonging and acceptance.

Summary and Conclusions

Content, process, structure, and developmental stages are all part of the life of a group, and all these elements need the vigilant attention of the group therapist. We discussed the essential nature of structure, and the significance of the therapist's role in maintaining structure to provide a safe and predictable environment for the group. Process is always observable, and more significant at some moments than others. Process comprises the words spoken, who is speaking and to whom, and body language and other nonverbal communications. We naturally attend to the content—what is said, the words used. However, the process—i.e., patterns of interaction, evolving leadership, and progression through developmental stages—is ongoing and should be a focus of attention when it contributes to the goals of the group or when a dysfunctional process is occurring. Observing process patterns is an essential exercise for the group facilitator and the group members. Understanding the developmental stages of groups is also important because the group therapist can better match the choice of interventions and facilitation to the current developmental level of the group (and individuals within the group).

CHAPTER 6

Facilitating the Group

What happens in this group should have happened in my family.

—Client nearing the end of treatment

The composition of the group and the structure that is established and maintained will shape what needs to happen in each session and how the group facilitator interacts with the group. Grounded in the ability to observe and identify group dynamics, effective facilitation is a matter of choosing when to respond and how best to respond at any particular moment in a session. The available research on group therapy does not demonstrate a direct causal link between facilitator actions and client outcomes; nor does it give us a manual for how to facilitate effective groups. Nevertheless, we can apply the extant literature for guidance on how to conceptualize group events and facilitate therapeutic opportunities.

In this chapter, we will emphasize the crucial importance of facilitating a *group-focused* group. In contrast with group therapy that focuses on one member at a time (what we call individual therapy in a group), group-focused group therapy focuses on group dynamics and the relationships within the group. By seeing each individual in the context of group interactions, we gain an enriched understanding of individual members and their problems and deficits.

LEAD, RUN, OR FACILITATE?

Your group leadership style is partly driven by how you view your role. Is your job to lead the group, run the group, or facilitate the group? To *lead* implies that you are the leader and the members are willing followers. To *run* implies that you are the authority and have sole responsibility for all that occurs (or fails to occur) in the group. To *facilitate* the group, however, implies assistance and collaboration in which the members retain the responsibility for their own change. Effective facilitation is the synthesis of the unique blend of your knowledge about your clients and the group processes, your expectations of the group at any moment in a session, your reactions to the content and process that are occurring, and your instinct—what we call the art of group facilitation.

How we facilitate is influenced by the social and professional context within in which we work. Given our heightened concern for public safety in this field, we often feel personal responsibility for our clients' success or failure in treatment. Assuming responsibility for their progress can push us (often unconsciously) into taking excessive control over the group process. This is difficult because we are so often faced with attitudes and behavior that make it hard to trust our sexual offending clients. *Is he lying? Is he denying? Is he deceiving me? Is he still engaged in deviant fantasies? Is he continuing to seek or groom victims?*

In addition to the internal pressure of feeling overly responsible, group therapists are inundated with information from the group. At any given time, there are dozens of observable events that can be clinically significant—verbal and nonverbal messages, personal reactions, exchanges between members, emotions expressed (or suppressed), and more. Part of the art of group facilitation is managing our own reactions to these internal and external forces, while we are choosing and applying the following techniques of effective facilitation.

Include Everyone and Get All to Participate

One of the primary therapeutic factors in group therapy is the experience of connection to the other group members (Yalom, 1995). It is essential to make a concerted effort to include every member in every session, if possible. This is especially important for the quiet ones—those who are reticent to participate because of shyness, insecurity, or avoidance. Even if you can do little more than give eye contact or a nod or another gesture of acknowledgment, you need to let every member know that he is acknowledged and valued. Your consistent efforts to encourage everyone to participate will contribute to the essential feeling of commonality in the group, which ultimately leads to cohesion. It says that every group member, no matter how small he may feel himself, is capable of helping his peers and making a valuable contribution to the success of the group. The altruistic experience of giving help to another member can be a powerful therapeutic boost to someone who feels insignificant, hopeless, lonely, and incompetent.

Greeting New Members

When a new member is placed in an ongoing, open-ended group, it is essential that each existing member is given the opportunity to welcome the new member, introduce himself, and learn something about the new member. Remember also that every time a new member joins a group, the process reverts to the initial developmental stage issue of trust. The entry of a new person naturally changes the dynamic of the group; all members need to feel out the change of balance and learn to trust the new member. This process is, of course, less difficult for established groups with strong cohesion. As the group leader, you can draw upon the existing group cohesion to reassure the new member that he is welcome to join the shared experience of the group and reassure the current members that the group is still safe and strong. The group therapist needs to be attentive to and encourage participation from the new member.

The next example illustrates one method of welcoming a new member.

Welcoming a New Member

An outpatient group had been meeting weekly for two years. Because this was an open group, new members occasionally joined as older members completed treatment and moved on. The group went through its usual ritual of welcoming Jack, the newest member, and introduced themselves. When invited to introduce himself, Jack said he was nervous and uncomfortable and not sure what to say. The more experienced members chimed in, "It's okay. We've all been there. It gets easier after you've been in group for a while." There was a warm round of laughter that helped Jack feel welcome and accepted.

Saying Good-Bye to Departing Members

Saying good-bye is as important as saying hello. When a member leaves the group, it is important to give everyone the opportunity to say good-bye and acknowledge the personal meaning of having known him. This highlights the lasting impact and value of relationships, even if it includes the sadness of losing a bond. This action models respect in relationships and illuminates the importance of attachments when members leave the group.

In addition to modeling social skills, the acts of greeting new members and saying good-bye to departing members emphasizes the high value of relationships and belonging. It helps the men to process both the anxiety of new relationships and the feelings of loss when members leave the group, while also being reassured of their continued place in a strong and supportive group.

The next example shows a group experience of cohesion and reflections on the impact of the group.

"I'm Going to Miss Coming Here"

Roy was ready to finish treatment and leave the group. As Roy spoke about how much he valued the group, Lenny suggested that Roy could simply extend his time and not leave. Roy responded, "Maybe the group could put me on speakerphone and I could join you from work." Everyone laughed. Stan looked at Roy and joked, "Now that you're leaving, who is going to keep me in line?" Several group members raised their hands. Again the group laughed. Lenny picked up on Stan's comment and spoke more seriously. "It's going to be very different. Who will take the torch of confronting us when we need it?" Roy responded that he had a lot of confidence in the group's ability to do well without him, emphasized how much he had learned and gained from the group, and concluded by saying, "I'm going to miss coming here and being with people who have been through the same wringer."

In this brief closing ritual, Roy was able to acknowledge his indebtedness to the group and say good-bye, while the group was able to acknowledge the contributions made by Roy and say their good-byes. Their humor and camaraderie in saying good-bye reflected their bonds and connectedness. The group was able to process the loss of Roy's important role of "calling a spade a spade" and challenging the group when needed. As group members reflected on how far Roy had come and what he had accomplished, they accepted the responsibility of taking the torch and felt a strong sense of hope—the therapeutic factor of *instillation of hope*. They also experienced the therapeutic factor of *altruism* as they reflected on how much they were able to help one another, and how Roy felt good about his contribution to the group. There was also a reflection of the developmental stage process as the group reflected on how many of them had difficulty with trust when they first started the group and how Roy had been able to develop trust in the group over time.

Facilitate Member-to-Member Interaction and Shared Goals

The group therapist should maintain a consistent focus on group interactions and relationships in the present moment. This means that interventions should be directed to the group, rather than individual members, and should bring the group process to the foreground. Facilitating active group interaction generates energy and engagement, and builds trust, cohesion, and commitment. Here are some techniques that you can use to foster interaction among the members in the group:

1. Make interventions that draw attention to, or elicit, interaction among group members.
2. When a member speaks directly to the therapist only, redirect his question or communication to the whole group to elicit their response.
3. Be cautious about allowing one member to dominate the discussion or to be the center of attention for an extended period. Instead reframe the individual's problem as one that is likely shared by others and encourage other members to react and contribute.
4. Recognize and point out themes that are shared by or pertinent to multiple members, such as similar problems, situations, beliefs, feelings, and experiences.
5. Draw attention to the positive feelings and bonding that ensue after members support or help one another, for both the givers and receivers.
6. Although each member may have his own unique set of individual goals, there will be a lot of commonality in goals among the members. When something is pertinent to one member's goal, it will probably be pertinent to several members. Draw attention to the shared connection.

Roving Eye Contact

Roving eye contact (REC) is a very active, continuous, and purposeful facilitation action by the group therapist that is a crucial foundation for effective observation and intervention (Jennings & Sawyer, 2004; Jennings & Deming, 2013). REC, which is frequently little more than a fleeting glance, continuously reminds each group member that he is not alone, that this is a group experience, and that he is connected to others in the group, like it or not. Through REC, every group member gets repeated, tangible attention, regardless of his level of verbal engagement in the group. At the same time, through simple observational learning, group members begin to use roving eye contact themselves, which literally opens their eyes to the presence and individuality of the other people in the group and the relatedness within the group. By continually attending visually to one group member after another, the group therapist can enhance the range, depth, and utility of verbal and nonverbal behavioral data about the group, which improves assessment and intervention, while also role modeling and reinforcing prosocial interaction for the group. Thus REC naturally counteracts egocentric behavior and thinking, and, in conjunction with other interventions, can promote empathy, listening skills, and relatedness. REC also counteracts the tendency for the therapist (and the group members) to focus too intensely on the individual currently speaking rather than maintain awareness of the vitally important social relations and interactions within the group.

Active Facilitation
Active facilitation means that the group leader is thoroughly engaged in every word, nuance, and communication among members in a dynamic way that enables him or her to take an active role when needed, or a more observant stance when the group is working well on its own. Being active does not mean talking or intervening more often. It means being attuned to what is happening in the here and now and being ready to intervene immediately to inhibit harmful exchanges or illuminate a salient exchange or emotional moment. It means intervening as often as needed so that the group stays focused on the task, topic, or issue under discussion, and helping members to engage emotionally and interpersonally.

Being active is being both engaged and strategic. At times being active is being educational when the group needs information. At other times being active means asking the group to pause to absorb the impact of an intensely emotional event. It is essential to the maintenance of a group-centered group that the facilitator is active when needed and less active when the group is interacting effectively. An active role also models a secure attachment style, countering the insecure attachment styles that characterize most sexual abusers (as discussed in chapter 7).

Facilitate to Manage Six Deficits in Group Composition
The traits and capacities of individual group members assigned to a particular group have a significant impact on overall group functioning. As discussed in chapter 4, sexual offenders tend to be deficient in many of the six recommended criteria for group composition (see table 4.1 in chapter 4). In this section, we will present strategies and facilitation techniques that can help mitigate the negative impact of individual deficits in each of the six criteria:

1. Motivation to change and improve.
2. Skills and capabilities to participate in reciprocal group interactions.
3. Ability to express emotions effectively.
4. Recognition of the interpersonal nature of their problems.
5. Capacity for empathy.
6. Capacity to give and receive feedback.

Motivation to Change

In this field, many of our court-ordered and involuntary clients are not motivated for treatment and can be at various stages of motivation to change. When working with groups with disparate levels of motivation, there is a risk that those who are eager to engage in treatment may resist taking personal risks in front of less motivated members. This dynamic stifles cohesion and prevents the group from advancing to higher levels of openness and trust. In this situation, the facilitator can try to reverse the dynamic so that the engaged members can help motivate the less engaged clients. setting an example of growth and success. Encouraging the more motivated members to engage in their treatment work while facilitating feedback from other motivated members will role model the potential benefits of engagement for less motivated members. Another facilitation intervention is to periodically invite the group to discuss these differences in motivation by asking the more motivated members to describe what they have gained and still hope to gain from the group. This can take the form of having the member recall his own lack of motivation or feelings of hopelessness when he first began treatment and how the group helped him to make changes.

Capability to Participate in Reciprocal Interactions

In this field, it is not uncommon that we must accept members into our groups who may be decidedly lower in their level of intellectual, social, and psychological functioning. The group research indicates that, when possible, we should exclude clients who are psychotic, have cognitive impairments, or have severely limited interpersonal skills. These clients often have a difficult time in groups. They are likely to have the most disturbed attachment histories, and can easily be disruptive or marginalized non-contributors. Under these conditions, active facilitation is needed to mitigate the distracting traits and reinforce positive, engaged member-to-member interactions.

It is disruptive when such a member has difficulty following the focus of the topic being discussed and then makes comments or gives feedback that is off topic or misses the point of the conversation. As an example of this problem, we discussed the case of Aaron in chapter 5. Aaron was a 69-year-old group member with cognitive deficits who often struggled to comprehend the topic of discussion and caused disruption when he would lose his focus or misunderstand.

One facilitation strategy is to appeal to the altruism of the group members by eliciting their compassion and support to help the struggling member. In this case, the group therapist tried to turn the disruption into an opportunity for the group to pull together to assist Aaron. For example, the leader could say, "What can we do to help Aaron?" or "Is there a different way to explain this so that Aaron can understand?" This facilitation intervention encourages cooperative problem solving and reinforces nonjudgmental acceptance of others.

Or the therapist may apply the technique of active facilitation by educating or giving guidance to the group members to improve their skills in giving constructive feedback to one another. Or, finally, another technique is to point to Aaron's good intention to help another group member, even if he may have misunderstood or missed the mark with his comment. This reframes Aaron's deficit and the disruption into an positive expression of his caring and his desire to contribute to the group.

Ability to Express Emotions

Expressing emotion is another area where sexual abusers often have difficulty. Many, perhaps most, have a constricted emotional range and may speak in an overly controlled and intellectualizing style that has little emotional energy. During the group, they may feel and react strongly inside, but tend to hide or hold it in with tight controls. When they do emote, however, it can burst out in extreme forms, such as an eruption of anger and rage. They may avoid emotion because it feels like a loss of control and is associated with feelings of pain and fear from childhood.

There are three general approaches to facilitating a group in which the members are passive, emotionally constricted, and/or intellectualizing. First, when faced with a poorly composed group like this, the group leader can try to increase the diversity of emotional styles in the group. As we saw in the case example in chapter 4, one therapist dreaded his Tuesday-night group because the group was composed almost entirely of men with avoidant personality styles, who withheld emotions and barely participated. The overly homogeneous group lacked members who could be more interactive and able to express emotions. The result was low energy and poor cohesion. Recognizing the composition problem, the group therapist brought in more energetic members and moved some of the constricted members to another group.

Second, the group therapist can use the reassurance of structure and rules to maintain a climate that feels safe enough to increasingly risk emotional disclosure and expression. Third, when there is a dearth of emotional disclosure, the group leader should draw attention to the emotional dimension in member interactions. The leader should try to include all members in the group interactions and reward members with praise after they risk feeling and expressing emotions. He or she can also gently encourage members to feel emotions by redefining moments of silence as opportunities to simply sit and feel inwardly.

Recognition of Interpersonal Nature of Problems

When sexual abuse clients begin group therapy, they are often unaware of the interpersonal basis for their problems. They may be acutely aware of their isolation, shame, and loneliness, but they do not yet see how sexual offending behavior can be rooted in these same interpersonal deficiencies. Many may externalize responsibility for their actions or their situation. The group therapist should try to facilitate the member-to-member interactions to create relational experiences for the men and help them experience the rewards of genuine connection in an accepting group. The therapist can also role model the importance of personal responsibility. and use interventions that help to (re)define their problems as interpersonal.

Capacity for Empathy

The capacity for empathy varies among men with sexual abuse problems, but it is generally presumed that most are severely lacking in empathy, especially with regard to their victims. In fact, there have been major debates in this field as to whether empathy should even be a target of treatment given the lack of any consistent research evidence that empathy is related to risk for reoffense. Others argue that this inconsistency merely reflects the diversity and unreliability of the measures of empathy that have been used.

Our clinical opinion is that empathy and altruism are extremely important therapeutic factors that occur frequently in sexual offender-specific group therapy. The key is being alert to expressions of empathy and caring when they occur in group in order to draw attention to them and label them as such. Our clients often make supportive statements or gestures, but need help to recognize their emotions of caring and being cared for. The group therapist needs to take advantage of opportunities to support empathic engagement to the extent that clients are capable. This can be done by drawing attention to such events and labeling them as empathy. It can also be facilitated with questions like, "If you [the group] were in Paul's shoes, how would you feel right now?" or "If you care about how Paul is feeling, what might you say to him?"

In the next case example, the group was unexpectedly empathic in a shared and emotionally intense moment.

Facilitating Member-to-Member Empathy

Paul had been convicted of sexual abuse of a 15-year-old neighbor girl. He denied much of the offense and spent four years in prison. He also had numerous contacts with the law for driving violations, driving under the influence, and drug possession. Paul began the group session by saying that his probation officer was going to apply sanctions because he had been caught abusing meth by a random drug screen. "I should've known better. I was doing so well. I was on the right track." Even though the violation had nothing to do with his sexual offense, Paul now faced a serious chance of being sent back to prison.

The group queried him about what had happened. Paul explained that he "just happened" to meet some friends at the local bar, who then "just happened" to invite him over to their apartment, where they "just happened" to be abusing speed. Although it was clear that Paul had made a series of poor choices, he continued to externalize responsibility for his actions as if everything was unplanned and things "just happened."

It would have been easy at this point for the group leader or the group members to confront Paul about his responsibility for making bad choices. And chances are good that Paul would have responded defensively with more rationalizations and the group would have again felt frustrated and disconnected. But then one member said something that picked up on the deeper emotional current in the group at that moment.

Tony turned to Paul and said, "I sure hope it doesn't happen because we're gonna really miss you." The group therapist seized upon this rare instance of emotion and empathy by simply restating Tony's words and asking the group how they felt. Mike responded with something even more heartfelt and surprising when he spoke directly to Paul, saying, "I feel bad for you. I feel like it's my fault." Mike explained that he had talked to Paul in the parking lot after the previous group session and Paul had invited Mike to talk about cars. "If I had just stopped to talk with you, maybe you wouldn't have gone to that bar in the first place." Mike suggested that Paul had been feeling lonely and that that was the reason he made the poor choice to hang out with the drug-abusing friends. "I could have been your friend," Mike added, "but I let you down."

Until this particular night, this group had lacked much cohesion and the sessions were often disjointed, dull, and lacking in emotional expression and empathy. By expressing direct concern for Paul during his crisis—rather than directly challenging his poor decision making—the group discovered a deeper layer of caring. For the first time, group members were talking personally and openly with one another and they began to bond as a group.

Giving or Receiving Feedback

It is common to observe significant differences in sexual offenders' ability to give and accept feedback. Therefore, it is sometimes necessary for the group leader to be directive and educational about the methods of constructive criticism—especially with newly formed groups or new members. It may also be useful to systematically go around the room to elicit feedback from each group member so that there is more equal participation and all members have the experience of learning to give constructive comments to one another.

When clients struggle to engage one another verbally or to engage in reciprocal give-and-take, active facilitation calls for the leader to engage those members by role modeling and inviting silent members to respond and become more engaged. This can be accomplished by first posing a question to the whole group, then asking individual members to offer their thoughts, and then reinforcing their efforts with praise. By encouraging all members to contribute, each member has the experience of talking as an equal and making a contribution. By engaging members in giving feedback and reacting to what others say in the group, the group leader gives them the positive experience of having something valuable to offer to others, thereby activating the experience of altruism.

Applying Five Established Group Principles to Sexual Offender Groups

Sawyer and Jennings (2014) applied the empirically investigated principles identified by Burlingame et al. (2002) to group work with sexual offenders to illustrate the applicability of general group therapy research to this field. The five principles can be translated into five essential leader actions:

1. Maintain clear and consistent structure.
2. Facilitate member-to-member interaction.
3. Engage in actions that foster cohesion.
4. Facilitate and manage verbal interactions.
5. Facilitate the emotional climate.

Maintain Clear and Consistent Structure

As we discussed in chapter 4, *pre-group preparation* is a foundational task that sets the stage for an effective group structure. Client preparation comprises educating members about how group therapy works, teaching the expectations of being a member of a therapy group, educating the client on how to engage in the group as a constructive contributing member, and allaying fears and anxiety about the group experience. When prepared, the client is better able to benefit from facilitated member-to-member interactions and be more receptive to cohesion as it evolves in the group.

The ongoing maintenance of structure continues to be the most basic and essential action of a group therapist. This includes clear boundaries, such as starting and ending times, commitment to attendance, participation, confidentiality, limited contact outside the group, timely payment of fees, focus on treatment goals, and respectful support of other members' pursuit of their treatment goals. Structure is essential for consistency, safety, and long-term stability of the group and assures that all group members are treated equally.

Even something as seemingly minor as starting the group at the scheduled time and clearly ending on time is very important. For example, starting group five or ten minutes late sends the message that you or tardy members do not respect and value the group's time. Group members who come prepared to work on their treatment goals, in particular, will be frustrated by wasting the first 10 minutes in idle waiting. Likewise, allowing the group to continue beyond the set stopping time shows disrespect for the members' time and sets a negative example of the importance of time management. Breaking time boundaries also communicates a devaluing of the group's precious treatment time, insensitivity to the members, and conveys a dismissive or avoidant attitude toward the group.

Facilitate Member-to-Member Interaction

Facilitating group member engagement with one another is the foundation for cohesion, which is a crucial therapeutic factor in all groups. Member-to-member interactions provide the energy of group. When group facilitators focus on one member at a time, and when interactions occur solely between the group therapist and individual members, the group becomes stilted, boring, demotivating, and disconnected. Members tune out and passively wait to be called on by the group therapist. As shown in figure 6.1, this is therapist-centered group therapy.

Figure 6.1 Therapist-Centered Group

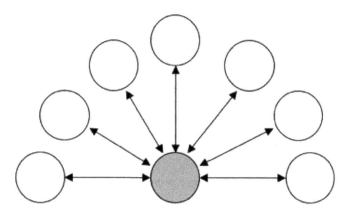

Instead, in group-centered group therapy (see figure 6.2), the leader should continually facilitate interactions among the members (especially by urging members to respond to one another directly) and by routinely *addressing and referring to the group as a whole*. Talking to the whole group (e.g., "What is the group's reaction to what John said?" or "What does the group think?") engages the group members as equals. Speaking to the members as a group, not as individuals, empowers all to join and contribute and helps them to connect with one another. This is illustrated in the next case example.

Figure 6.2 Group-Centered Group

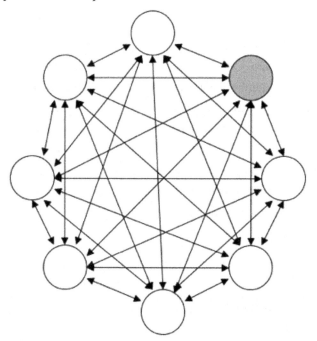

Facilitating Member-to-Member Interaction

Paul asked for time to present his assignment on creating a safety plan. When he finished, the therapist waved her arm across the group and said, "What does the group think about what Paul said?" Henry spoke first, telling the therapist what he thought Paul should do. Bart agreed with Henry's critique, but he, too, addressed his comments to the therapist. The group therapist gently interrupted their feedback by using hand gestures to redirect Henry and Bart to look at Paul. "This is good, but say it to Paul." The members quickly grasped the idea and spoke directly to Paul.

Directing the group to talk directly to Paul shifted the focus from the therapist as the "director" and empowered the group members to become more engaged with one another. It conveyed the fact that every member's ideas are valued and every member has wisdom to share—and connected them to one another.

Engage in Actions That Foster Cohesion

Cohesion has been reliably correlated with client progress (Burlingame, 2011), as well as reduced symptoms and the quality of the group climate. Facilitating cohesion may be the leader action that has the most significant positive and long-term impact on the effectiveness of a group. Cohesion is the glue in groups, and a key mechanism of change. It occurs when members experience caring for other members and the group as a whole. When members are engaged with one another, they become invested in one another's success. This fosters trust, which is the container for self-disclosure and risk taking, which, in turn, facilitates learning new ways of relating and progress toward treatment goals. The group leader can foster cohesion by facilitating each of the four simultaneous alliances that constitute cohesion: therapist to group; member to member; member to group; and member to therapist.

Therapist to group The therapist can facilitate this aspect in two ways. First, as shown in the sexual offender-specific group research (see chapter 2), the leader should express the four therapist characteristics of warmth, empathy, encouragement, and guidance, and avoid the use of confrontation. Second, the therapist can use interventions that engage the whole group and that draw group members together as a whole, such as, "What is the group feeling right now?" or "What is the group's reaction?"

Member to member The leader can facilitate this aspect of cohesion by facilitating verbal interactions and emotional engagement directly between members. For example, the leader could connect members using simple clarifications, such as, "What did you hear Mike say to you?" or "How do you feel about what Jack offered?"

Member to group Each member has a relationship with the whole group and the group has a relationship with each member. The therapist can facilitate this aspect of cohesion with interventions that subsume the group as a whole, such as, "What can the group offer to Ted in this moment?" or "There's a lot of sadness in the group right now."

Member to therapist Cohesion also occurs between individual members and the therapist. Sometimes giving personal attention to an individual during the group session can be helpful, such as giving extra reassurance or support to a new member or a member in crisis. But we strongly urge group therapists to use it selectively and, when used, to be mindful of how other group members are responding to that individualized attention (as evidenced in their facial expressions and body language or subsequent comments).

Facilitate and Manage Verbal Interactions

The facilitation and timing of verbal interactions has been found to contribute to group cohesion and effective group process. Member-to-member interaction is influenced by how the leader manages verbal interactions between members and between leader and members. In fact, group therapy researchers have studied the micro-processes of verbal interaction within groups and have identified several empirically supported interventions that yield optimal results.

1. **The therapist role models desired behavior** The group leader is the primary role model for the use of appropriate language, tone, and emotional intensity. The facilitator supports positive group interaction while discouraging unhealthy or inappropriate conflict.
2. **The therapist responds in the moment** In general, the group leader should respond to the group with in-the-moment observations or interventions in a manner that demonstrates empathy, warmth, and understanding. It is better for the group therapist to respond to the group in the moment rather than waiting and commenting later or in a future group. This might sound like, "John, what are you feeling right now after what the group just said to you?"

3. **Facilitate feedback between members** In addition to facilitating member-to-member communication as described above, the group therapist must be ready to give guidance to those verbal communications. There are numerous opportunities for the therapist and members to give feedback, correct thinking errors, challenge attitudes, or offer support, yet in any given moment a client may not be prepared to hear or accept the particular feedback being offered (and/or the giver of that feedback may not be skilled enough to deliver his feedback in a positive way). The group therapist assesses both the ability of a given member to receive feedback in that moment, and the ability of the giver to articulate feedback in a constructive fashion. This includes intervening to give specific instructions to group members in how to give feedback and how to receive feedback, as well as suggesting alternative ways of verbalizing feedback. Or it may entail guidance in helping members to respond to one another directly.
4. **Interrupt injurious feedback** Member-to-member relationships can be emotionally charged, and communication can result in intentional or unintentional emotional injury. In this respect, it is essential that the group leader actively intervene to ensure that harm is limited, relationships are not damaged, and the experience is understood in a reparative way.
5. **Reinforce appropriate self-disclosure** The group leader encourages and nurtures emotional disclosure from the members. This is done, first, by identifying and discussing the members' fears and concerns about revealing highly personal information that may be embarrassing, painful, or emotionally overwhelming, and by reaffirming the safety and trust of the group. It includes praising efforts to disclose, as well as interrupting self-disclosure that is inappropriate, ill timed, threatening, or excessive. Another technique is helping members to self-disclose in the here and now (which heightens emotion and energy) rather than "storytelling" in the past tense (which stifles emotion).

Facilitate the Emotional Climate

Emotional climate is one of the foundational elements of cohesion in groups and is related to the therapeutic factor of catharsis, which is the experience of relief from emotional distress through the free and uninhibited expression of emotion. Maintaining the emotional climate is using the supportive relationships of the group to facilitate the constructive expression of emotions by members. By consistently conveying the empirically based therapist qualities of warmth, empathy, understanding, and guidance, the leader sets the emotional tone for the group. The leader role models attentive listening to show that all members are equally valued and that their concerns are of equal importance. To nurture the emotional climate, the leader offers support and, at times, challenges the members in ways that they feel understood by the leader and the group. As shown in the following example, the group therapist is aware of the effects of emotional expression on all members, both direct and vicarious, and facilitates opportunities for cathartic emotional expression.

In these case examples, the group coalesced around two members' cathartic moment.

Catharsis and a Reassuring Silence

The group had been meeting for many months. Stan was one of the most verbal and emotionally expressive members, in many ways the emotional leader. He started the group session with very emotional news, stating, "I am a wreck, my cancer is back." He showed a visible tumor on his neck to the group, and struggled to express his fear and anguish with emotionally choked words. The group showed their support by listening attentively, but when Stan finished, the group sat silent for a long time.

The group therapist facilitated by asking, "What is the group feeling right now after hearing Stan's bad news?" Paul said, "That sucks man, I feel for you." Others said the same, or nodded sympathetically. Then George spoke with tears in his eyes. "I'm really scared, too. My dad is going into the hospital tomorrow for surgery, but he wouldn't tell me why, so I don't know how bad it is. He could die . . ." The group fell into a new silence, but one that felt reassuring and strong rather than overwhelmed. Several showed their own tears. The group therapist allowed the positive silence to continue, saying only, "We don't need any words to feel the caring in our group."

In this highly emotional session, Stan and George experienced catharsis by being able to freely express the fear and loneliness of facing an unknown future. At first, the group was uncomfortable with the intimacy and intensity of the emotions and could offer little more than verbal expressions of empathy. Then George added even more emotion to the moment. The group leader acknowledged the positive nature of the silence and simply encouraged the group to sit with their reactions, thus giving the group the opportunity to feel the intimacy and intense emotions more deeply. Contrary to their usual pattern of emotional suppression, the group learned that they were able to tolerate these very intense emotions—and they, too, experienced catharsis in the session.

Let's consider another example of facilitating the emotional climate of a group. In this case, the therapist facilitates the experience of tolerating conflicting emotions.

Learning to Experience and Contain Intense Emotions as a Group

Roy asked for time to work on his treatment goal of processing his own personal abuse in childhood. He began by telling a disjointed story about his alcoholic father, who died when Roy was 12. He described his father as emotionally unpredictable, sometimes caring, but sometimes verbally abusive. With a distinct rise in emotion, Roy blurted out that he was angry at his father, but then quickly stifled his emotion and insisted that he also loved and admired him. He rambled on about how his father would pick him up from school and take him for a drive, eventually ending up at a bar. While it was initially fun to play video games in the bar, he came to dread and fear his father's drunken driving on the ride home. As he told his story, he vacillated between nervous laughter and tearfulness, between anger at being mistreated and neglected and longing for his father's love.

Other members of the group began to relate to both emotional states. Some members acknowledged their fear of their fathers, while others expressed only positive memories. But most, like Roy, had strong mixed feelings about their fathers. Roy reiterated his emotional confusion between feeling both anger and love for his father. He confessed that he was relieved when his father died, but then spent the next ten years feeling guilty and depressed over his father's passing.

The group therapist intervened at this point by asking Roy and the other members to sit quietly with the conflicted emotions and to stop asking questions or analyzing Roy's relationship with his father. Learning to contain and experience intense emotions without resorting to defensive avoidance was a challenge for many of the members. Instead, the group therapist directed the group to simply feel the sensations of their shared conflicting emotions—without words or analysis. Group members experienced connectedness and emotional catharsis as they shared the dilemma of conflicted feelings for their fathers, and they also learned how difficult it was to stay in the moment with those feelings.

Facilitating Silence in Groups

Silence is a common and important event in group therapy. It can be negative or positive and can mean different things at different times. That is why the next section of this chapter on facilitation will focus on managing silence in the group.

Being Comfortable with Silence

The first and most basic facilitation skill for silence is simply learning to be comfortable with it. For most people, not just members of therapy groups, the experience of an extended moment of silence with other people is anxiety provoking and uncomfortable. There is a strong impulse for someone to say something, anything, as soon as possible, to break the awkward silence. The same is true for ourselves as group leaders. One of the first lessons we learn as therapists is to tolerate silence and wait long enough for the client to initiate, or in this case wait long enough for the group members to initiate.

Silence Can Be Emotionally Energizing

The good news is that, in most cases, silence can be a positive therapeutic tool. Although the anxiety of silence might seem and feel negative for the individual, a certain amount of anxiety and discomfort helps to heighten members' alertness and attention in the group, which generates energy. In particular, silence tends to facilitate inner awareness of bodily felt sensory states, such as feelings and emotions, which helps bring the members into the here and now. The challenge for the group therapist is knowing when and how to facilitate silence for a therapeutic purpose, and when to intervene and break silence (see table 6.1). We'll look at some examples and talk about both.

Group Capacity for Silence Is Developmental

Like interpersonal trust and cohesion, the group's capacity to tolerate and use silence therapeutically is a developmental issue that builds over time. For a new group, and for new members in an established group, the novel experience of silence can be quite anxiety provoking and even aversive. Therefore, the group therapist needs to be careful about allowing an extended silence with new members and new groups. They need some time to build familiarity and trust and to have accumulated some positive experiences of group silence over time.

TABLE 6.1 POSITIVE AND NEGATIVE SILENCE

When to Facilitate Positive Silence:	When to Intervene During Negative Silence:
• To facilitate emotional and feeling experience (rather than intellectualizing and thinking).	• To relieve anxiety for a new group or new group members in the earliest developmental stages.
• To give the group members greater autonomy to help one another figure out situations and manage problems.	• To reassure a new group that is fearful, distrusting, and dependent on the group leader.
• To facilitate the shared experience of feelings that facilitate cohesion and bonding.	• To stop the use of silence as a gesture of defiance or hostility.
• To provide an opportunity to feel without words.	• To help a group that is struggling to process or make sense of an extremely emotional or intense event.
• To provide an opportunity to feel vulnerable yet safe.	• To reduce volatility when the group is too emotionally charged and needs to refocus on thinking and rational control.
• To energize the group.	• To break silence as boredom.

In this example, silence is more anxiety provoking for a new group in the first stages of group development.

Silence Is Harder for a New Group

A new group was started and had been meeting weekly for only a few weeks. The initial members were told to expect other men to join the group in the coming weeks. The sessions started with a brief check-in during which the members would provide a status report of how the week had been and relate any significant events. The members were hesitant, tended to talk briefly and without emotion, and often gave perfunctory descriptions of "doing fine" or "doing okay." To date, no one had shared anything very personal about their sexual offense issues or risk factors. When the check-in was fin-

ished, no one spoke. The group leader asked if anyone wanted to take time to work on a treatment goal or assignment. Silence followed. The therapist allowed the silence to continue for a brief period, then normalized the experience by explaining that it was sometimes hard to share personal information in front of the group.

Group silence may be a natural reflection of a new group's lack of trust, fear of a new situation, and dependency on the leader. At the beginning of a new group, there is reliance on the leader to give direction and to manage the process. As a group builds trust and cohesion and becomes more emotionally expressive, however, the group is increasingly comfortable with silence as a good thing. In new groups, active facilitation is used to encourage members to be assertive and establish their place in the group while also affirming the agreed-upon group protocol (group agreement).

Silence Can Be an Expression of Being Emotionally Overwhelmed

Silence sometimes occurs after a very emotional event in the group. The group therapist needs to be alert to the context and meaning of the silence in order to know how to, or whether to, intervene verbally. When silence is a moment of shared empathy or shared compassion, there may be no need to speak at all. Allowing the group to sit quietly with their own emotional reactions can be experienced as a moment of intense intimacy and wholeness.

There are other times, however, when a group is silent out of frustration, or is feeling overwhelmed and unsure about how to respond to a conflict or tense situation. In these moments, the most beneficial approach is to encourage the group members to stay engaged and talk to each other about the conflict, strain, or frustration of the moment. This is an opportunity to ask whole-group questions, such as, "What is the group thinking right now?" or "What are you all feeling right now?" or "What just happened?" This can be a valuable opportunity for members to learn and practice communication and self-control as they work through the conflict and emotions of the moment. This, in turn, further strengthens their social coping skills and deepens their relationships.

In the next example, silence is used as an opportunity to internally experience emotion.

Using Silence to Process Emotions

Finally, after many months, George brought a goal to present to the group. He disclosed the story of how he was arrested for arranging to have sex with an underaged girl whom he had solicited online. George related a long story about his lonely childhood and adolescent years. He explained how he had craved attention and approval from his parents, mostly his father, and how he continually acted out to get what he wanted at home and at school. He adopted a selfish and callous attitude of "I don't care." He became sexually active in his early teens and the thrill of sexually conquering girls gave him a feeling of power and superiority over his peers. But there was never any relationship or feelings of caring for the girls. "It was only about the number, not the quality." As George told this story, he spoke in an emotionless monotone, but he was also visibly uncomfortable in front of the group.

After George finished, the group was silent for quite a while. The group therapist could sense the tension, but opted to let the silence continue. Charles offered a rather brief analytical response, saying, "I can see how you learned that acting out was not getting you what you needed from your parents. I think I did that, too." Charles also spoke without emotion, and the tense group silence resumed. At this point, the therapist concluded that the group needed some help to process or articulate the emotional aspect of their communication. She focused on the missing emotion with this intervention: "Both George and Charles just talked about acting out as kids to get what they needed from their parents—and then acting out sexually as adults to get what they needed. What is the feeling or emotion that we all need—as kids and as adults? Is that what we may be feeling right now in the group?"

Allowing the group to sit silently with the discomfort was an opportunity to revisit the longing emotions of their childhood and teenage years and to see how, in this moment, they were still suppressing their needs for attention and the lonely emptiness of their day-to-day lives—the same negative emotional states that seemed to trigger their sexual acting-out behavior.

Facilitating the emotional climate is an essential leader action. In this emotional moment the group appeared unsure of how to respond. Illuminating the moment without distracting analysis or intellectualizing allows the group to experience empathic emotion together. The therapist role models by sitting silently and could have invited the group to respond by simply stating what they were feeling in the moment, allowing spontaneous emotional reaction and reflection to occur. The shared experience enhances cohesion and facilitates member-to-member interaction.

In the next example, the therapist engaged the whole group and facilitated member-to-member interaction; gave feedback in real time; and provided support and positive comments (Burlingame et al., 2002), all of which contribute to cohesion.

Using Silence to Strengthen Cohesion

After a brief check-in, the therapist asked, "Who would like to start?" Dan immediately volunteered. "I'll go first." He pulled out a sheet of paper and proceeded to read a list of observations that he had made about his chronic feelings of loneliness. This topic was significant for him because he had identified loneliness as a catalyst and precursor to his sexual offense behavior, his long-standing problem with drug abuse, and his recent pattern of searching for porn on the Internet (which violated the conditions of his probation and treatment). Dan read his list of loneliness experiences from the page with no emotional expression. He avoided eye contact with anyone in the group as he read, and seemed very disconnected from the group. As he finished, Dan had a pained expression on his face, perhaps sadness or depression. The group sat silent, unsure of what to say to Dan. It was as though Dan was distancing himself from the group rather than approaching them as a way of relieving his loneliness.

As the silence continued, the group therapist used roving eye contact to assess the group's reaction to Dan's communication. Rather than focus on the content of Dan's loneliness list, the therapist pursued the emotional importance of feeling lonely—here and now—while surrounded by potentially supportive peers. Here was a member who was clearly yearning for connection and a group that was failing to respond with acceptance and connection. The therapist asked Dan, "Do you feel connected to the group right now?" Dan immediately answered, "No."

This exchange evolved into a long conversation between Dan and the group about feeling lonely in a group of people, what loneliness means, how it occurs in relationships, and some possible antidotes. Some group members could relate with Dan and shared their own examples of feeling lonely. All of the group members offered expressions of encouragement. It became apparent that Dan subtly rejected and was unable to internalize the connections the group offered to him. By the end of this group session, all of the group members engaged more actively than typically would happen. The group in many ways tried to relate to Dan and joined in the experience of exploring their own sense of loneliness in a way that would relate to him while also observing the difficulty he had in internalizing their support. Unfortunately, in the end he did not appear to appreciate the genuine nature of their support; nor was he able to feel any affective relief. In fact, he left the session frustrated and unsure as to how to proceed.

Co-Facilitation

Many sexual abuse treatment programs use group co-therapists and many programs do not. We recognize that you may have little or no choice in whether you have a partner in leading your groups. For some programs, it is cost-prohibitive to have two clinicians in the group. Likewise, this may not be possible for a solo clinician who operates alone in a private practice setting. (Note: For professional ethical reasons, we strongly advise the use of co-therapists to promote the experiential training of novice clinicians who are new or inexperienced in leading sexual offender-specific treatment groups. As discussed in chapter 3, supervisors and programs have an ethical obligation to help novice clinicians to gain competency in group as a new area of practice.)

Advantages of Using Co-Therapists

If it is possible to use co-therapists, there are many benefits to doing so. Sharing responsibilities for the group can help to ease the stress and workload of group therapy. Co-therapists can support each other when a particular group or group session is especially difficult. If either group therapist is struggling during a given session (e.g., tired, under the weather, under attack from a hostile group member, momentarily confused, or whatever), the other therapist can take a stronger role. It also helps the group to feel safer and more secure when there are two leaders in the room—especially during an intense group session.

Having two sets of eyes also increases your ability to recognize significant clinical events in the group, both for individual members and for the group as a whole. Two therapists are better able to monitor the abundant direct and indirect communications occurring in the group. Two group leaders are also able to offer more than one perspective and can be models of different styles of communication.

Another advantage is that you can discuss your plans for the group before the session begins. Is there a particular curriculum topic or lesson to be presented? Are there any unresolved issues from the prior session? Is anyone in crisis? Are any members engaging in problematic behavior that needs to be addressed, and if so how do you plan to manage it together? Is either of you having a difficult day and needing the other to be aware and take a stronger role during the session?

Most of all, having a co-therapist is a chance to share in the pleasure, inspiration, and poignancy of the many great group sessions that you will have—and also a chance to share the annoyance and strain of the occasional, but hopefully rare, "bad" group sessions that you will have.

Research on Co-Facilitation

To the best of our knowledge, there does not appear to be any research showing that co-therapists are more clinically effective than single group leaders, nor is there research showing any added advantage to using a male–female, male–male, or female–female pairing of group co-therapists with sexual abusers. There is the obvious fact that solo group therapists are more cost-efficient than co-therapists, but we still believe that co-therapists are worth the added expense because using co-therapists can be a valuable way to both rejuvenate staff and reduce burnout and turnover.

There is some evidence in the general group therapy research literature that consistent messaging between co-therapists is a critical factor in effective co-facilitation. In other words, when there are two clinicians, it is essential to have close collaboration. Co-facilitation is a relationship. If the two co-therapists have very different leadership styles or conflicting perspectives about group treatment, those differences can be expressed as tension and incompatible messages that can cause confusion, mistrust, and other potential harm to the group. It is expected that clinicians will have different personal styles of group facilitation; this is not an inherently serious problem—unless the styles conflict. When co-therapists have strong differences in leadership styles, philosophies of treatment, or ideas about how to facilitate the group, these differences should be a topic of discussion before or after group sessions. The co-therapists should have ongoing dialogue to identify potential conflicts, to sort out what is occurring in the group, and to achieve a common understanding of how to manage their stylistic differences during the group.

The next case example illustrates the negative impact of unresolved cotherapist differences.

When Co-Facilitator Collaboration Is Lacking

The outpatient group was started by Paul and had been meeting for more than a year before Daniele joined as a co-therapist. Initially, Paul took on a lesser role and usually observed, allowing Daniele to become more involved. Although Paul and Daniele talked in advance about the group structure and treatment goals, they talked very little about their differing treatment styles. As the weeks progressed, their differences became more apparent. Paul was generally more laid-back and nondirective, and sought to encourage interaction among the group members, while Daniele pressed the members to do their goal work and liked to focus attention exclusively on one member at a time to be sure that he was understanding and applying the concepts accurately. As a result, Paul and Daniele were giving different messages to the group about how or when to talk to one another, how to finish treatment goals, the meaning of treatment concepts, and what was considered "good enough" work on a goal to achieve completion. Paul was encouraging the group members to interact, support, and challenge one another, while Daniele was discouraging interaction as a distraction to the systematic accomplishment of each individual's specific treatment goal work.

The growing frustration burst out one day when Paul asked the group how they felt about Harry's tearful confession that he had relapsed into deviant fantasies of children. Before any members could respond, however, Daniele pressed Harry to explain the thinking errors that led to his failure. Harry spoke sharply to Daniele: "I know what I think. What helps me the most is hearing what the others think and getting another perspective." The other members nodded, and Harry turned to Paul with a pleading expression. Although Paul disagreed with Daniele's approach, he felt his best option was to support his co-therapist by saying, "Harry, why don't you answer the question first, and then we can see what the other group members may think?"

The case example shows two co-therapists who had some extreme differences in group leadership style and treatment philosophy and how it had a negative impact on the group. Perhaps these differences were just too extreme for this particular pairing to ever work well together, but they clearly should have had some frank and open discussions of their differences from the beginning. In fact, such a discussion prior to the first group session may very well have led to a decision against co-facilitation at all.

On the other hand, mutual discussions could have helped them to understand the strategy behind each other's interventions, and they could have adjusted their approach in ways that complimented their respective strengths. For example, Daniele could have helped Paul to appreciate the importance of individual responsibility in mastering the principles of cognitive restructuring, while Paul could have helped Daniele to see the value of facilitating member-to-member interaction for increasing the members' individual motivation to learn and apply those principles. In any case, the lesson to be learned is that co-therapists need to regularly communicate with each other about the group and to proactively talk about any incongruities in their approach that could be problematic.

SUMMARY AND CONCLUSIONS

Having covered the fundamentals of group composition, structure, dynamics, and developmental stages (as covered in chapters 4 and 5), this chapter builds upon that knowledge by presenting multiple techniques and principles for facilitating groups. The chapter begins with some basic group skills, such as welcoming, inclusion, roving eye contact, and active facilitation, all of which emphasize the primary importance of facilitating member-to-member interaction. Clear and consistent structure is a cornerstone of effective groups. It is the working agreement and the space within which the group operates. It is the safe and predictable boundaries that help to promote engagement and interpersonal risk taking. Within this container, member-to-member interaction occurs and the members can feel secure in the surroundings. Facilitating interaction, verbal and emotional, is an essential leader action.

The next section of the chapter presented techniques for managing six characterological and behavioral deficits that are contraindicated for group therapy in the general group literature—but which we cannot avoid because they are so common to our clinical population of sexual abusers. These are deficits in emotional expression, empathy, motivation to change, social reciprocity, awareness of interpersonal issues, and the ability to give and take feedback/criticism. The next major section presented five principles of group facilitation to promote a secure structure and a positive emotional climate that can foster engagement, member-to-member interaction, and cohesion. Member engagement is strongly related to goal progress and group cohesiveness.

Before closing, the chapter discussed another major challenge in conducting sexual offender-specific groups—silence—and provides guidelines for both intervening in and facilitating silence for therapeutic benefit. Finally, the chapter concluded with a discussion of issues regarding co-facilitation of groups that can help you work effectively with a co-therapist.

CHAPTER 7

Using Group Therapy to Treat Insecure Attachment

It makes me feel better to know that someone else understands and I'm not alone.
—Reflection from a new group member

Attachment theory has been one of the most influential ideas in the field of sexual offender-specific treatment. First articulated by Marshall (1989), it hypothesizes that negative experiences of childhood, particularly the inability to form trusting and secure relationships with one's caregivers in early life, can contribute to the development and maintenance of sexually abusive behavior. Marshall's theory has inspired a great deal of research to identify areas of deficiency that may distinguish sexual abusers from other types of offenders and non-offenders. Before reviewing the empirical support for the theory, however, we'll look at Marshall's central idea.

Marshall's Theory of the Insecure Attachment of Sexual Abusers

Marshall's theory posits that "insecure" attachments to one's parents can impair both self-confidence and trust in others, and thereby harm the individual's ability or desire to engage in developmentally appropriate relationships as adolescents and later as adults. Lacking the experience, skills, and values needed to seek and establish effective and intimate relationships, the individual becomes increasingly isolated and lonely, which sets the stage for sexual aggression, inappropriate sexual behavior, deviance, and sexual abuse. In essence, the insecurely attached individual engages in abusive or developmentally inappropriate behaviors in a maladaptive attempt to fulfill his intimacy needs and/or to express his negative or angry feelings toward others.

The attraction of applying Marshall's attachment theory to the treatment of sexual abusers was that it offered an etiology that could explain the development of different types of deviance and sexually abusive behavior from a common root cause. For example, fearing rejection from peers, one insecure adolescent might turn to young children as an inappropriate way to meet intimacy needs and overcome loneliness, while another insecure adolescent or young adult might turn to sexual violence to forcibly fulfill his needs for human bonding. At first, the theory that sexual abuse could be parsimoniously grounded in early attachment deficits presented a seemingly straightforward research paradigm. It implied that, at the broadest level, adolescent and adult sexual offenders should have higher rates of insecure attachment than nonsexual offenders and normal populations, as well as attachment-related deficiencies, such as isolation, loneliness, and intimacy deficits. Second, it might be possible to show that different types of insecure attachment corresponded with different types of sexual offending. In this chapter we will summarize the research on attachment and how that research applies to those who sexually abuse. We will then demonstrate how knowing the attachment style of group members can guide your understanding of their behavior in group and inform your interventions.

Biological Basis of Attachment Theory

The idea of attachment theory began with John Bowlby's biological observations of primates. He argued that the primary survival purpose of attachment behavior is to keep the infant in close proximity to the mother for protection from predators and exposure. As the infant develops his or her independence, the mother then serves as a secure base from which the infant can explore the surrounding environment, gradually testing and increasing independence skills and thus extending his or her explorations. Developmental psychologist Mary Ainsworth (Ainsworth, Blehar, Everett, & Wall, 1978) operationalized Bowlby's theory with human infants in a laboratory where she observed mothers and their 12-month-old toddlers. In this controlled "strange situation," she measured the interactions between the mothers and their toddlers, specifically focusing on the management of separation anxiety. At the two extremes, an insensitive or cold mother might allow the toddler to stray too far, while an overprotective or anxious mother might not allow the toddler enough freedom to explore. Alternatively, the more anxious toddler might cling excessively to the mother and need to be encouraged to test a greater distance, while another more adventurous toddler might need closer attention to keep within a safe distance.

Based on her observations, Ainsworth merely categorized the infants into three groups, which later became labeled as types of secure attachment and types of insecure attachment: The *preoccupied-anxious ambivalent* type feels separation anxiety when separated from the mother and does not feel reassured when the mother returns. *Anxious-avoidant* attachment is when the infant avoids the caregiver. *Disorganized* attachment is when there is an overall lack of attachment behavior or no discernible pattern.

Secure and Insecure Attachment Styles

Subsequently, Bartholomew and Horowitz (1991) added a fourth attachment style by developing a descriptive framework for adults across the two dimensions, view of self and view of others (see table 7.1).

TABLE 7.1 BARTHOLOMEW AND HOROWITZ'S FRAMEWORK

		View of Self	
		Positive	Negative
View of Others	Positive	**Secure** Secure adults have positive views of themselves, their partners, and their relationships. They are self-confident, realistically trusting of others, and comfortable with both intimacy and independence, balancing the two needs.	**Preoccupied-Anxious** Preoccupied-anxious adults are bothered by self-doubt and struggle with trusting others. They are consumed with seeking and holding on to close relationships. They are continually worried about rejection and abandonment, seek approval, and are overly dependent. They often show high emotionality and impulsiveness in their relationships. [Most often child molesters]
	Negative	**Dismissive-Avoidant** Dismissing adults desire a high level of independence and self-sufficiency. They downplay the importance of relationships and avoid attachment. They have overinflated views of self and critical or poor view of others. They are emotionally constricted and suppress feelings and deal with perceived rejection by further distancing themselves or disparaging the other. [Most often rapists and incest offenders]	**Fearful-Avoidant** Fearful-avoidant adults have low self-confidence and tend to mistrust others. They have conflicted feelings between desiring close relationships and being uncomfortable with intimacy. They tend to view themselves as unworthy. Like dismissive-avoidant adults, they also tend to seek less intimacy and suppress emotional expression. [Most often child molesters]

Another way to conceive of the same four attachment styles is to use the two dimensions of avoidance and anxiety. This schema also yields two avoidant types of insecure attachment and two anxious/fearful types (see figure 7.1).

Figure 7.1 Four Attachment Styles

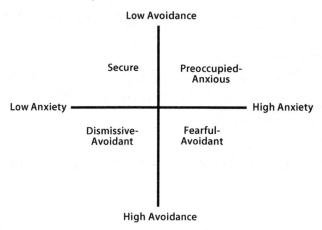

Research Supporting the Theory of Insecure Attachment

While Marshall's application of attachment theory has generated a great deal of research interest and further theorizing in the sexual offender field, how well has the research supported this theory? The following review summarizes the empirical results.

Rates of Insecure Attachment

The rate of secure and insecure attachment in normal populations has been estimated to be two-thirds secure and one-third insecure (Rich, 2004). Ward, Hudson, and Marshall (1996) estimated that 55 to 65 percent of the general population is secure, while Grattagliano et al. (2015) found 53 percent of its normal comparison group to be securely attached.

Several studies indicate that adult sexual offenders are generally more likely to have insecure adult attachment styles than non-sexual offenders and non-offenders (Jamieson & Marshall, 2000; Sawle & Kear-Colwell, 2001; Smallbone & Dadds, 1998; Stirpe, Abracen, Stermac, & Wilson, 2006), while one study found that adolescent sexual offenders showed higher rates of fearful-avoidant and preoccupied attachment styles than their non-sexual offending peers.

Ward et al. (1996) found that 69 percent of rapists and 78 to 82 percent of child molesters had insecure attachment styles, while Hudson and Ward (1997) and Grattagliano et al. (2015) both found that 79 percent of a mixed population of sexual offenders had insecure attachment styles. Marsa, O'Reilly, Carr, Murphy, O'Sullivan, Cotter, and Hevey (2004) found that child molesters were four times more likely to have an insecure style and eight times more likely to have a fearful-avoidant attachment style (59 percent) than nonviolent, violent non-sexual, and non-offenders. These findings are summarized in table 7.2.

TABLE 7.2 RATES OF INSECURE ATTACHMENT STYLES

	Dismissive-Avoidant	Fearful-Avoidant	Preoccupied-Anxious	Study
Child molesters		59% 8x higher		Marsa et al., 2004
Mixed sex offenders	57%	24%	17%	Lyn & Burton, 2004
	35%	33%	12%	Hudson & Ward, 1997
	Highest Incidence			Grattagliono et al., 2015
	2x higher		2x higher	Stirpe et al., 2006

Loneliness

According to attachment theory, sexual offenders resort to sexual violence and child molestation as inappropriate ways of meeting their needs for attachment and belonging. The research is generally quite strong in showing that sexual offenders, as a group, report higher rates of loneliness than non-sexual offenders and non-offenders. Nine studies show that sexual offenders experience more loneliness (Awad, Saunders, & Levene, 1984; Bumby & Marshall, 1994; Fagan & Wexler, 1988; Kazemi, Nayar, & Pogosjana, 2012; Marshall, 1989; Mulloy & Marshall, 1999; Saunders, Awad, & White, 1986; Seidman, Marshall, Hudson, & Robertson 1994; Tingle, Bernard, Robbin, Newman, & Hutchinson, 1986). Within the attachment styles themselves, Hudson and Ward (1997) found that preoccupied and fearful-avoidant sexual offenders had higher loneliness scores than dismissive-avoidant and securely attached. For our purposes, the frequency of loneliness reported by sexual abusers underscores the special therapeutic value of group therapy in providing meaningful connections to other group members.

Intimacy Deficits

Attachment theory posits that sexual offenders, as a group, would show problems with intimacy, such as greater fear of intimacy and poor intimacy skills. While one study showed no differences in intimacy skills between sexual offenders and non-sexual offenders (Ward, McCormack, & Hudson, 1997), many more showed strong support for pervasive intimacy deficits of sexual offenders (Bumby & Hansen 1997; Bumby & Marshall, 1994; Kazemi et al., 2012; Lisak & Ivan, 1995; Marshall, 1989; Miner, Robinson, Knight, Berg, Swinburne-Romine, & Netland, 2010; Miner, Swinburne Romine, Robinson, Berg, & Knight, 2016; Mulloy & Marshall, 1999; Seidman et al., 1994). Within attachment types, Hudson and Ward (1997) found that the two types of sexual offenders that avoid attachment (the fearful-avoidant and dismissive-avoidant types) showed more fear of intimacy than the preoccupied type, who are obsessed with finding and retaining close relationships. Lyn and Burton (2004) also found that sexual offenders show more attachment anxiety than non-sexual offenders and non-offenders. In terms of sexual offender types, Bumby and Hansen (1997) found that child molesters had more fear of intimacy and intimacy deficits than rapists, while Kazemi et al. (2012) found that child molesters had more intimacy deficits than other types of sexual offenders.

There is, however, contradictory research. Two studies found no evidence of social skills deficits in adult sexual offenders (Marshall, Barbaree, & Fernandez, 1995; Stermac & Quinsey, 1986), and one found no deficits for juvenile sexual abusers compared with delinquents (Seto & Lalumiere, 2010).

Even though the research is quite strong in showing various social deficiencies for sexual offenders, it is important to note that a major meta-analysis of 82 studies found that intimacy deficits were not major predictors of recidivism and effect sizes for both loneliness and poor social skills were not significant (Hanson & Morton-Bourgon, 2005). Nevertheless, to the degree that social and intimacy skills are important, group therapy is an ideal modality for observing, learning, practicing, and improving such skills.

Isolation

Attachment theory also posits that insecure attachment styles would cause sexual offenders to be more socially isolated and less socially competent than non-sexual offenders. Five studies have shown sexual offenders to be more isolated (Fagan

& Wexler 1988; Marshall 1989; Miner & Munns, 2005; Miner et al., 2010; Seto & Lalumiere, 2010; Tingle et al., 1986) and one study showed they are less socially competent (Overholser & Beck, 1986) than comparison groups of non-sexual adult and juvenile offenders and controls. Once again, group therapy is ideal for breaking the characteristic isolation, secrecy, and shame of those who sexually abuse.

Negative Family Upbringing

Since poor parenting would be expected to harm secure attachment, attachment theory would predict that sexual offenders would tend to have more negative parenting and family upbringing than non-sexual offenders and non-offenders. In two studies, Smallbone & Dadds (2000; 2001) showed that insecure parent–child attachment relationships were related to aggressive and antisocial dispositions in adults, including inappropriate sexual expression. Three studies found that sexual offenders described both of their parents as cold, distant, uncaring, indifferent, unsympathetic, rejecting, hostile, aggressive, or emotionally detached (Awad et al., 1984; Hazelwood & Warren, 1989; Smallbone & Dadds, 1998). Four studies found that sexual offenders report low levels of parental care, consistency, and supervision, and high levels of harsh control, rejection, and neglect compared with non-sexual offenders and non-offenders (Craissati, McClurg, & Browne, 2002; Marsa et al., 2004; McCormack, Hudson, & Ward, 2002; Tingle et al., 1986), while Marshall and Mazzucco (1995) found *no* difference in perceived parental rejection between child molesters and non-offenders.

Similarly, several studies found that sexual offenders, compared with differing comparison groups of non-sexual offenders and non-offenders, experienced higher rates of parental neglect, violence, and disruption (Bard, Carter, Cerce, Knight, Rosenberg, & Schneider, 1987; Craissati et al., 2002; Kazemi et al., 2012), including higher rates of sexual abuse (Milner & Robertson, 1990), higher rates of physical abuse (Grattagliano et al., 2015; Kahn & Chamber, 1991; Seidman et al., 1994), and higher rates of loss, separation, or disruption of primary caregivers (Ryan & Lane, 1991; Prentky, Knight, Sims-Knight, Straus, Rokous, & Cerce, 1989). Of note, one study by Craissati et al. (2002) found no difference between rapists and non-offenders in rates of parental neglect, violence, disruption, and disturbed bonding.

In terms of frequency of negative upbringing, Levenson, Willis, and Prescott (2014) gave the Adverse Childhood Experience scale to 679 sexual offenders and found that, compared with men in the general population, sexual offenders reported 3 times the rate of child sexual abuse, 2 times the rate of physical abuse, 13 times the rate of verbal abuse, and 4 times the rate of emotional neglect and coming from a broken home.

From our perspective, the prevalence of childhood trauma and abusive family upbringing plays out in group therapy in many ways, such as problems with appropriate boundaries, feelings of shame and self-disgust, and alienation. Perhaps most of all, we see that childhood abuse and trauma causes profound difficulties with trust. In fact, fundamental distrust and guardedness is common for this population and presents a major challenge for a new group in the initial stages of development. By providing a consistently safe social environment, group therapy is a rare but powerful opportunity for these men to begin to open up, lower their guards, and experience acceptance and trust.

Father and Mother Relationships

A number of studies also show some interesting patterns in sexual offenders' relationships with their fathers and mothers. In four studies, sexual offenders described their fathers as cold, distant, uncaring, unsympathetic, and rejecting (Grattagliano et al., 2015; Lisak & Roth, 1990; McCormack et al., 2002; Smallbone & Dadds, 1998; Tingle et al., 1986) and three studies found higher rates of fathers who were hostile, abusive, and violent (Kahn & Chambers, 1991; Lisak & Roth, 1990; Smallbone & Dadds, 1998). These studies used non-sexual offenders or controls as comparison groups. Two studies found that self-reported college rapists and juvenile sexual offenders viewed their fathers more negatively than their mothers (Lisak & Roth, 1990; Tingle et al., 1986) compared with non-offending peers. In terms of sexual offender type, two studies found that rapists had more distant relationship with fathers than child molesters (Tingle et al., 1986) and perceived their fathers more negatively than their mothers (Hazelwood & Warren, 1989), while a third study showed that child molesters showed the highest levels of disturbed bonding with parents, especially their mothers (Craissati et al., 2002). At the same time, three studies found that sexual abusers had more disturbed bonding, poor communication, and frequent arguments with their mothers than nondelinquent adolescents (Blaske, Borduin, Henggeler, & Mann, 1989) and controls and other offender groups (Craissati et al., 2002; Tingle et al., 1986).

Attachment Style Corresponds to Sexual Offender Type

Ward et al. (1996) hypothesized that rapists tend to have a dismissive-avoidant attachment style, which leads to devaluation of others, hostility, and sexual coercion of adult partners, while child molesters tend to have preoccupied-anxious attachment, which leads to seeking approval by engaging in sex with children who are perceived as less threatening than same-aged peers. Most of the research has generally supported this hypothesized correspondence between attachment style and offense type.

At least six studies have shown that rapists tend to have a dismissive-avoidant attachment style (Baker & Beech, 2004; Lyn & Burton, 2004; McCormack, 2002; Smallbone & Dadds, 2001; Stirpe et al., 2006; Ward et al., 1996), and two studies have shown that incest offenders are more likely to have dismissive attachment (Lyn & Burton, 2004; Stirpe et al., 2006). The picture of child molesters is less consistent. Two studies found that child molesters are more likely to have a fearful-avoidant style (Jamieson & Marshall, 2000; Marsa et al., 2004), and two other studies found that child molesters are more likely to have a preoccupied attachment style (Lyn & Burton, 2004; Stirpe et al., 2006). Several other studies found that child molesters are more likely to have either a fearful-avoidant *or* preoccupied style (McCormack et al., 2002; Proeve, 2003; Ward et al., 1996; Ward, Hudson, Marshall, & Siegert, 1995; Wood & Riggs 2008). At the same time, there are at least five studies that have detected no relationship between insecure attachment style and offense type (Baker & Beech, 2004; Marshall, Serran, & Cortoni, 2000; Proeve, 2003; Smallbone & Dadds, 1998; Smallbone & McCabe, 2003), while two studies found only partial support for the hypothesis that child attachment style predicted adult attachment style (Smallbone & Dadds, 2000; 2001). These studies reduce the strength of the research on this aspect to moderately weak.

Other research has detected more specific deficits related to offender type and insecure attachment style. Wood and Riggs (2009) found that child molesters with insecure attachment style had more negative perceptions of self/others/future and more cognitive distortions about adult–child sex, while those with a preoccupied style had better treatment outcomes than those with fearful-avoidant and dismissive-avoidant styles. Hudson and Ward (1997) found that sexual offenders with a fearful-avoidant style showed the highest hostility toward women while those with dismissive-avoidant style had strongest belief in rape distortions, and that child molesters and nonviolent sexual offenders were less angry than rapists and violent sexual offenders.

Finally, in what may be the most rigorous research study to date, Miner et al. (2014) found that adolescent anxious attachment to parents was *not* directly related to sexual offending. Instead, they found that adolescents who were the highest in anxious attachment were most likely to commit acts of child sexual abuse (rather than adult or peer sexual violence), *but* this was mediated by the amount of time spent with friends and perceived isolation from peers. Thus, even though adolescents with anxious attachment tend to have a poor internal model of self-esteem and poor personal agency, those who are able to maintain age-appropriate peer relationships are buffered from inappropriate sexual behavior and violence (Miner et al., 2014).

Indeed, we believe that Miner's research points to the great potential value of group therapy with sexual offenders. To the degree that a therapy group can be a source of healthy peer relationships, we believe that it can help to mitigate and reduce the risk of sexual abuse.

Summary of Sexual Abuser Attachment Research

Table 7.3 summarizes the relative strength of the supporting research for each area of research about attachment deficits and related problems.

TABLE 7.3 ATTACHMENT RESEARCH SUMMARY	
Attachment Factors and Aspects	**Strength of Supporting Research**
Higher rates of insecure attachment	Moderate
Higher rates of loneliness	Very strong
Greater intimacy deficits	Very strong
More social isolation	Strong
Less social competency	Weak
Negative parents and family upbringing	Moderately strong
Poor father relationship	Moderately strong
Poor mother relationship	Moderate
Attachment style corresponds to offense type	Moderately weak

CASE STUDIES SHOWING THE THREE ATTACHMENT TYPES

Given what the research tells us about insecure attachment styles, how do we expect these styles to be manifested in a sexual offender therapy group? Let's begin by looking at three case studies that illustrate the three types of insecure attachment and how they were expressed in group. As you read each story, try to discern his insecure attachment style (answers are presented at the end).

Case 1. Joseph

Joseph was habitually neglected and physically abused as a child by both parents. In the chaos and unpredictability of his family home, he developed a sense of constant vigilance and anxiety. As an adolescent and young adult he was constantly on the lookout for slights from his peers, friends, and romantic partners. He had a series of intense, short-lived courtships until he married the first woman who was willing to stay with him for more than a few months. Feeling that he must hold on to his wife at all costs, he frequently asked for reassurance that he was loved or reacted emotionally to any perceived rejection or devaluation. Over time his wife grew tired of his emotional demands and insecurity and increasingly distanced herself. Resentful, Joseph began to focus on her preteen stepdaughter, seeking closeness and companionship, and becoming increasingly physical in his displays of affection. Ultimately he was arrested for sexual abuse of the girl.

Behavior in group: Joseph is eager to do all the right things and presents as a highly motivated patient. He is frequently self-blaming and ashamed of his incest crime. He is meek and obedient. He never expresses any negativity to anyone in the group and withdraws into silence when there is any tension or conflict between members. He is careful and cautious to abide by his parole conditions and passes polygraphs.

Case 2. Chico
Chico reported that his mother was verbally abusive and routinely slapped him in the face for minor disciplinary issues. His mother went through a series of unstable live-in boyfriends, most of whom ignored Chico, except for one who showed him a lot of attention. This boyfriend allowed Chico to drink beer and smoke weed and then started to "share the fun" of watching pornographic videos. This escalated into teaching masturbation, then mutual masturbation, and then the man coerced Chico into oral and anal sex. When the sexual abuse was discovered, his mother threw the boyfriend out, but blamed Chico for participating and continued to taunt him with comments about being queer and homo. As a teen, Chico avoided sports or peer friendships and prided himself on becoming his own man, including earning money as a laborer. He had no male friends—"who needs 'em"—and complained that white girls were "too stuck up" and "racist" to date a Latino. He got into trouble as a juvenile for fighting and for forcing an intellectually disabled neighbor to fellate him in a garage. Chico continued to live with his mother as a young adult. He was arrested twice for attempted rape, but convicted of a lesser crime only once. After serving a prison sentence, he returned to live with his mother. He had no future goals, no friends, and set up his own house within his mother's house by converting the garage into an apartment. He described his mother as "my cook—it's the only thing the fat bitch is good for"—and portrayed himself as the "executive of the estate."

Behavior in group: In his first group meeting, Chico turned his chair around backward and mounted it like a horse. He politely corrected this when asked, but thereafter always pulled his chair back from the circle and/or turned it cockeyed. Chico presented as cold and serious. He displayed little interest in the discussion, rarely spoke, and showed no emotion.

Case 3. Nathan

Nathan remembered feeling like an outcast even in his earliest years. He was weak and uncoordinated and ashamed of a birthmark on his neck, so he tended to shy away from playing with other boys. Lacking any particular talent or interest in sports or school, he continued to avoid his peers and spend more time alone. At age 14, Nathan was pleased when another boy actively sought him out for friendship. Nathan liked the feeling of companionship, but he felt anxious and held back from closeness. The other boy persisted in calling him to get together, but Nathan made no reciprocal effort and the friendship faded. He described this with tearful affect. Nathan obsessed about loving a particular girl at his high school, but never dared to speak to her. He felt lonely and desired friendship, but it was easier to stay in his room and watch TV or play video games. Then he discovered pornography. He described it as "magic" because he could pretend to be with a girl even though there was no girl. He spent hours obsessing with pornography and compulsively masturbating. He began exploring other types of pornography and found that he was most strongly aroused by child pornography. He never sought contact with real children, nor peers, but he was eventually caught and charged with possession of child pornography.

Behavior in group: From his first group, Nathan presented as bland and emotionless. He was always highly attentive and curious about the other members, who seemed to like him and welcomed his questions about their problems and relationships. Nathan admitted that he was a virgin, but rarely disclosed anything else of a personal nature. When pushed by other members, he would just shrug and say, "There's nothing to tell. I don't do anything or go anywhere. I don't have any victims, so there's nothing to say."

Determining Attachment Styles

As you have likely figured out, each case study demonstrates one of the three types of insecure attachment. Joseph is preoccupied-anxious, Chico is dismissive-avoidant, and Nathan is fearful-avoidant. Remember, however, that attachment, like any trait, exists on a continuum. Few sexual offenders will be clearly one type or another like these examples. Nevertheless, it is enough to have a good working hypothesis of the predominant styles of your group members. It is usually easier to identify members with predominantly avoidant-dismissive and preoccupied-anxious styles. It is harder to distinguish someone with avoidant-fearful attachment because, by its very nature, the person shows an ambivalent and fluctuating approach/avoidance that makes it harder to discern his attachment pattern.

Using Self-Report Attachment-Style Measures

You can also use a brief self-report measure to help determine the predominant attachment styles of your group members. The gold standard of attachment measures is the quasi-clinical, semi-structured Adult Attachment Interview (AAI), in which the respondent reflects on childhood attachment experiences and the possible impacts on his own personality and behavior (Hesse, 2008). But the AAI requires a one-hour interview and four hours of transcription and coding. Fortunately, two brief self-report scales are available. Although they may be less valid than the AAI, they can be administered easily. The Adult Attachment Scale (AAS) is an 18-item self-rating scale, but it yields only three adult attachment styles: Secure, Anxious, and Avoidant. Therefore, we recommend the Relationship Scales Questionnaire (RSQ). With 30 items, the RSQ is a bit longer, but it includes items from the AAS and, most important, it yields measures of all four attachment styles: secure, dismissing-avoidant, fearful-avoidant, and preoccupied-anxious (Griffin & Bartholomew, 1994).

The RSQ can be part of your initial assessment of a new group member to discern his attachment style. It can also be repeated over the course of group therapy, thus providing a potentially valuable pre-, mid-, and post-treatment measure of treatment change. Be aware that few offenders will be purely one type; still, having a sense of an offender's predominant style is enough to be useful. Even an offender whose score indicates an overall secure attachment style may still show a tendency toward one of the insecure styles.

THE IMPACT OF ATTACHMENT STYLE ON GROUP THERAPY

Understanding each group member's primary attachment style is useful in treatment in several ways.

- Attachment style impacts the perception of the therapeutic climate and therefore treatment outcomes.
- Knowing attachment styles helps you to know what to expect.
- You can adjust interventions to different attachment styles.
- Your own attachment style can interact with the offenders' attachment styles.

Impact of Attachment Style on Perception of Therapeutic Climate

There is strong research with non-offenders that shows that the client's attachment style directly impacts his or her perception of the therapeutic climate in both individual and group therapy (Dozier, 1990; Eames & Roth, 2000; Goldman & Anderson, 2007; Korfmacher, Adam, Ogawa, & Egeland, 1997; Mallinckrodt, Gantt, & Coble, 1995; Parish & Eagle, 2003). It has also been shown that a positively perceived therapeutic climate promotes positive treatment outcomes with both non-offenders (Gillaspy, Wright, Campbell, Stokes, & Adinoff, 2002; Martin, Garske, & Davis, 2000), and sexual offenders (Beech & Fordham, 1997; Beech & Hamilton-Giachritsis, 2005; Marshall & Burton, 2010). A meta-analysis of 17 non-offender attachment studies showed that secure attachment is strongly related to greater alliance, while insecure attachment is related to poorer therapeutic relationships (Diener & Monroe, 2001). We also know that group therapy can actually facilitate more secure attachment (Kilmann, Urbaniak, & Parnell, 2006; Keating, Tasca, Gick, Ritchie, Balfour, & Bissada, 2014; Maxwell, Tasca, Ritchie, Balfour, & Bissada, 2014; Tasca, Balfour, Ritchie, & Bissada, 2007). Therefore, improving attachment is expected to improve the client's attitude and receptiveness to treatment, again yielding better outcomes.

One team of researchers conducted an interesting study that shows a direct relationship between attachment styles and perceptions of the therapeutic climate with 277 incarcerated sexual offenders in group therapy (Garbutt & Hocken, 2014; Garbutt & Palmer, 2015). Using Moos's Group Environment Scale, they found that securely attached sexual offenders showed significantly positive perceptions of Leader Support, Task Orientation, Self-Discovery, and Order and Organization, while the three insecure styles showed different patterns:

Those with *avoidant-dismissive attachment* also showed *positive* perceptions of Leader Support (defined as help, concern and friendship shown by the therapist to group members) and Task Orientation (defined as placing emphasis on completing and concrete practical tasks, decision making, and training). This suggests that the dismissive-avoidant offenders are very sensitive to therapist qualities of warmth and caring, but they also like to keep group discussions focused on practical tasks like homework.

In contrast, those with *preoccupied-anxious attachment* showed significantly *negative* perceptions of Leader Support. This suggests that, for all their anxiety and efforts to gain approval, acceptance, and caring, the preoccupied offenders tend to perceive the therapist as *not* caring and *not* giving enough of the support they seek, or see themselves as unworthy of receiving it. This basic insecurity is, of course, likely to fuel more attention seeking.

Finally, those with *avoidant-fearful attachment* showed significantly *negative* perceptions of Self-Discovery (defined as how much the group encourages the members to discuss personal problems). This makes sense in terms of their essential ambivalence about both closeness and emotional expression. They fluctuate between getting close and emotional and then withdrawing into guardedness and distrust.

Knowing What to Expect

Knowing the attachment styles of your group members can give you a preview of what to expect from an individual, especially in the early stages of group treatment. For example, you will know who is more likely to jump right in and participate (and whether that may be less-than-optimal behavior for that member) and who is more likely to be guarded and hold back. Over the longer term, you will have an appreciation for what will recur as the most difficult issues for that member in group (because of his particular attachment style) and an enhanced appreciation for the progress he is making.

Adjusting Interventions to Different Attachment Styles

Most important, knowing attachment styles will give you a better idea of how to adjust your interventions to be more effective with differing individuals. Take, for example, a member who is always quiet and rarely participates. The group becomes accustomed to his silence and just carries on as if he is not there. What happens when he finally does speak up in group? Suddenly everyone is staring at him, intensely curious to hear what he will say—which makes it even harder for him to speak. If the silent member is *dismissive-avoidant*, you may want to explicitly reinforce his participation by pointing out how much his contribution was valued by the group or how it really helped another member. This is important for men with this attachment style because they lack awareness or appreciation for the value of connection and caring. But if the silent member is *fearful-avoidant*, you would *not* want to make such a big fuss over his contribution. Too much attention and too much praise may overwhelm the fearful-avoidant member and unintentionally cause him to retreat back into withdrawal and guardedness. He needs to more gradually test the waters before he can trust the group, so you should be less forceful.

How Your Attachment Style May Interact with Other Styles

If you have an understanding of your own personal attachment style, you may have a better grasp of your particular comforts and discomforts in group and you may know how your own style may positively or negatively interact with other styles. You can take the RSQ yourself and see what your style may be. You might find that you are predominantly anxious, or secure with an anxious tendency. You might be avoidant, or secure with an avoidant tendency. Knowing your attachment style may help you manage your own behavior and how you interact with other styles of attachment.

For example, two studies show that higher degrees of therapist attachment anxiety tend to reduce therapist empathy (Rubino, Barker, Roth, & Fearon, 2000) and weaken the therapeutic alliance (Black, Hardy, Turpin, & Parry, 2005). But another study showed that anxious therapist attachment can actually improve client-rated alliance at the beginning of treatment, yet hinder the alliance over the long term (Sauer, Lopez, & Gormley, 2003).

Two studies found that more avoidant clients functioned better and were more satisfied with preoccupied-anxious (but secure) therapists, while more anxious clients did better with more avoidant (but secure) therapists. This suggested a complementary attachment configuration (Mallinckrodt, 2000). Contrarily, Mohr, Gelso, and Hill (2005) found that counselors with fearful-avoidant or dismissive-avoidant attachment styles showed more negative feelings when working with preoccupied-anxious clients.

Using Group Therapy to Treat Insecure Attachment

Given what the research tells us about insecure attachment styles, how do we expect to see these styles expressed in a sexual offender therapy group? What are the best strategies for managing these patterns? In this final section on attachment, we will look at how you can anticipate and adjust your interventions to best facilitate positive change and manage problems related to each of the three insecure attachment styles. The good news is that you will not need to master three different approaches—there are several fundamental interventions that will, by virtue of being group-focused, be effective with *all* three types. Let's start there.

Facilitate Cohesion as the Secure Base

Group cohesiveness is considered the most fundamental factor from which all the other therapeutic factors flow (Yalom, 1970; 2005), and as we have seen in chapter 2, there is strong empirical support for the therapeutic power of cohesion in sexual offender groups. A cohesive group is one in which all members feel a sense of belonging, acceptance, and validation, and where they can work together, supporting and challenging one another. In terms of attachment, group cohesion is the secure base.

A cohesive group is analogous to the "good mother" who fosters secure attachment in the child. It is like the toddler who learns to manage his anxiety and maintain trust in his mother, while venturing farther and farther to explore the world and build independence. A healthy, cohesive group is the secure base from which the members can safely explore and test new behaviors, attitudes, and ways of genuine relating. This is accomplished while simultaneously learning to recognize and manage their internal distrust and anxieties about disapproval and rejection, ultimately, to become more feeling, self-confident, and meaningfully connected.

Group Must Be a Safe and Protected Place
The group members need to have a reasonable expectation that they will be respected and valued in the group, and will not be subject to humiliation or attack. The group therapist has the vital role of establishing a consistent climate of group safety. This is done by establishing and maintaining the protective structure of rules and expectations (see chapter 4). It is also done by intervening as necessary to stop or reframe behavior in the group that may threaten safety and security—most especially by preventing or mitigating acts of intimidation, threat, or uncontrollable anger.

Highlight the Occurrence of Connection
The group therapist can also strengthen the shared perception of the group as a safe and secure place by pointing out events that show trust and mutuality. Given their characteristic isolation and loneliness and their poor familial upbringing, sexual offenders will, as a group, have little experience with healthy interpersonal relationships of trust, respect, and caring. More often than not, they have learned to be distrustful and detached, and operate in a self-absorbed and selfish manner. They actually need help from the group therapist, who by using group-focused interventions can help them to recognize when events in group have shown the occurrence and positive effects of acts of altruism, caring, respect, universality, bonding, and trust. Over time, they can begin to incorporate these accumulating experiences of connection and trust.

Reframing Negative Expressions of Connection
Given the attachment deficiencies of sexual offenders, it is inevitable that they will frequently blunder in their efforts to help others and to accept help from others. This is a major focus for the group therapist. As described in chapter 2, the research from the five Levenson studies showed that "helping others in my group" and "getting help and support from others" were ranked as most important by the highest percentage of sexual

offenders across all groups and settings" (Levenson & Prescott, 2009; Levenson et al., 2004, 2009, 2010, 2014). Thus the group therapist must first stay attuned to the dynamics among the group members (who likes who, who dislikes who) and recognize when someone is trying to help, and when the intended recipient is rejecting or missing that help.

The dyadic nature of helping means that there is often a double lesson to be learned by the group—in both giving constructive criticism and receiving it. For example, Joe gets angry at Bill and says, "You're just lying to yourself, Bill. You're gay. We all know it. We accept it. Why can't you?" Bill winces then snaps, "'Cuz I'm not," and clenches his jaw in silence. This could be a good opportunity for the group therapist to step in, first to protect Bill (and any group member) from an overly harsh confrontation by reaffirming the group's rules about respect, and second to reframe the event as an attempt to help and an expression of bonding and acceptance. "Let's stop for second and look at what just happened. One thing the group shares is a commitment to being respectful. Joe may have stated it too strongly this time, and Bill has a right to disagree and feel hurt or offended, but it appears to me that Joe may have been saying something important for the whole group. He said, 'We accept it.' Whether Bill is gay or not, the more important thing that Joe is saying is that he and the group *care* about Bill and accept him. That it's okay for Bill—and anyone—to be his real self and be accepted. What does the group think?"

This intervention accomplishes multiple things. It reaffirms the group's commitment and rule of being respectful. Joe (and the group) receive some guidance about how to give more sensitive and appropriate feedback. Bill gets feedback that, contrary to his fears, the group accepts him as a gay man. The group sees that anger and strong emotions can be processed safely within the group. And an apparent angry confrontation is revealed, instead, as an expression of caring and acceptance.

Interventions Specific to Insecure Attachment Styles

In this section we summarize the way that each insecure attachment style is likely to be expressed in the group therapy situation and how interventions might be focused accordingly.

Avoidant-Dismissive Attachment Style
Presentation in Group
- Presents as self-sufficient and not needing any help from other group members or the therapist.
- Reports no problems and/or everything is under control.

- Shows discomfort with needing or depending on other group members and with others needing or depending on him.
- Emotionally constricted and underreactive, he rarely expresses emotions or feelings and is usually serious and stoic. He places little value on emotions and avoids feelings.
- Fails to recognize, disregards, or devalues expressions of caring, friendship, or connection among group members.
- Sensitive to the demand for engagement and closeness.
- May distance himself or disdain the group as self-protective avoidance.
- Despite his appearances to the contrary, he may be very attentive to experiences of warmth and caring from the group leader and the group (Garbutt & Palmer, 2015).
- Is more comfortable when group discussions are focused on practical tasks like homework (Garbutt & Palmer, 2015).

Recommended Interventions
- Increase his awareness of and appreciation for the value of group and connections by pointing out occurrences of closeness, bonding, and caring in the group, as well as the positive feelings that result from such experiences.
- Reinforce the value and importance of his belonging in the group by strongly emphasizing his participation and pointing out how much his contributions are valued by the group.
- Encourage him to allow himself to feel more, and to feel more deeply, to up-regulate his emotional state.
- Reinforce his expression of emotions and the positive results of doing so to increase awareness of the value of feelings.
- Point out instances of others helping others to help increase his positive view of others as competent and show that needing others is not a weakness.
- Reinforce instances in which he gives help to others, which show his need to connect and what it is like to be needed and valued himself.

Preoccupied-Anxious Attachment Style
Presentation in Group
- Often seeks approval and acceptance and emotional support from group members.
- Overly reliant on praise from therapist and other members.
- Readily willing to reveal his personal weaknesses, failures, and crises as a way to command attention from the group.

- Overreacts emotionally to positive and negative events.
- Vigilant to any statements or behavior that suggest rejection, disapproval, or dislike from the therapist or group.
- Comes early and lingers late to gain as much personal attention as possible.
- Eager to please the therapist and group, he presents as the perfectly cooperative client, always trying to say the right words, give the right answer, and do homework the best.
- Attentive and jealous of others when they receive praise.
- Prone to negative perceptions of leader support, he tends to presume he is not worthy of and/or not receiving enough caring and support (Garbutt & Palmer, 2015)

Recommended Interventions
- Point out instances of closeness, bonding, and caring in the group that are gained naturally and *without* having to be elicited through displays of neediness.
- Point out instances in which he acted with strength, independence, and competence on his own to increase self-sufficiency and self-confidence.
- Emphasize instances in which he helped others through his own competence and deemphasize instances in which he received help by acting needy and weak.
- Redirect the group away from focusing on him during episodes in which he overreacts emotionally to gain approval and attention.
- Help him learn to tolerate a certain degree of anxiety about abandonment (and to self-soothe) by (1) nonverbally acknowledging awareness of his immediate distress and (2) *not* turning the group's attention to his problem, or by reframing the issue as something important to the whole group.
- Strongly reinforce instances in which he speaks positively of himself and his competency or progress in treatment.
- Given his tendency to be overly reactive, it is generally better to *discourage* impulsivity and expression of strong emotions in favor of more thoughtful, reflective (rational) thinking.

Avoidant-Fearful Attachment Style
Presentation in Group
- May present as guarded and reluctant to share or open up until others have disclosed first—and have done so safely.
- Usually likes to participate in the positive interactions of the group, but can sometimes hold back or sit in silence, especially when there is negativity or tension.

- May test the waters for quite a long time by using vague, limited, tentative, or unemotional revelations of his true feelings and issues—checking whether the therapist and the group can be trusted.
- May show emotional withdrawal and guardedness after experiencing a moment of *positive* bonding or closeness with others in the group.
- Vigilant to any experience suggesting that he is being looked down on as weak or inferior and, if so, reacts with anger, withdrawal, and guardedness.
- Shows fluctuations and ambivalence about trusting and opening up, sometimes getting close and then backing away if others get too close.
- May have intense feelings, but is often reluctant or fearful of showing those emotions and vulnerabilities.
- Will be uncomfortable and prone to negative perceptions of the group when it discusses personal problems in too much depth (Garbutt & Palmer, 2015).

Recommended Interventions

- Reinforce times when he takes the risk of opening up and trusting the group.
- If his openness results in being ignored or a negative outcome, draw the group's attention to the event so that his effort is acknowledged and reinforced.
- Reinforce times when he gives support and helps others through his competence.
- Emphasize that receiving support and help from others is natural, not a weakness or humiliation.
- Draw attention to instances in which he (and the group) have weathered through an emotionally intense or negative episode and maintained basic trust, safety, and respect.
- Reinforce his self-esteem and sense of social belonging by pointing out how much his participation and contributions are valued by the group.
- Reinforce emotional expression and closeness/engagement with others.

SUMMARY AND CONCLUSIONS

This chapter reviewed the empirical research supporting the theory that sexual offenders, as a group, have significant deficits in forming and maintaining attachment with others. Studies show that, compared with non-sexual offenders and non-offenders, sexual offenders appear to be more isolated and lonely, less socially competent, lack intimacy skills, and have a higher rate of abusive and negative family upbringing. According to an influential theory by Marshall (1989), sexual offenders are insecurely attached and may therefore seek inappropriate relationships with children or commit sexual violence in maladaptive attempts to fulfill their social intimacy needs and/or to express their negative or angry feelings toward others.

In terms of the three insecure attachment styles, child molesters tend to show the preoccupied-anxious or fearful-avoidant style, while rapists and incest offenders tend to show the dismissive-avoidant style. Identifying the particular insecure attachment styles of group members can provide valuable insights into why individuals behave in particular ways in the therapy group, and you can adjust your interventions to be more effective with different attachment styles. At the same time, there are strategies that work well with all styles of insecure attachment. Above all, group therapists should maintain group as a safe and protected place and consistently foster the development of group cohesion to create a "secure base" from which members can safely explore and test new behaviors, attitudes, and ways of genuine relating.

CHAPTER 8

Managing Resistance and Other Common Problems in Sexual Offender Groups

The group helped me see that there is a way out.

—Client at the end of treatment

Treatment groups are composed of individuals who enter treatment at different stages of change and who have different personal strengths, deficits, and needs. A group is a dynamic social organism that is the accumulation of each member's unique contributions over time. These traits mean that the group has a "personality" that we work with each session. Groups have moods, experience shifts in dynamics, and may experience change in fits and starts. Sometimes groups get stuck in a developmental stage, in conflict, or in fear of intimacy, or they are just plain obstinate.

In this chapter, we will explore some common challenges we encounter when working with complex groups and their individual and group dynamics.

Resistance

Resistance to psychotherapeutic treatment has been discussed in the literature since the 1920s (Kemper, 1994). As long as therapists have been trying to help clients to change for the better, they have been frustrated by clients who resist that change, whether it is desired by the client or not, at various points during treatment. Resistance has been described as a psychological mechanism or method of defending oneself against emotional distress and unwanted thoughts or feelings. It can be seen as both conscious and intentional opposition, or as unconscious sabotage of positive change.

Expressions of Resistance

Resistance can be expressed directly and indirectly. A client may declare, "This is not a problem" or "I do not want to look at this issue"—or he can feign agreement and then simply not do what is being asked of him. In group therapy, there are a variety of ways that clients can "resist" treatment and the therapist, such as arriving late, canceling sessions, "forgetting" homework or treatment assignments, changing the group discussion to some irrelevant topic, making jokes, failing to pay for services, or supporting another resistant client who may be giving the therapist a hard time in the group.

In all these forms, we typically think of resistance as an entirely negative and pathological process that is detrimental to treatment—at least when viewed from our perspective as therapists. In our field, we may too often attribute a malevolent intent to clients who deny the severity of their offense-related problems and regard such "resistance" as an expression of antisocial behavior and increased risk of future sexual offending. What if we view the same behavior from the perspective of the client? Mitchell (2015) asserts that so-called "resistance" is simply the fact that the client is currently unable to make a desired change. Inability to change may be the result of many different processes, only some of which may be malevolent, and some of which could be seen as normal. He lists the following reasons for resistance in therapy:

1. **Fear of failure** The client has a strong need for success and competency and is afraid of looking weak, inferior, or incompetent by failing at the therapeutic task.
2. **Fear of taking risks** The client generally plays it safe in life and sees counseling as a highly risky endeavor that could have negative consequences, such as embarrassment, failure, and loss of control.
3. **Manipulation** The client enjoys the power of controlling or manipulating others (and/or the power of noncooperation) and experiences power in manipulating (or not complying with) the therapist.
4. **Passive-aggressive behavior** The client may distrust or feel angry with the therapist or with the therapist-as-a-representation of some other adult or authority, such as a parent or the criminal justice system that convicted him (e.g., transference).
5. **Shame** The client may feel deeply ashamed of his weakness, deficiency, incompetence, or deviancy, and therefore fears social rejection.
6. **Desire to maintain a valued relationship** Sometimes a client may not want to improve to a level that could result in the loss of a much-valued relationship. "If

I get better, then I will not be able to come to my sessions anymore and I'll lose all of this attention and support from my therapist."

7. **Exhaustion** Resistance could be an indication that the client is psychologically drained and currently lacks the energy to take on the tasks that will lead to change.
8. **Personality style** Some people are characterologically averse to changes in their routines, habits, and lifestyle, and instinctively respond to change with resistance.
9. **Client enjoys resisting** Some people enjoy the stimulation of a good argument, or enjoy disagreement as a way of exerting their power or showing off their intelligence.

Resistance as a Normal Expected Response

Resistance can also be seen as normal when it is seen as situational. A person who is rigid and pigheaded in one situation may be flexible and open-minded in another. Beutler, Moleiro, and Talebi (2002) distinguish between *state resistance*, which varies with the situation, and *trait resistance*, which is more characterological and stable, and therefore more likely to lead to relationship problems. They observe that a person who is high in trait resistance "is easily stimulated to behave with opposition to a situation. High trait-like resistance may or may not lead to broader psychopathology, but easy arousal of resistance behavior is likely to be disruptive to relationships in social activities." They describe resistance as an underlying reaction to feeling threatened with the loss of free behavior. As such, resistance can be viewed as a relatively normal opposition to a perceived threat of loss of personal freedom.

Morris (2014) asserts that resistance is normal, even predictable in the therapy process, and that we can learn from patterns of resistance in our groups. "When we invite a group of people to come together, agree to a contract, and engage each other in a way that will help them develop intimacy, we are asking them to do something that is quite terrifying. Really."

Reactance as a Form of Resistance

In the field of social psychology, Brehm (1966) proposed his theory of "psychological reactance" that applies to everyday life. *Reactance* is defined as a negative internal state that is aroused by a perceived threat to one's freedom of action, which then motivates the individual to act in ways to restore that loss of freedom. For example, a probation officer tells a client that he is not allowed to own or use a computer in order to prevent him from viewing Internet pornography. The client feels irritated at this loss of freedom and may then act in ways to restore that freedom, such as using a smartphone instead, or concealing the purchase of a computer, or using the computer at the local library. Likewise, many sexual offender clients feel reactance when they are first ordered into sexual offender-specific counseling or when they are first required to disclose their sexual offenses to the group. They may respond with active or passive refusal to cooperate or change. This could take the form of denial, minimization, rationalization, and blaming.

Blaming the System
Kirmayer (1990) makes the point that many clients do not attribute their resistance to their own behavior in psychotherapy, but instead blame external factors and view themselves as victims of circumstance or the malevolence of others. For example, when a client blames the probation officer for applying a blanket sanction that is persecutory, rather than as a strategy to help him exercise self-control over his deviant impulses. In our field, we frequently encounter resistance in the form of blaming when group members are newly mandated for treatment by the court. Involuntary clients often express their anger at the injustice of the conviction (including outright denial of having committed any offense), blaming the court system, and complaining, "I don't need any treatment for a problem I don't have."

Several strategies can help with blaming resistance of this kind. One is simple education about the reality of the criminal conviction and the opportunity that treatment offers. You can clarify that the client can choose to leave treatment and return to court to dispute the treatment order, but emphasize that treatment is separate from the courts and is designed to help them. This technique entails going with resistance rather than fighting it. Another technique is to invite other group members to share their own initial reaction to being court-ordered into treatment and how they gradually came to a new understanding of how treatment was helpful and why they now view the group as a positive support. (It is also helpful to the veteran group members to look back at their own course of change and see how much progress they have made.) This shared experience evokes Yalom's (1970) therapeutic factor of *universality* and becomes a potential source for the *instillation of hope* for the new member. Both of these factors can build trust among group members and enhance group *cohesion*.

Higher Levels of Resistance Expected in Early Stages of Group
Higher levels of resistance are commonly seen in groups in which the early-developmental-stage issues of trust have not been fully worked through and cohesion is still weak. It is easy to forget that the new court-mandated client is entering the treatment group with the same apprehensions as any person entering into a new

experience with a group of strangers. In other words, *we should expect to observe higher levels of resistance in the early stages of group development and with new clients; this is relatively normal behavior.* We should expect new clients to hesitate and show reluctance to disclose their offense behavior and to display the various behaviors of blaming, denial, minimization, lying, avoidance, and rationalization. We should understand that this heightened level of "resistance" is reflective of the early developmental stage of the group and it is *not* necessary (and probably counterproductive) to immediately confront or challenge such behavior at this early point in treatment. There will be plenty of opportunities to challenge resistance behaviors later in treatment—at a point when the client feels safe and accepted in group and is more open to feedback and criticism. It will be remembered from the research in chapter 2 that confrontation is contraindicated in sexual offender-specific treatment and viewed as not helpful by the clients. We can be sure that confrontation is even more certain to fail in the early stages of group.

Missed Sessions as Resistance

Typically, when a court-ordered client misses a group session in our field, we clinicians tend to react in an authoritarian and disciplinary fashion. We are trained to regard this behavior as a potentially serious violation of the conditions of probation/parole and/or mandated treatment. Although we have a unique dual responsibility to the client *and* to community safety (see chapter 3), we nearly always take the latter role of authority when this occurs. This response, of course, leaves us with only punitive options, such as reporting the behavior to the parole officer, or suspending or discharging the client from the group.

While sanctions may be a legitimate and appropriate response, what if we viewed a missed session *from the therapeutic perspective* rather than the accountability stance? In other words, what if we looked at the missed session as a form of resistance, the meaning of which is yet to be discovered? Has the client missed a group to avoid a particular issue or treatment goal? Did he miss this group after an episode of crying or intense emotion in the previous session? Perhaps he is still feeling shamed, vulnerable, embarrassed, overwhelmed, or afraid of losing control. Does the missed session seem irresponsible or oppositional, or is it consistent with his overall lifestyle of disorganization? Could it be the result of a multitude of life stressors that have overwhelmed the client, making therapy attendance yet another source of unbearable stress? Is it a financial issue?

Based on your familiarity with and recent observations of the client prior to the missed session, you should be able to judge whether the missed session is an instance that can be handled therapeutically. If this is a recalcitrant client who has not engaged in group treatment and frequently ignores or breaks rules, then you probably are correct in applying limits and sanctions. On the other hand, if this is unusual behavior from a client who has been actively invested in the group, you may want to explore the possible meaning of the missed session to help him remain engaged in the group.

Coming from a strictly therapeutic perspective, Councilman and Gans (1999, p. 174) remind us that a group can feel very different when a particular member is not present: "Just as in cooking where omission of a single ingredient can significantly alter the flavor of a dish, every member contributes to the chemistry of the group. Much can be learned about a member's role by how the group changes (or does not change) in his or her absence."

We believe that the same approach is entirely valid for sexual offender-specific groups. By viewing the group as a whole entity in itself, and by being attuned to the member-to-member relationships, the group therapist can observe how the absence of one member impacts upon the group as a whole and other members within the group, which can provide valuable clinical data about the members. The impact of a missed session is especially true in a well-established group with good cohesion. When it is possible and advisable, we believe that a missed session can become a topic to explore together as a group—as a discussion of a structural rule issue or as a psychological issue. How did members feel about Jack missing the group? How was the group different? What does that reveal about the group? By shifting perspective from the single individual who missed the group, it is possible to see the broader impact on the group, which can reveal much to the members about their relatedness, while directly reinforcing trust and cohesion in the group.

Managing Other Common Problems in Sexual Abuser Groups

Now let us look at three other types of problems that you may encounter in sexual abuser groups: subgrouping, scapegoating, and boundary violations. For each problem, we will suggest interventions to manage and reduce its negative impact on group process.

Subgrouping

Subgroups occur when two or more group members form an overt or covert alliance around a particular issue, or against the group, the group leader, or other group members. Subgroups sometimes form when certain members feel disconnected from the group or when members seek to gain power over other group members or the leader. Early recognition of subgrouping behavior is the first step. For example, you might notice several group members join together to dispute a program rule or challenge the therapist's authority (e.g., "We think this homework is a waste of time"). You might observe a pattern in which several group members join together to criticize or mock another member. You might notice how several group members always agree about some negative theme or repeat an issue that has already been discussed and resolved. Or you might observe the tendency of particular members to readily follow the opinions of one dominant member.

When you see such a pattern, the next step is to discern the purpose or meaning of the subgrouping process. The technique of mapping the group interactional patterns (see chapter 9) is one you can use to identify potential subgroups and to clarify which members are inside or outside the subgroup. Think about the possible advantages that the subgroup members may be seeking to gain from their subgroup alliance. What is the function of the subgroup? Is it a way to avoid an emotional issue or distract the group from a particular issue? Is it a way to gain power and dominate others? Is it a way to conspire together to engage in some illicit or deviant behavior outside the group? Is it two or three members who share a close affinity because of similarities in age, education, race, or occupation? Is the group divided into a subgroup of members who are highly motivated and engaged in treatment and a subgroup of those who are unresponsive to treatment?

The next case example illustrates a sequence of responses by the group therapist.

An Alliance of Blaming

Bart insisted that he had been "entrapped" by law enforcement when he was caught chatting online with an officer whom he thought was a teenage female. Mike promptly added that he, too, had been the victim of similar entrapment. He claimed that he was unfairly lured into the chat room and insisted that the officer was the one who pressured him to meet for sex at the motel. A third group member, who was convicted of statutory rape, joined in the subgroup, stating, "We're not sexual offenders. We're just regular guys. How can you expect a guy to say no if a girl offers to screw him? It's not fair."

This exchange marked the beginning of a subgrouping of members who were angry at the court system (and at the group leader as a representative of that system). They were allied in using blame and externalization as a defense against the deep shame of being labeled as sexual offenders. The subgroup was functioning as a way to support one another and salvage their badly damaged self-respect. They were also the three newest members of this ongoing group.

The group therapist decided to go with the resistance by first validating their feelings of outrage and resentment, as well as their pain and dread over being labeled as sexual offenders. She pointed out that, even if they had been lured or tricked, they had a choice to act or not act. She then turned the question to the entire group. Andre, one of the longest-running members, responded by admitting that he had said the same things when he was first arrested because he didn't want anyone to think he was a sexual offender. But he knew all along that he "did what he did" and he deserved to get into trouble.

The general response to subgrouping is to block the interactional dynamic and work toward engaging the subgroup with the whole group. This can be accomplished by interrupting the subgrouping alliance, reaffirming the value and importance of participation from all members, and then inviting the larger group to respond to the topic or issue at hand. In this example, the group therapist was trying to invite the subgroup of resistant new members into the larger group. She did this by first acknowledging their feelings, showing that all group members shared their pain of being labeled as sexual offenders, and, most important, demonstrating that the group accepts them as fellow people who have made mistakes.

Scapegoating

Scapegoating in a treatment group occurs when one or more group members are picked on, blamed, ignored, excluded from participation, or somehow treated differently than other group members. Scapegoating is often a symptom of mistrust or fear within a group that lacks familiarity and cohesion among the members. It can also be a response to feeling threatened by the introduction of a new member or the acting-out behavior of a particular member who is disrupting the group. Scapegoating pushes members apart, increases guardedness, and inhibits members from getting to know one another beyond a shallow level.

When any group member is treated differently from the rest of the group, it affects the equality and cohesion of the entire group. If any one member is targeted or treated differently—whether it is positive (such as excessive praise, favoritism, or extra privileges) or negative (such as being shamed, chastised, or ignored)—all members feel the impact. They realize that the group is not safe or fair and that they may also be at risk of being targeted or rejected. In turn, this apprehension reduces risk taking, personal disclosure, and expression of affect.

Scapegoating sometimes occurs when more powerful members dominate the discussion and aggressively assert their opinion in ways that shut down or put down other members. In groups composed of mixed offenders, scapegoating may also take the form of one type of sexual abuser asserting that his offense was not as bad as another member's (see chapter 4). For example, an exhibitionist or voyeur may say his offense was not as bad as a contact offense; or a rapist may say his crime was not as bad as molesting a child; or a child pornography user may say he never touched a child. Comparisons like this are used to gain status by scapegoating and lowering the status of another member. Some members may avoid dealing with their own issues by using scapegoating to shift attention to another member with "worse" offenses or deviancy.

The general approach for averting and discouraging scapegoating is to facilitate member-to-member interaction and foster mutual understanding by finding common traits and experiences that are shared among the members (the therapeutic factor of universality). If a member has been sharply interrupted or shut down by other members, you can intervene to protect the equality and safety of the group by enabling the scapegoat to say what he had wanted to say. You can also redirect the whole group (not the just the problem member) to revisit the scapegoating interaction to illuminate and discuss what happened. It is a way to bring awareness to the group about the importance of respectful behavior and equality, to show how disrespect or insensitivity can harm the trust and mutuality of the group, and to explore better ways to express criticism or feedback.

Boundary Violations—In and Out of Group

Boundary violations are a common and complex challenge in sexual offender-specific treatment groups. Boundary violations can occur between members, between members and the group, or between members and the group leader. Boundary violations can seem minor or inconsequential, such as arriving late for a session; or can be overt and extreme, such as acts of verbal, physical, and emotional intimidation or intrusion. Boundary violations can also extend to behavior beyond the group room, such as a group member harassing another member or attempting a sexual seduction or engaging in a sexual relationship. The meaning and significance of boundary violations varies depending on the nature of the situation.

In the following case example, a friendship outside the group became unhealthy.

A Friendship Outside of Group Goes Bad

The group had been meeting for more than a year and there were many indications of strong cohesion. Group members were progressing in treatment, openly talking about their offenses, making significant personal disclosures, and asking for group time to work on goal assignments or get help with important personal issues.

Over the months, Mike and Stan formed a close connection. Mike was in his 50s, struggling with feelings of self-disgust and fear of rejection related to his lifelong pedophilic attraction to preteen boys. Stan was in his 20s, openly gay, and had been sexually abused as a child. They found commonality in their histories with their fathers and the parallels in their lives. They had talked in group about occasionally meeting outside of group for coffee or lunch.

In this session, however, Stan complained about an incident at a restaurant in which Mike openly stared at a young boy and remarked that he found the boy attractive. At first, Stan thought that Mike was simply being honest about his struggle against his pedophilia, but then he became very uncomfortable because he felt that Mike was indulging in his sexual attraction for boys. Mike apologized to Stan, explaining how he did not realize how his behavior would be upsetting to others and should be recognized as a serious warning signal of risk. The group praised both Mike and Stan for being forthcoming about the situation. Rather than chastising or rejecting Mike for his inappropriate behavior, the group remained supportive by helping Mike to reaffirm his goal and strengthen his tactics for managing his pedophilic risk. After getting feedback from the group, the two men decided to stop meeting outside of group and Mike sought extra individual help for reducing and controlling his urges.

As we discussed in chapter 4, it is essential that boundary expectations are explained to all group members at the beginning of the group, and repeated as appropriate throughout the course of treatment, to prevent minor and major transgressions. Rules about boundaries are a standard structural element of the group agreement. In fact, many sexual offender treatment programs prohibit contacts outside of group, citing the risk of "criminal associates." The general group therapy literature also advises against extra group contacts, but for a different reason. Group agreements often prohibit extra-group relationships so that all of the psychic, emotional, and sexual energy in the group is retained within the group sessions. In the case example above, the program allowed extra-group contacts, but only if the members clearly inform the group about their contacts and maintain personal boundaries. This rule helps to assure transparency and prevents the development of secret relationships that can create subgroups and harm group process and cohesion. By establishing and periodically reinforcing the group agreement, the group therapist can rely upon the agreement to proactively address minor or major violations when they occur.

FACILITATING DIFFICULT GROUPS

Effective group treatment requires a reasonable amount of engagement from the members. Excessive levels of passivity, avoidance, hopelessness, apathy, hostility, or other negative attitudes can suck the energy from the group room and crush the spirits of the group leader. In this section, we will talk about ways to manage negative group dynamics and facilitate engagement.

The Passive Group

In this example, a group with multiple structural problems felt no incentive to actually engage in their own treatment.

Waiting to Be Called On

A social worker named Tom took over an existing group that was part of an outpatient treatment program for sexual offender parolees and probationers. The group met each week at the local parole office. The 12 group members sat around a rectangular table in an open break room. Occasionally, a probation officer or office worker would enter the room unannounced to retrieve his or her lunch from the refrigerator or to make a cup of coffee. This was frequently disruptive to the group and greatly annoying to the new group therapist.

> *Tom quickly discovered that the prior group leader had been extremely directive and authoritative. Members were accustomed to waiting until they were called on to participate. A few members never spoke at all. Most did not know what treatment goals they were working on and had little idea of how they were progressing in treatment. Tom found that he had to prompt the men to participate and, when they did talk, they would speak directly to him as if no one else were in the room. Tom administered the Cohesiveness Subscale and was not surprised to find that the group scored extremely low.*

First, Tom faced a host of *structural problems* when he took over this group (see chapter 4). With so many interruptions, the open room was completely unsuitable for protecting the privacy and integrity of the group. The table felt like a giant barrier. The group itself was too large to allow time and attention for the members. There was a group agreement in place, but no one remembered what it was because it had never been discussed or reinforced by the group leader. Moreover, the men lacked any clearly defined individual treatment goals.

The second big problem was the *need to facilitate group process* and meaningful interaction (chapter 6). The men were passive, disengaged, and guarded. They were conditioned to wait and respond to the therapist when called upon. They were like strangers to one another. Communications were stiff, unemotional, and impersonal.

Tom realized that he had to begin by building the structural rules in order to establish a therapeutic space where the members could begin to feel safe. By working with the program director, Tom was able to split the group into two smaller groups, scheduling one group at a time of day that would not be interrupted and moving the other group to a smaller room that assured privacy. He acted as if the group was a newly formed group in the first stage of development (chapter 5). Tom made the group agreement into a topic of discussion for an entire session. All group members were given new copies of the treatment goals and educated about the goals of the group and expectations of members. Treatment expectations were defined and group members were educated to speak with one another as they presented their treatment goal work. The treatment group structure was followed each session.

Once the structural boundaries were well established, Tom was able to address the passivity and disengagement that were legacies of the prior therapist. Tom consistently reinforced member-to-member interactions, redirected members to speak to one another rather than himself, and presented questions to the group as a whole. Over time group members learned to talk to one another and to take more responsibility for their own treatment progress. After 10 weeks, Tom administered the Cohesiveness Subscale again and found a dramatic increase in cohesion.

The Anti-Group: Managing the Dark Side of Groups

In his book *The Anti-Group: Destructive Forces in the Group and Their Creative Potential*, Nitsun (1996) argued that all groups contain inherent destructive "anti-group" dynamics, which can undermine the therapeutic climate of the group. As distinguished from hostility expressed *within* the group, anti-group forces can be seen as hostility directed *toward* the group itself. The anti-group begins with (1) fear, distrust, doubt, or dislike of groups, and/or (2) naturally occurring conflicts or adverse experiences in the group, which can lead to further withdrawal or hostility to the group. Sometimes these anti-group forces can be managed with relative ease, but in other cases they can destroy a group.

Contrary to the overly optimistic image of group psychotherapy as an all-accepting corrective experience for the disappointments and hurts of past experience, Nitsun asserts that some groups are unsafe, hostile, and harmful because of unmanaged anti-group forces. But anti-group is not a purely negative force that will inevitably harm the group. Instead anti-group actually provides the dynamic counter-resistance against change that is necessary for taking risks, exploring issues, and experiencing psychological growth. Anti-group is also a natural and predictable expression of the stages of development of the group.

"The successful handling of the anti-group represents a turning point in the development of the group. By helping the group to contain its particular anti-group, not only are the chances of destructive acting out reduced, but the group is strengthened, its survival reinforced and its creative power liberated" (Nitsun, 1991, pp. 7-8).

Nitsun identifies 10 inherent characteristics of therapy groups that can give rise to anti-group attitudes and reactions among members. In table 8.1, we have suggested the type of group facilitation that can best manage each aspect of anti-group.

TABLE 8.1 MANAGING ANTI-GROUP ATTITUDES	
Characteristics Eliciting Anti-Group	**Strategies to Manage Anti-Group**
Group is **(1) a collection of strangers** and it **(4) occurs a public arena:** Some people dread or fear the idea of talking in front of strangers and are especially averse to revealing private thoughts in front of a group.	Fully prepare each individual for the group experience, explaining what to expect, and allaying common fears of being attacked or embarrassed. Restrict the size of the group to an appropriate number and ensure that the group room is private and uninterrupted (chapter 4).
The group experience is **(2) unstructured** and **(8) unpredictable:** Some people desire strong guidance or direction. Unforeseen events, unexpected emotional upheavals, and changes in membership cause anxiety that is expressed toward the group.	Frequently draw upon the security and predictability provided by the group agreement and structure to provide reassurance. Use the structure of treatment goals to keep the group focused and directed (chapter 4).
Each group is **(3) created by its members:** Each group is unique, but what if the available members lack the skills, empathy, and engagement to create an effective group? It can feel like the blind leading the blind. For example, in chapter 4, we saw a group composed of so many avoidant members that it could not generate interaction.	Some groups desire and need stronger leadership from the group facilitator to help them find and maintain their focus (chapter 6). Facilitate member-to-member interaction to foster engagement. (chapter 6). Also, attend to the composition of the group and make changes accordingly to facilitate interaction (chapter 4).
Group is a **(5) plural entity** and **(6) complex experience:** Some people are overwhelmed by too many people at once. Moreover, there is a great deal happening psychologically at any given time in group, which can be confusing and cause sensory overload.	Take moments to focus on the here and now and summarize what is happening in the session, especially if the session has been fast-paced, intense, or highly emotional among members. Pause the group to calm down, take quiet time to reflect on what has happened, and reassure the group that it can tolerate intense emotions.
Group **(7) creates interpersonal tensions:** Group members are often worried about being accepted, judged, embarrassed, attacked, or put in the position of hurting someone else. They may conflict over all sorts of interpersonal issues, such as dominance, jealousy, submission, rivalry, pressure to conform, rejection, criticism, and antisocial attitudes.	Intervene promptly when necessary to protect members from attack (chapter 6) and help the group review and process the conflictive event in order to understand how negative emotions can be experienced and safely managed within the group.
Group is **(9) an incomplete experience:** The group can only handle so much participation, and members may not be able to get enough attention to their individual problems.	Use roving eye contact to be alert to the nonverbal behavior of new members, silent members, and members who are reticent to participate or unable to get a word in edgewise. Facilitate opportunities for the individual to participate and praise the value of his contribution (chapter 6).
Groups **(10) fluctuate in progress:** Groups have periods of progress, stasis, and regression.	Be cognizant of the developmental stage of the group and continually facilitate in ways that protect and promote cohesion and move the group beyond developmental stage stagnation (chapters 5 and 6).

The Stuck Group

Groups are dynamic human organisms that continually evolve in response to changes in membership and the various moods, personality traits, relationship styles, and social/relational abilities of the individual members. But sometimes even a well-functioning group can go through a period that feels stagnant, lethargic, negative, or "stuck." It might feel as if the group has lost momentum or lost direction. There is no sense of progress, and the group is just not working together effectively. Leader actions fail to energize and move the group forward. When a group gets stuck, so does the group facilitator.

When this happens, it may be a good time to step back from the group and get a fresh perspective on what is happening or not happening, and why. Stepping back can literally mean moving your chair to the edge of the circle and sitting back to observe the process. By allowing yourself the freedom to stop active leadership, you can attend more closely to here-and-now observation. Allow yourself to quietly listen and watch the group. You may not say anything for most of the session.

There will be plenty to observe. Individual and group level interactions, reactions, and verbal and nonverbal communications will generate a plethora of data to absorb, assess, digest, and respond to in the moment or at some later time. Observe who is talking, the content of what they are saying, which group members respond, and who remains silent. Observe who provides leadership, who is emotionally present, who is making eye contact, and who seems distracted or disengaged. Use roving eye contact to observe the facial expressions, postures, and body language of the members, particularly those who are not participating verbally. What patterns do you observe? Are there indications of resistance from some, and what is the meaning? Do the same members remain silent, while other members repeatedly speak up and engage?

Later, based on your observations, see if you can identify patterns and synthesize the data into a conceptualization of the group. You can draw an interactional diagram or mapping of the group dynamics that you've observed (chapter 9). Who are the most and least active? Did you see any subgroupings, alliances, or patterns of dominance or avoidance? If the pattern is that most members do not take risks or seem reluctant to freely participate, it is often helpful to revisit the developmental stage of the group. You can assess the level of trust among members by asking how they feel about the group at this point in time and how they view their role and contribution to the group. You may want to consult with a colleague to gain another perspective.

As illustrated in the next case example, being "stuck" has different causes, such as being disengaged.

The Disengaged Group That Was Going Nowhere

The Wednesday group mostly comprised younger men on probation, who were living with parents or family members, and had marginal employment histories. All had graduated high school and showed average intelligence. All but one had been arrested for non-contact offenses, which included voyeurism and child pornography. The group sessions were routinely dull and uneventful. The members rarely initiated discussion and needed frequent prodding and encouragement from the therapist to participate or respond. When members presented work on their treatment goals, the other members offered little feedback and rarely asked questions. Their lack of engagement in the group seemed to mirror their lack of engagement in life outside of group. They were living week-to-week on limited incomes and had no goals or career ambitions. They were traveling at no particular pace toward no particular destination, and with little confidence in their capacity to make positive changes.

With so many young, passive males, this group had an obvious composition problem. The excessive homogeneity stacked the deck against interaction. The group therapist was advised to bring in one or two active, assertive members who could enliven the group and role model a very different style of relating. (It was also suggested that she try to move one or two of the current passive members into a different group.) Even with the hoped-for change in chemistry, the group therapist needed to intensify her leadership and use frequent active facilitation to continually prompt and encourage the members to participate. Like men with avoidant-fearful attachment styles (see chapter 7), these young men were too passive, alienated, and disconnected to seek out social connections, but this was *exactly* what they needed and could potentially gain from an effective group. The therapist needed to consistently reinforce their participation and point out how their contributions had positively impacted other members and the group. The therapist emphasized what they shared in common and tried to facilitate their interest in one another. As they engaged more and more with one another, the group members were able to experience the positive feelings that derive from cohesion and altruism (the value of giving to others). This, in turn, strengthened their self-confidence and self-esteem and helped activate their hopes for the future.

Managing Our Own Issues

There's no way around it. It is difficult to deal with men who sexually abuse others. It is hard to listen to stories of brutality, violence, selfishness, exploitation, depravity, and misery on a daily basis. We are challenged professionally, emotionally, and spiritually to retain our humanity and compassion and our belief that we can make a positive impact. In this section, we will talk about some of the danger signals and ways to protect and care for yourself in the field of sexual abuse treatment.

The "Ick" Factor—Countertransference

When you allow yourself to quietly observe the group, you can also take note of your personal reactions and feelings about the various members. Do you like or dislike particular clients? Do you feel disdain, anger, disgust, or other negative attitudes toward some members? As mental health professionals, we are committed to remaining objective and to honoring the therapist–client relationship by acting on behalf of the needs of our clients—unless there is a risk of harm, in which case we must also act to protect others. But we are human and it is inevitable that we may experience negative feelings about our clients, especially in this field where our clients have perpetrated horrible acts of abuse and engage in deviant sexual behavior and fantasies that repulse us. While we are trained to be objective and client-centered, our negative reactions can become intrusive and reduce our ability to respond empathically or with measured directness. Our negative countertransference can impair our clinical judgment and ability to fully engage in the therapeutic process. Our clients may display all sorts of qualities that can be repugnant, annoying, or simply exhausting. One client may be dirty and unkempt, another may avoid eye contact, while yet another stares inappropriately. One client may be brash and boastful, while another is weak and needy. One client may talk incessantly, while another says almost nothing. Such clients challenge our capacity for empathy and patience, or even our tolerance for being treated in a disrespectful manner.

Burnout

In this field, we often talk about burnout, compassion fatigue, stress, countertransference, and just plain getting tired of doing the seemingly unending work of the treatment of sexual abuse perpetration. We may feel the daily stress of working in harsh forensic and correctional facilities or the pressure from probation/parole and the courts. Day after day, week after week, year after year, we hear painful stories of abuse, trauma, damaged lives, loss of freedom, lost jobs, and loss of hope. We bear witness to the repeated bad decisions and malicious acts perpetrated by callous individuals, many of whom were victims of childhood emotional, physical, and sexual abuse.

We work with clients who live day-to-day at the bottom of Maslow's (1954) hierarchy of needs. They struggle to make ends meet, suffer from homelessness caused by local residency restrictions and landlords who refuse to rent to sexual offenders or felons, and cannot find employment because of blanket policies that prohibit the hiring of felons. We watch our clients as they try to change their lives, while society remains lost in irrational fears and continues to put up more barriers. We are challenged to help our clients come to terms with their psychological and sexual pathology, their dark desires, and their malevolent lack of empathy. Our work is hard enough, but we must also deal with a hostile, or at best unsupportive, public arena where we have to defend our chosen work over the dinner table at social gatherings.

Given all this stress and strain, burnout is a potential problem. How do we sustain our clinical curiosity? How do we maintain our clinical objectivity and high professional standards? How do we maintain our belief in the capacity of our clients to make meaningful changes? Burnout saps your energy. It colors your conceptualizing of every client and every situation, and can eventually lead you to some self-destructive behaviors. To prevent burnout, it is important to talk regularly with peers you can confide in and unload some of your negative emotions and worries. Make a point of doing activities that give you pleasure, such as traveling, comedy shows, dancing, and socializing with friends and family. Take care of yourself in any way possible. If you are feeling burned out, it is okay to ask for help. If that does not work, talk to your supervisor and explore the possibility of a new job in your agency, or another program, or even a different clinical field.

Raising (or Lowering) Expectations

As a supervisor and longtime clinician, Steve has had many experiences, alone and with other therapists, where frustration increased as a group appeared to flounder and struggle with seemingly simple social interactions. Some of the examples in this chapter, such as the passive group and the disengaged group, illustrate the frustration of dealing with members who sit in silence and offer nothing after a member has presented an assignment and asked for feedback. When frustrated with groups like these, Steve has sometimes realized that this is the best that a given group can do at this juncture in its development. Some groups are simply limited in their capacity. Some members truly do not have any idea what to say or how to respond, and doubt that they can make any kind of meaningful contribution. When faced with this challenge, the group therapist must be very active. This includes direct coaching, role modeling responses, demonstrating emotional expressiveness and enthusiasm, and giving frequent praise for any efforts by members to participate and interact. But perhaps the most helpful strategy for reducing frustration for Steve, or for any group leader, can sometimes be to *lower one's expectations* for a particular group. It is neither an insult to the group nor giving up on it if you lower your expectations to a more realistic, achievable level. It is respectful and clinically sound to meet the group where they are at, and match your facilitation to their level of social and interpersonal functioning. In social work, it is called person in context.

Conversely, sometimes it can be helpful to reconsider your overly pessimistic expectations when dealing with difficult groups. For example, the disengaged group was emotionally and psychically "dead" for many months. In the spirit of "consultation with self," Steve reconsidered each member in terms of his strengths and weaknesses. In the process, Steve was reminded of how poor composition can be detrimental to the potential of a group, but it also became clear that several of the members had excellent potential for growth—*if* given the right group environment. By systematically altering the composition of the group, and by finding ways to accentuate the strengths of individual members, Steve was able to *raise* his expectations for the group and facilitate more improvement.

Changing Leadership Style for an Advanced Group

After many years and thousands of group hours, there are times when group work can feel dull and routine. When a group is stable, making progress, and doing the work they came to do, the therapist needs to guard against getting lazy and less involved, or even trying to stir things up by asking provocative questions. Instead, this is a time when your role as facilitator changes from active leadership to less active but important new ways of facilitating more advanced levels of group interaction and growth. This is an opportunity to listen for nuance and more subtle language and themes in the group. Group interventions can focus more on the here and now, facilitating richer emotional experiences, deepening intimacy among members, and giving the group members more and more opportunity to self-direct and resolve problems together by themselves. Freed from the need to actively direct the group, the group therapist has greater flexibility to focus more closely on complex interactions, or simply to sit back and enjoy watching the members exercise their increasing skills for interpersonal cooperation and conflict management.

When a group advances to this higher level of functioning (i.e., the mature stage of group development), the new challenge for the group therapist is to withhold intervention and trust that the group members have the cohesiveness, self-sufficiency, and skills to manage more emotional and complex conflicts. This means having enough confidence in the group to intentionally risk some chaos and, frankly, allow members to struggle and fail. In effect, the group therapist is conducting a controlled experiment to test how the group manages the situation. The challenge for the group therapist is to stay calm and restrain the natural urge to come to the rescue as things get more and more disorganized or heated. The results can then be a rich topic for discussion and exploration.

Summary and Conclusions

This chapter was designed to help group therapists to manage many of the common problems that can present in sexual offender-specific group therapy. The first section dealt with the fundamental issue of resistance and described the many ways that so-called resistant behavior can be expressed or displayed in group. In fact, we have offered some new ways of conceptualizing resistance as a natural and normal response to group treatment, especially when it is mandated rather than voluntary. This was followed by a section that provided methods for managing different types of resistant behavior, such as subgrouping, scapegoating, missed sessions, and boundary violations. The next section presented a series of difficult groups that are commonly found in work with sexual abusers. Here we talk frankly about managing the intense negativity and inertia of disengaged groups and anti-groups and how it can cause us to feel stuck and ineffective. Finally, we present some strategies for recognizing and addressing our own weaknesses as therapists, such as the recognizing the signs of our own burnout, countertransference, and unrealistic expectations.

Our goal throughout has been to empower, not discourage, group therapists by providing some practical strategies and skills to recognize and manage the occasional difficulties and problems that can happen to all of us in this field. Despite its challenges, however, group therapy with sexual offenders can be an exciting and enriching experience that yields incomparable moments of profound feeling, poignancy, hope, caring, and purpose—for socially ostracized men mired in loneliness, anger, shame, and despair.

CHAPTER 9

Tools for Measuring Group Processes

We can't have you get in trouble again.

—Group member to another member

WHY ASSESS WHAT IS HAPPENING IN YOUR GROUPS?

As shown by the empirical research in chapter 2, the quality of group functioning is directly related to individual treatment progress and goal attainment. In short, the better your group is doing, the better your clients are able to engage in and benefit from treatment—both in and out of group therapy. Yet many group facilitators rarely ask themselves, *How is my group doing?* Like its individual members, a given group has the potential to change and improve in many ways over time. Like its members, the group can also experience periods of clear progress, and periods of struggle and confusion. Sometimes the group changes in response to new members entering or long-term members leaving. Sometimes changes reflect the natural and predictable stages of development for any group, as from the beginning phase to the middle phase to the mature phase.

Ideally, as group therapists, we like to see our groups evolve toward increasing levels of trust, openness, compassion, emotional expressiveness, intimacy, social awareness, bonding, and, particularly for sexual offenders, toward a deep and meaningful acceptance of personal responsibility for prior abusive behavior and commitment to living a prosocial life without reoffending or sexual preoccupation.

It is not enough to simply focus on how the individual members are progressing in their respective treatment goals. We need to assess how the group is functioning as well, which, frankly, also includes looking honestly at our own performance as group facilitators. There are many benefits to assessing our groups, not the least of which is the fact that a better-functioning group will directly facilitate the individual progress of group members (Budman et al., 1993).

But how do you measure the quality of your group? How do you know if your group is doing well? Running a group requires a lot of concentration on a lot of moving parts. In any given session, the group leader is attending to the content and the process of the group, observing and facilitating group cohesion, managing problem behavior, and trying to keep the group members focused on the primary or key issue, topic, or goal. With so many things to attend to, it might seem overwhelming to add group assessment as well.

Group Mapping

One simple technique that can be implemented at any moment in any group is called *group mapping* (Sawyer & Jennings, 2014). The map, which can take the form of a circle showing where the members typically sit in the group room, may reveal "positions of power" and weakness in the group (Jennings & Deming, 2013). The map can be used to draw pattern lines among the members and/or the therapist, which can show where the most frequent interactions are occurring among which members (see figure 9.1). These could be positive or negative alliances, or conflict pairings, or triads, or other subgroups that are impacting the quality and cohesion of the overall group. The map can be used to visually reflect which members are most and least talkative, most and least participatory, most and least open or defensive. The map can also assess the degree of equidistant circularity of the group and help identify potential positions of power, such as commanding the best chair or sitting outside the circle (Jennings & Deming, 2013).

Fortunately, there are some easy and valuable measurement tools that you can use to assess a rich variety of group factors and processes. With the help of these tools, you can measure the current level of cohesion, relatedness, and engagement in the group; assess member relationships within the group; and measure changes in member attachment, overall member satisfaction, and more. As shown in the group therapy research from chapter 2, positive therapist qualities, satisfaction, cohesion, and engagement can all positively influence one another and yield better treatment outcomes. In chapter 7, we also learned how the different insecure attachment styles can impact group and how group is the ideal modality for enabling sexual abusers to make lasting improvement in their attachment capacity. Attachment, too, can be measured in groups by using some simple assessment tools.

Figure 9.1 Group Mapping

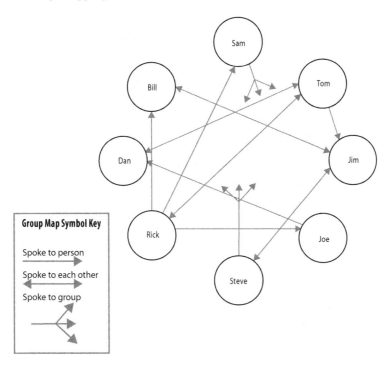

Multiple Benefits of Group Assessment

Using an instrument to periodically assess your group members' perceptions and experience of the group can provide an objective view of how well your group is functioning—one that is independent of your personal biases, clinical judgment, or countertransference. An instrument can be as brief as a few questions that measure very specific member self-perceptions, such as, "I stayed on task in the group today" or "I made a contribution to the group." Other instruments are more comprehensive and elaborate, yielding multiple subscale scores pertaining to various dimensions of group functioning, including member relationships, member-to-leader relationships, and member perceptions of the leader.

Whether you are a supervisor, therapist, researcher, clinical director, or program administrator, you can take advantage of available group measures to measure the quality and functioning of your groups. Measurement can come in the context of supervision, training, outcome research, program evaluation, individual client progress, or even self-evaluation, and you can measure your group(s) for many reasons:

- To assess the current level of cohesion, engagement, trust, satisfaction, etc., in the group.
- To establish a baseline for a given group for comparison of its level of functioning over time.
- To discern suspected or unrecognized problems, concerns, or dissatisfaction with the group leader or issues in the group.
- To assess how any given member is currently adjusting, progressing, and responding to the group and the treatment program.
- To identify or clarify particular subgroups and subrelationships or interaction patterns between and among members of group.
- To assess improvements in attachment over the course of group treatment.
- To assess progress (or lack of) in sexual offender-specific treatment.
- To measure performance/outcomes for research studies or internal program evaluation.
- To compare the therapist's and the group's perception of aspects of the group for level of congruence or incongruence.
- To identify and measure group developmental stages and compare to norms.
- To assess how well the group therapist is applying group facilitation skills.

Measures of Group Functioning

The field of group therapy has developed well over 20 different measures of group process, which are available for use (Burlingame, Fuhriman, & Johnson, 2001). We have selected an array of measures that can be used to assess and measure overall group functioning and/or that target specific dimensions and aspects of group process, including two tools designed especially for sexual offender-specific groups.

The GES (Group Environment Scale)

The Group Environment Scale (Moos, 1994) is a 90-item self-report scale that is completed by both group members and the group leader. It is used to assess the quality of the group therapeutic environment and to compare perceptions of the group members and leader(s). It contains 10 subscales measuring different aspects of group climate and functioning across three dimensions: Relationship Dimensions (Cohesion, Leader Support, and Expressiveness scales), Personal Growth (Independence, Task Orientation, Self-Discovery, and Anger and Aggression scales) and System Maintenance and Change (Order and Organization, Leader Control, and Innovation scales). While subscales are helpful in studying process variables, MacKenzie and Livesley (1986) recommend that it is important to do so in conjunction with a measure of the group as an entire system.

The GES is especially useful to us because it has been used in several studies of sexual offender treatment (e.g., Harkins & Beech, 2008; Beech & Hamilton-Giachritsis, 2005; Harkins, Beech, & Thornton, 2013; Davis, Marshall, Bradford, & Marshall, 2008). Beech and Fordham (1997) used this instrument to assess group functioning across multiple groups and sites. The findings are significant for the field as they found differences across groups and among leadership styles resulting in a different profile of a successful group. They also found differences between the group leaders' and members' scores, suggesting that leaders may perceive their role, relationship to the group, and contributions differently than the group members.

Steve found both similarities and differences between group member and leader perceptions when he used the GES and the GCQ (see below) in an unpublished study of adult outpatient treatment groups with multiple therapists. He found surprising consistency across groups and across time, as well as some significant differences among some groups. The results led to helpful discussions with the participating group therapists regarding their personal leadership style, decisions about group composition, facilitation philosophy, and group functioning.

The advantage of this measure is that it is well researched and provides multiple dimensions. Its shortcoming is its cumbersome size and length. Since the GES provides an individual profile of how a client views the group environment and his place in it, it is especially useful for clinicians whose primary interest is the individual, not the group as a whole.

The GCQ (Group Climate Questionnaire)

The Group Climate Questionnaire (GCQ; MacKenzie, 1981) is one of the most commonly used measures of group process in the group psychotherapy literature. One reason is that, with just 12 items, the GCQ has the advantage of ease of administration. The GCQ measures three dimensions: Engagement, Conflict, and Avoidance.

- **Engagement** is the extent to which the group members are connected to and actively participating in the group process. It includes items such as: "The members liked and cared about each other" and "The members revealed sensitive and personal information or feelings."
- **Conflict** is the degree of actual conflict in the group, such as: "The members rejected and distrusted each other" or "The members were distant and withdrawn from each other."
- **Avoidance** is measured by such items as, "The members avoided looking at important issues going on between themselves."

The three dimensions are interrelated. Thus, a group that is engaged and cohesive would facilitate open discussion of interpersonal conflicts, while a group that is not engaged might avoid conflict, withhold personal information, and show less caring among members. A group whose members are engaged, interact with one another, and do not avoid relationship conflict is correlated with higher levels of member satisfaction and change.

By providing a snapshot of group functioning at any given point in time, the GCQ can be used as frequently as weekly to assess group functioning. MacKenzie and Tschuschke (1993) found that relatedness was closely associated with cohesion and was correlated with positive outcome in inpatient psychotherapy groups. The GCQ can also be used to assess the three phases of group development. Kivlighan and Goldfine (1991) have determined the average score for each subscale for the initial Engagement phase, middle Differentiation phase, and final Individuation phase (see table 9.1). They found that engagement typically increases and avoidance decreases over the course of an effective group, while conflict is less intense in early group (when members tend avoid conflict) and late group (when members have learned to manage conflict, ostensibly after the going through the high levels of conflict of the middle phase). You can use these to assess how your group compares with established norms.

TABLE 9.1 AVERAGE GCQ SCORES ACROSS THE DEVELOPMENTAL PHASES OF A GROUP

GCQ Subscales	Group Developmental Phase (mean scores)		
	Engagement	Differentiation	Individuation
Engagement	3.48	3.78	3.95
Avoidance	2.16	2.18	1.67
Conflict	0.71	1.67	0.89

The TFI-8 (Therapeutic Factor Inventory–8)

The new TFI-8 was developed specifically to give group therapists a brief, reliable, and valid measure of the quality of group process (Tasca, Cabrera, Kristjansson, MacNair-Semands, Joyce, & Ogrodniczuk, 2014). Consisting of just eight self-rated items, the TFI-8 can be administered frequently and easily to continuously monitor the functioning of a group as a whole and to detect problems with any of the individual members.

The conciseness of the TFI-8 also reflects the growing conviction among group therapy researchers that therapeutic factors can be represented by a single higher-order group therapeutic factor (Burlingame, Fuhriman, & Johnson, 2002). Thus, instead of trying to measure and tease out the importance of multiple therapeutic factors—such as Yalom's 12 factors of cohesion, instillation of hope, universality, altruism, etc.—it is more practical and more reliable to conceive and measure a single group factor that encompasses multiple processes. Some group researchers believe that this single factor may be *expressed emotion* (Castonguay, Pincus, Agras, & Hines, 1998), while others think of it as *group cohesion* (Budman, Soldz, Demby, Davis, & Merry, 1993; Burlingame et al., 2002). The creators of the TFI-8 themselves "conceptualize the single TFI-8 factor as feeling *hopeful* about the processes of *emotional expression* and *relational awareness*, which then translate into and promote *social learning*" (Tasca et al., p. 10, italics added).

In fact, the TFI-8 originated as a 99-item TFI that was too cumbersome for practical use. Subsequently, the authors used factor analysis to condense the TFI to a shorter, more valid and reliable 23-item version in 2010, and then a 19-item version; both were very good at predicting positive outcomes. This process also led to the identification of four parallel group factors: instillation of hope, secure emotional expression, awareness of relational impact, and social learning. As shown in table 9.2, the TFI-8 retains these four subfactors in its eight items with two items for each factor.

The value of the TFI-8 is that it is very easy to use repeatedly to continually assess the therapeutic quality of the group and to immediately identify and address any disruptions within the group or an individual that requires a specific intervention in order to repair group functioning. As a tool, research indicates that the TFI-8 is more accurate in discriminating groups with low-to-moderate levels of the "single therapeutic factor," such as new or struggling groups, but less effective with well-functioning groups with high levels of cohesion and emotional expression.

Cohesiveness Subscale

This measure consists of nine rating items from the TFI-99. Rated on a seven-point scale from "not at all" to "extremely," it can be used in an ongoing fashion to establish a baseline and to monitor the level of cohesion of a group over time.

1. Even though others may disagree with me sometimes, I feel accepted in group.
2. We cooperate and work together in group.
3. I feel accepted by the group.
4. The members distrust each other.
5. I feel a sense of belonging in this group.
6. I feel good about being a part of this group.
7. Group members don't express caring for one another.
8. We trust each other in my group.
9. Even though we have differences, our group feels secure to me.

TABLE 9.2 THERAPEUTIC FACTORS INVENTORY–8	
TFI-8 Items	**Group Therapeutic Factor**
1. Because I've got a lot in common with other group members, I'm starting to think that I may have something in common with people outside group too.	Social Learning
2. I feel a sense of belonging in this group.	Secure Emotional Expression
3. In group I've learned that I have more similarities with others than I would have guessed.	Instillation of Hope
4. My group is kind of like a little piece of the larger world I live in: I see the same patterns, and working them out in group helps me work them out in my outside life.	Social Learning
5. I pay attention to how others handle difficult situations in my group so I can apply these strategies in my own life.	Awareness of Relational Impact
6. This group inspires me about the future.	Instillation of Hope
7. Even though we have differences, our group feels secure to me.	Secure Emotional Expression
8. By getting honest feedback from members and facilitators, I've learned a lot about my impact on other people.	Awareness of Relational Impact

Group Session Rating Scale (GSRS)

Ultra-brief measures have been developed for individual therapy to assess session-by-session *treatment progress* (e.g., Outcome Rating Scale by Miller, Duncan, Brown, Sparks, & Claud, 2003) and *alliance* (e.g., Session Rating Scale by Duncan, Miller, Sparks, Claud, Reynolds, Brown, & Johnson, 2003). Based on these two measures, Duncan & Miller (2007) created the Group Session Rating Scale as an ultra-brief measure of group therapy alliance. As shown in figure 9.2, this two-minute, four-item measure is a visual analog scale in which the client rates each item by making a mark on a 10-centimeter line. The group therapist measures and sums the lengths of the four lines to calculate the GSRS score of up to 40 points.

Figure 9.2 Visual Analog Scale

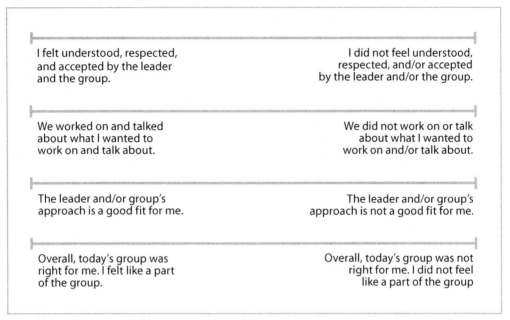

Quirk, Miller, Duncan, & Owen (2012) established the validity and reliability of the GSRS in relation to the other established group measures including the TFI-Cohesion scale and Group Climate Scale discussed above. Though brief, the GSRS was strongly correlated with measures of group cohesion, group climate, therapist-rated alliance, and client-rated alliance.

The GEM (Group Engagement Measure)

Macgowan and Levenson (2003) developed the psychometrics for the Group Engagement Measure (GEM) as the first and only measure of group process specific to sexual offender treatment. This 37-item instrument includes both therapist- and client-rated versions, which assess seven group engagement factors: attending, contributing, relating to worker, relating with members, contracting, working on own problems, and working on others' problems. Levenson and Macgowan (2004) also established correlations among the GEM, Group Attitude Scale, Sex Offender Treatment Rating Scale, and Facets of Sexual Offender Denial measure at the scale and subscale levels, and used the GEM in two additional studies (Levenson, Macgowan, Morin, & Cotter, 2009; Levenson, Prescott, & D'Amora, 2010).

Group Member Satisfaction Questionnaire

Levenson and her colleagues developed a comprehensive satisfaction questionnaire, which was used in a series of five published studies covering 582 sex offenders across multiple outpatient and inpatient civil commitment settings (Levenson & Macgowan, 2004; Levenson, Macgowan, Morin, & Cotter, 2009; Levenson & Prescott, 2009; Levenson, Prescott, & D'Amora, 2010; Levenson, Prescott, & Jumper, 2014). The satisfaction survey is divided into several subsections. One section asks the participant to rate the importance and perceived benefit of 20 different aspects or components that are common to sexual offender-specific treatment. Another section rates the perceived importance and benefit of five issues of group process. A third section includes eight items asking about satisfaction with group climate in areas such as comfort, structure, trust, and participation. A fourth section asks about program policies and rules. This questionnaire can be gleaned from the studies listed above.

RSQ (Relationship Scales Questionnaire)

The RSQ is not a group process measure, but it can be used to identify the particular secure or insecure attachment styles of individual members to better understand dynamics related to attachment issues (see chapter 7). There are several variations on the RSQ, but we recommend the version consisting of 17 items because it is the shortest and easiest to use (Griffin & Bartholomew, 1994). The RSQ can also be repeated after a significant period of group membership or at the end of treatment to measure improvements in attachment gained from group therapy and overall treatment.

Tools for Assessing Therapist Facilitation Skills

In addition to tools for assessing our group members and group processes, there are also tools for assessing how well we, as group therapists, are able to apply our group facilitation skills and knowledge.

GPIRS

The Group Psychotherapy Intervention Rating Scale (GPIRS) evaluates group leaders on the basis of their ability to perform interventions aimed at enhancing group cohesion. The GPIRS is an observer-rated, behavioral measure consisting of 48 items that assess therapist behaviors specific to setting and maintaining group structure, facilitating verbal interactions, and maintaining emotional climate. Each item is rated on a five-point scale from 0 for "intervention did not occur" to 5 for "excellent" use of the intervention. Examples are included in table 9.3.

TABLE 9.3 SAMPLE ITEMS FROM THE GPIRS		
Group Structure	Verbal Interaction	Creating and Maintaining a Therapeutic Emotional Climate
• Discussed group rules such as time, attendance, absences, tardiness, confidentiality, and participation. • Identified and discussed fears/concerns regarding self-disclosure.	• Facilitated appropriate member-to-member interaction. • Encouraged self-disclosure relevant to the current group agenda. • Balanced positive and corrective leader-to-member feedback.	• Maintained balance in expressions of emotional support and confrontation. • Encouraged active emotional engagement between group members. • Elicited verbal expressions of support among group members.

Of note, Chapman, Baker, Porter, Thayer, and Burlingame (2010) used the GCQ in their validation research of the GPIRS and found significant correlations between leader intervention scores and group member perceptions of group climate and verbal interaction scores, as well as correlations between group leader interventions aimed to gain balance between confrontation and warmth and the group members' rated levels of group cohesion.

IC-SWG

The Inventory of Competencies in Social Work with Groups (IC-SWG) was developed to assess the group leader's knowledge of essential group therapy techniques and confidence in their group practice (McGowan, 2012). The 70-item inventory measures two domains for each item: how important the item is for successful group work, and how confident the respondent is about demonstrating the skill in practice. Some examples from the IC-SWG items include the following:

- Prepares members for the group in appropriate ways.
- Selects the group type, structure, processes, and size that will be appropriate for attaining the purposes of the group.
- Establishes rapport with individual members and the group as a whole.
- Identifies difficulties and obstacles that interfere with the group and its members' abilities to reach their goals.
- Models and encourages honest communication and feedback among members and between members and workers.

The IC-SWG can provide feedback on competency in group skills to the group leader, his or her supervisor, and even the program administrator who has responsibility for the quality of the services being provided. The tool does not assess specific group processes, but it can provide valuable information about the structure of the group environment and overall facilitation process as observed from an outside or extra-group perspective.

Summary and Conclusions

There are many reasons that you may want to measure the quality and functioning of your group, including its levels of cohesion, engagement, and satisfaction. Measuring a group can be used to establish a starting baseline for pre- and post-treatment and for measuring effectiveness and outcomes. It can be a great way to assess how individual members, and the group as a whole, are progressing (or struggling) over the course of treatment. It can reveal how well the perceptions of the group therapist align with those of the group members. As summarized in table 9.4, there are many comprehensive and brief measures to choose from to meet your needs.

TABLE 9.4 SUMMARY CHART OF GROUP MEASURES

Name of Instrument or Tool	Size	Areas/Aspects of Group Measured
GES Group Environment Scale-R (Moos, 1994)	90 items 10 subscales	Measures overall group climate, including 10 areas such as cohesion, therapist issues, structure, task orientation, etc.
GCQ-SF Group Climate Questionnaire–Short Form (Mackenzie, 1983)	12 items 3 subscales	Measures group members' perceptions of the group therapeutic climate, including engagement, conflict, and avoidance. Also measures developmental phases of group.
TFI-8 Therapeutic Factors Inventory–8 (Tasca et al., 2014)	8 items 4 factors	Quick, easy, valid, and reliable assessment of overall group climate.
TFI-99 Therapeutic Factors Inventory–99 (Tasca et al., 2014)	99 items 4 factors	Measures group climate, particularly areas of instillation of hope, secure emotional expression, awareness of relational impact, and social learning
Cohesiveness Subscale [from the TFI-99 by Tasca et al., 2014]	9 items	Quick measure of cohesion drawn from the TFI-99.
GEM Group Engagement Measure (Macgowan & Levenson, 2003)	37 items 7 factors	Created specifically for measuring level of engagement of sexual-offender-specific groups.
Group Member Satisfaction Questionnaire (Levenson & McGowan, 2004)	90 items	Created specifically for measuring client perceptions of and satisfaction with various aspects of sexual-offender-specific groups, group process, and treatment.
RSQ Relationship Scale Questionnaire (Griffin & Bartholomew, 1994)	17 items	Identification of individual secure or insecure attachment styles and changes over time in response to group experience.
GSRS Group Session Rating Scale	4 items	Ultra-brief global measure of alliance within the therapy group that can be delivered session by session.
GPIRS Group Psychotherapy Intervention Rating Scale (Chapman et al, 2010)	48 items	Observer-based assessment of group therapist behaviors/skills in facilitating group structure, member interaction, emotional climate, and therapist qualities.
IC-SWG Inventory of Competencies in Social Work (McGowan, 2012)	70 items	External rating of therapist's knowledge of essential group therapy techniques and level of confidence.

References

Abel, G., Becker, J., Mittelman, M., Cunningham-Rathner, J., Rouleau, J., & Murphy, W. (1987). Self-reported sex crimes of nonincarcerated paraphiliacs. *Journal of Interpersonal Violence, 2*, 3–25.

Ainsworth, M., Blehar, M., Everett, W., & Wall, S. (1978). *Patterns of attachment: A psychological study of the strange situation*. Hillsdale, NJ: Lawrence Erlbaum.

Allam, J., Middleton, D., & Browne, K. (1997). Different clients, different needs? Practice issues in community-based treatment for sex offenders. *Criminal Behavior and Mental Health, 7*, 69–84.

American Counselling Association. (2014). *Code of ethics*. Alexandria, VA: ACA.

American Group Psychotherapy Association. (2002). *AGPA and NRCGP guidelines for ethics*. Retrieved May 17, 2010, from www.agpa.org

American Group Psychotherapy Association. (2007). *Guidelines for group psychotherapy practice*. New York, NY: AGPA.

American Psychological Association. (2010). *Ethical principles of psychologists and code of conduct*. Retrieved May 28, 2010, http://www.apa.org/pubs/index.aspx.

Andrews, D., & Bonta, J. (2007). *Risk-need-responsivity model for offender assessment and rehabilitation*. Ottawa, Canada: Correctional Services of Canada.

Association for the Advancement of Social Work with Groups. (2006). *Standards for social work practice with groups* (2nd ed.). Retrieved October 11, 2014, iaswg.org

Association for the Treatment of Sexual Abusers (2001). *Professional Code of Ethics*. Beaverton, OR.

Association for the Treatment of Sexual Abusers. (2014). *Practice guidelines for the assessment, treatment, and management of male adult sexual abusers*. Beaverton, OR: ATSA.

Association of Social Work Boards. (2008). *Continuing education requirements*. Retrieved May 18, 2010, from www.aswb.org

Awad, G., Saunders, E., & Levene, J. (1984). A clinical study of male adolescent sexual offenders. *International Journal of Offender Therapy and Comparative Criminology, 28*, 105–155.

Aylwin, A. (2010). *The therapeutic alliance in sex offender treatment: The juxaposition of violence and care* (Doctoral dissertation). University of Alberta, Edmonton, Alberta, Canada.

Baker, E., & Beech, A. (2004). Dissociation and variability of adult attachment dimensions and early maladaptive schemas in sexual and violent offenders. *Journal of Interpersonal Violence, 19*, 1119–1136.

Bard, L., Carter, D., Cerce, D., Knight, R., Rosenberg, R., & Schneider, B. (1987). A descriptive study of rapists and child molesters: Developmental, clinical, and criminal characteristics. *Behavioral Sciences and the Law, 5*, 203–220.

Bartholomew, K., & Horowitz, L. (1991). Attachment styles among young adults: A test of a four-category model. *Journal of Personality and Social Psychology, 61*, 226–244.

Bauman, S., & Kopp, G. (2004). An integrated humanistic approach to outpatient groups for adult sex offenders. *Vistas Online* (American Counseling Association), 2004.

Beech, A., & Fordham, A. (1997). Therapeutic climate of sexual offender treatment programs. *Sexual Abuse: A Journal of Research and Treatment, 8*, 219–237.

Beech, A., & Hamilton-Giachritsis, C. (2005). Relationship between therapeutic climate and treatment outcome in group-based sexual offender treatment programs. *Sexual Abuse: A Journal of Research and Treatment, 17*, 127–140.

Beutler, L., Moleiro, C., & Talebi, H. (2002). Resistance. In J. Norcross (Ed.), *Psychotherapy relationships that work* (pp. 129–144). New York, NY: Oxford University Press.

Black, S., Hardy, G., Turpin, G., & Parry, G. (2005). Self-reported attachment styles and therapeutic orientation of therapists and their relationship with reported general alliance quality and problems in therapy. *Psychology and Psychotherapy: Theory, Research and Practice, 78*, 363–377.

Blaske, D., Borduin, C., Henggeler, S., & Mann, B. (1989). Individual, family and peer characteristics of adolescent sex offenders and assaultive offenders. *Developmental Psychology, 25*, 846–855.

Bowlby, J. (1969; 1982). *Attachment and loss: Vol. 1. Attachment.* New York, NY: Basic Books.

Brehm, J. (1966). *A theory of psychological reactance.* New York, NY: Academic Press.

Brown, N. (2003). Conceptualizing process. *International Journal of Group Psychotherapy, 53*, 225–244.

Budman, S., Soldz, S., Demby, A., Davis, M., & Merry, J. (1993). What is cohesiveness? An empirical examination. *Small Group Research, 24*, 199–216.

Bumby, K., & Hansen, D. (1997). Intimacy deficits, fear of intimacy, and loneliness among sexual offenders. *Criminal Justice and Behavior, 24*, 315–331.

Bumby, K., & Marshall, W. (1994). *Loneliness and intimacy deficits among incarcerated rapists and child molesters*. Paper presented at the 13th annual Association for the Treatment of Sexual Abusers conference, San Francisco, CA.

Burlingame, G., Fuhriman, A., & Johnson, J. (2002). Cohesion in group psychotherapy. In J. Norcross (Ed.), *Psychotherapy relationships that work* (pp. 71–88). New York, NY: Oxford University Press.

Burlingame, G., Fuhriman, A., & Mosier, J. (2003). The differential effectiveness of group psychotherapy: A meta-analytic perspective. *Group Dynamics: Theory, Research, and Practice, 7*, 3–12.

Burlingame, G., McClendon, D., & Alonso, J. (2011). Cohesion in group psychotherapy. In J. Norcross (Ed.), *Psychotherapy relationships that work* (2nd ed., pp. 110–131). New York, NY: Oxford University Press.

Burlingame, G., Strauss, B., & Joyce, A. (2013). Change mechanisms and effectiveness of small group treatments. In M. Lambert (Ed.), *Handbook of psychotherapy and behavior change* (pp. 640–689). New York, NY: Wiley & Sons.

Burtenshaw, R. (1997, August). An ethnic comparison of the ranked value of Yalom's therapeutic factors among chemically dependent incarcerated adult males in group psychotherapy. *Dissertation Abstracts International, 58*(2-A).

Campbell, C., & Gordon, M. (2003). Acknowledging the inevitable: Understanding multiple relationships in rural practice. *Professional Psychology: Research and Practice, 34*, 430–434.

Castonguay, L., Pincus, A., Agras, W., & Hines, C. (1998). The role of emotion in group cognitive-behavioral therapy for binge eating disorder: When things have to feel worse before they get better. *Psychotherapy Research, 8*, 225–238.

Chapman, C., Baker, E., Porter, G., Thayer, S., & Burlingame, G. (2010). Rating group therapist interventions: The validation of the Group Psychotherapy Intervention Rating Scale. *Group Dynamics: Theory, Research, and Practice, 14*, 15–31.

Clark, P., & Erooga, M. (1994). Groupwork with men who sexually abuse children. In T. Morrison, M. Erooga, & R. Beckett (Eds.), *Sexual offending against children: Assessment and treatment of male abusers* (pp. 102–128). New York, NY: Routledge.

Connor, D., Copes, H., & Tewksbury, R. (2011). Incarcerated sex offenders' perceptions of prison sex offender treatment programs. *Justice Policy Journal, 8*, 1–23.

Cook, D., Fox, C., Weaver, C., & Rooth, F. (1991). The Berkeley Group: Ten years' experience of a group for non-violent sex offenders. *British Journal of Psychiatry, 158*, 238–243.

Costell, R., & Yalom, I. (1972). Institutional group therapy (of sex offenders). In H. Resnik & E. Wolfgang (Eds.), *Sexual behaviors: Social, clinical, and legal aspects* (pp. 305–330). New York, NY: Little, Brown.

Counselman, E., & Gans, J. (1999). The missed session in psychodynamic group psychotherapy. *International Journal of Group Psychotherapy, 49*, 3–17.

Cox, F., Ilfeld, F., Squire-Ilfeld, B., & Brennan, C. (2000). Group therapy program development: Administrator collaboration in new practice settings. *International Journal of Group Psychotherapy, 50*, 3–24.

Craissati, J., McClurg, G., & Browne, K. (2002). Characteristics of perpetrators of child sexual abuse who have been sexually victimized as children. *Sexual Abuse: A Journal of Research and Treatment, 14*, 225–240.

Davis, A., Marshall, L., Bradford, J., & Marshall, W. (2008). *Group climate in a program for seriously mentally ill sexual offenders.* Paper presented at the 27th Annual Research and Treatment Conference, Association for the Treatment of Sexual Abusers, Atlanta, GA.

Diener, M., & Monroe, J. (2001). The relationship between adult attachment style and therapeutic alliance in individual psychotherapy: A meta-analytic review. *Psychotherapy, 48*, 237–248.

Dies, R. (1986). Practical theoretical, and empirical foundations for group psychotherapy. In A. Francis & R. Hales (Eds.), *The American Psychiatric Association annual review* (Vol. 5, pp. 659–677). Washington, DC: American Psychiatric Press.

Di Fazio, R., Abracen, J., & Looman, J. (2001). Group versus individual treatment of sex offenders: A comparison. *Forum on Corrections Research, 13*, 56–59.

Dozier, M. (1990). Attachment organization and treatment use for adults with serious psychopathological disorders. *Development and Psychopathology, 2*, 47–60.

Drapeau, M. (2005). Research on the processes involved in treating sexual offenders. *Sexual Abuse: A Journal of Research and Treatment, 17*, 117–125.

Drapeau, M., Körner, C., Brunet, L., & Granger, L. (2004). Treatment at La Macaza Clinic: A qualitative study of the sexual offenders' perspective. *Canadian Journal of Criminology and Criminal Justice, 46*, 27–44.

Duncan, B., & Miller, S. (2007). *The Group Session Rating Scale*. Jensen Beach, FL: Author.

Duncan, B., Miller, S., Sparks, J., Claud, D., Reynolds, L., Brown, J., & Johnson, L. (2003). The Session Rating Scale: Psychometric properties of a "working" alliance scale. *Journal of Brief Therapy*, 3, 3–12.

Eames, V., & Roth, A. (2000). Patient attachment orientation and the early working alliance: A study of patient and therapist reports of alliance quality and ruptures. *Psychotherapy Research*, 10, 421–434.

Erikson, E. (1968). *Identity: Youth and crisis*. New York, NY: Norton.

Fagan, J., & Wexler, S. (1988). Explanations of sexual assault among violent delinquents. *Journal of Adolescent Research*, 3, 363–385.

Fehr, S. (2002). *Introduction to group therapy: A practical guide* (2nd ed.). New York, NY: Hayworth Press.

Fowler, C., Burns, S., & Roehl, J. (1983). The role of group therapy in incest counseling. *International Journal of Family Therapy*, 5, 127–135.

Frey, C. (1987). Mini-marathon group sessions with incest offenders. *Social Work*, 32, 534–535.

Frost, A. (2000). *New connections: The engagement in group therapy of incarcerated men who have sexually offended against children* (Doctoral dissertation). University of Canterbury, Christchurch, New Zealand.

Frost, A. (2004). Therapeutic engagement styles of child sexual offenders in a group treatment program: A grounded theory study. *Sexual Abuse: A Journal of Research and Treatment*, 16, 191–208.

Frost, A., & Connolly, M. (2004). Reflexivity, reflection, and the change process in offender work. *Sexual Abuse: A Journal of Research and Treatment*, 16, 365–380.

Frost, A., & Daniels, K. (2006). Disclosure strategies among sex offenders: A model for understanding the engagement process in groupwork. *Journal of Sexual Aggression*, 12, 227–244.

Ganzarain, R., & Buchele, B. (1990). Incest perpetrators in group therapy: A psychodynamic perspective. *Bulletin of the Menninger Clinic*, 54, 295–310.

Garbutt, K., & Hocken, K. (2014). *Treatment implications of sex offenders' attachment styles*. Paper presented at the 33rd Annual Research and Treatment Conference, Association for the Treatment of Sexual Abusers, San Diego, CA.

Garbutt, K. & Palmer, E. (2015, in press). Client attachment and the perceived environment in sexual offender treatment. Unpublished manuscript.

Garlick, Y., Marshall, W., & Thornton, D. (1996). Intimacy deficits and attribution of blame among sexual offenders. *Legal and Criminological Psychology*, 1, 251–258.

Garrett, T., Oliver, C., Wilcox, D., & Middleton, D. (2003). Who cares? The views of sexual offenders about the group treatment they receive. *Sexual Abuse: A Journal of Research and Treatment, 15*, 323–338.

Gillaspy, J., Wright, A., Campbell, C., Stokes, S., & Adinoff, B. (2002). Group alliance and cohesion as predictors of drug and alcohol abuse treatment outcomes. *Psychotherapy Research, 12*, 213–229.

Goldman, G., & Anderson, T. (2007). Quality of object relations and security of attachment as predictors of therapeutic alliance. *Journal of Counseling Psychology, 54*, 111–117.

Grattagliano, I., Cassibba, R., Costantini, A., Laquale, G., Latrofa, A., Papagna, S., Sette, G., Taurino, A., & Terlizzi, M. (2015). Attachment models in incarcerated sex offenders: A preliminary Italian study using the adult attachment interview. *Journal of Forensic Science, 60*, 138–142.

Griffin, D., & Bartholomew, K. (1994). The metaphysics of measurement: The case of adult attachment. In K. Bartholomew & D. Perlman (Eds.), *Advances in personal relationships: attachment processes in adult relationships* (Vol. 5, pp. 17–52). London, UK: Jessica Kingsley.

Gutheil, T., & Gabbard, G. (1993). The concept of boundaries in clinical practice: Theoretical and risk-management dimensions. *American Journal of Psychiatry, 150*, 188–196.

Halse, A., Grant, J., Thornton, J., Indermaur, D., Stevens, G., & Chamarette, C. (2012). Intrafamilial adolescent sex offenders' response to psychological treatment. *Psychiatry, Psychology and Law, 19*, 221–235.

Hanson, R., & Morton-Bourgon, K. (2005). The characteristics of persistent sexual offenders: A meta-analysis of recidivism studies. *Journal of Consulting and Clinical Psychology, 73*, 1154–1163.

Harkins, L., & Beech, A. (2007). A review of the factors that can influence the effectiveness of sexual offender treatment: Risk, need, responsibility, and process issues. *Aggression and Violent Behavior: A Review Journal, 12*, 615–627.

Harkins, L., & Beech, A. (2008). Examining the impact of mixing child molesters and rapists in group-based cognitive-behavioral treatment for sexual offenders. *International Journal of Offender Therapy and Comparative Criminology, 52*, 31–45.

Harkins, L., Beech, A., & Thornton, D. (2013). The influence of risk and psychopathy on the therapeutic climate in sex offender treatment. *Sexual Abuse: Journal of Research and Treatment, 25*, 103–122.

Hazelwood, R., & Warren, J. (1989). The serial rapist: His characteristics and victims (conclusion). *FBI Law Enforcement Bulletin, 58,* 18–25.

Heil, P., Ahlmeyer, S., & Simons, D. (2003). Crossover sexual offenses. *Sexual Abuse: A Journal of Research and Treatment, 15,* 221–236.

Hesse, E. (2008). The Adult Attachment Interview: Protocol, method of analysis, and empirical research. In J. Cassidy & P. Shaver (Eds.), *Handbook of attachment: Theory, research and clinical applications* (pp. 552–598). New York, NY: Guilford Press.

Holdsworth, E., Bowen, E., & Brown, S. (2014). Offender engagement in group programs and associations with offender characteristics and treatment factors: A review. *Aggression and Violent Behavior, 18,* 102–121.

Houston, J., Wrench, M., & Hosking, N. (1995). Group processes in the treatment of child sex offenders. *Journal of Forensic Psychiatry, 6,* 359–368.

Hudson, K. (2005). *Offending identities: Sex offenders' perspectives of their treatment and management.* Cullompton, UK: Willan Publishing.

Hudson, S., & Ward, T. (1997). Intimacy, loneliness, and attachment style in sexual offenders. *Journal of Interpersonal Violence, 12,* 323–339.

International Association for the Treatment of Sexual Offenders (2016). Standards of Care for the Treatment of Sexual Offenders. https://www.iatso.org/index.php?option=com_phocadownload&view=category&id=4&Itemid=24. Retrieved May 9, 2016.

Jamieson, S., & Marshall, W. (2000). Attachment styles and violence in child molesters. *Journal of Sexual Aggression, 5,* 88–98.

Jennings, J. (1987). History and issues in the treatment of battering men: A case for unstructured group therapy. *Journal of Family Violence, 2,* 193–213.

Jennings, J. (1990). Preventing relapse versus "stopping" domestic violence: Do we expect too much too soon from battering men? *Journal of Family Violence, 5,* 43–60.

Jennings, J., & Deming, A. (2013). Effectively utilizing the "behavioral" in cognitive-behavioral group therapy of sex offenders. *International Journal of Behavioral Consultation and Therapy, 8,* 7–13.

Jennings, J., & Deming, A. (2016). Review of the empirical and clinical support for group therapy specific to sexual abusers. *Sexual Abuse: A Journal of Research and Treatment.* Advance online publication. doi:10/1177/1079063215618376.

Jennings, J., & Murphy, C. (2000). The male–male dimensions of male–female battering: A new look at domestic violence. *Journal of Men and Masculinity, 1,* 21–29.

Jennings, J., & Sawyer, S. (2003). Principles and techniques for maximizing the effectiveness of group therapy with sex offenders. *Sexual Abuse: A Journal of Research and Treatment, 15,* 251–267.

Johnson, D., & Lokey, J. (2007, Summer). Individual psychology approaches to group sex offender treatment. *Professional Issues in Psychology.* Retrieved from http://www.shsu.edu/piic/summer2007/lokey.htm

Kahn, T., & Chambers, H. (1991). Assessing re-offence risk with juvenile sexual offenders. *Child Welfare, 70,* 333–345.

Kazemi, E., Nayar, M., & Pogosjana, M. (2012). A critical review of the current literature on intimacy deficits and sexual offending. In B. Schwartz (Ed.), *The sex offender* (Vol. 7). Kingston, NJ: Civic Research Institute.

Keating, L., Tasca, G., Gick, M., Ritchie, K., Balfour, L., & Bissada, H. (2014). Change in attachment to the therapy group generalizes to change in individual attachment among women with binge eating disorder. *Psychotherapy, 51,* 78–87.

Kemper, B. (1994). Dealing with resistance in group therapy. *Perspectives in Psychiatric Care, 30,* 31–36.

Kilmann, P., Urbaniak, G., & Parnell, M. (2006). Effects of attachment-focused versus relationship skills-focused interventions for college students with insecure attachment patterns. *Attachment and Human Development, 8,* 47–62.

Kirmayer, L. (1990). Resistance, reactance and reluctance to change: A cognitive attributional approach to strategic interventions. *Journal of Cognitive Psychotherapy, 4,* 83–104.

Kivlighan, D., & Goldfine, D. (1991). Endorsement of therapeutic factors as a function of stage of group development and participant interpersonal attitudes. *Journal of Counseling Psychology, 38,* 150–158.

Knox, L. (2009). *Juvenile sex offenders: A consideration of attachment deficits in the etiology of offending.* Unpublished manuscript, Department of Psychology, Portland State University, Portland, OR.

Korfmacher, J., Adam, E., Ogawa, J., & Egeland, B. (1997). Adult attachment implications for the therapeutic process in a home visitation intervention. *Applied Developmental Science, 1,* 43–52.

Levenson, J., & Macgowan, M. (2004). Engagement, denial, and treatment progress among sex offenders in group therapy. *Sexual Abuse: A Journal of Research and Treatment, 16,* 49–63.

Levenson, J., Macgowan, M., Morin, J., & Cotter, L. (2009). Perceptions of sex offenders about treatment: Satisfaction and engagement in group therapy. *Sexual Abuse: A Journal of Research and Treatment, 21,* 35–56.

Levenson, J., & Prescott, D. (2009). Treatment experiences of civilly committed sex offenders: A consumer satisfaction survey. *Sexual Abuse: A Journal of Research and Treatment, 21*, 6–20.

Levenson, J., Prescott, D., & D'Amora, D. (2010). Sex offender treatment: Consumer satisfaction and engagement in therapy. *International Journal of Offender Therapy and Comparative Criminology, 54*, 307–326.

Levenson, J., Prescott, D., & Jumper, S. (2014). A consumer satisfaction survey of civilly committed sex offenders in Illinois. *International Journal of Offender Therapy and Comparative Criminology, 58*, 474–495.

Levenson, J., Willis, G., & Prescott, D. (2014). Adverse childhood experiences in the lives of male sex offenders: Implications for trauma-informed care. *Sexual Abuse: A Journal of Research and Treatment.* Advance online publication. doi:10.1177/1079063214535819.

Lisak, D., & Ivan, C. (1995). Deficits in intimacy and empathy in sexually aggressive men. *Journal of Interpersonal Violence, 10*, 296–308.

Lisak, D., & Roth, S. (1990). Motives and psychodynamics of self-reported, unincarcerated rapists. *American Journal of Orthopsychiatry, 60*, 268–280.

Liungman, C. (1991). *Dictionary of symbols.* Santa Barbara, CA: ABC-CLIO.

Long, L., & Cope, C. (1980). Curative factors in a male felony offender group. *Small Group Behavior, 11*, 389–398.

Longo, R. (2004). An integrated experiential approach to treating young people who sexually abuse. *Journal of Child Sexual Abuse, 13*, 193–213.

Lyn, T., & Burton, D. (2004). Adult attachment and sexual offender status. *American Journal of Orthopsychiatry, 74*, 150–159.

MacDevitt, J., & Stanislaw, C. (1987). Curative factors in male felony offender groups. *Small Group Behavior, 18*, 72–81.

Macgowan, M. (2012). A standards-based inventory of foundation competencies in social work with groups. *Research on Social Work Practice, 22*, 578–589.

Macgowan, M., & Levenson, J. (2003). Psychometrics of the Group Engagement Measure with male sex offenders. *Small Group Research, 34*, 155–160.

MacKenzie, K. R. (1981). Measurement of group climate. *Journal of Group Psychotherapy, 31*, 287–296.

MacKenzie, K. (1983). The clinical application of a group climate measure. In R. Dies & K. MacKenzie (Eds.), *Advances in group psychotherapy: Integrating research and practice* (pp. 159–170). New York, NY: International Universities Press.

MacKenzie, K., & Livesley, W. (1984). Developmental stages: An integrating theory of group psychotherapy. *Canadian Journal of Psychiatry, 29*, 247–251.

MacKenzie, H., & Livesley, W. (1986). Outcome and process measures in brief group psychotherapy. *Psychiatric Annals, 16,* 715–720.

Maletzky, B. (1999). Groups of one. *Sexual Abuse: A Journal of Research and Treatment, 11,* 179–181.

Mallinckrodt, B. (2000). Attachment, social competencies, social support and interpersonal process in psychotherapy. *Psychotherapy Research, 10,* 239–266.

Mallinckrodt, B., Gantt, D., & Coble, H. (1995). Attachment patterns in psychotherapy: Development of the Client Attachment to Therapist Scale. *Journal of Counseling Psychology, 42,* 307–317.

Marsa, F., O'Reilly, G., Carr, A., Murphy, P., O'Sullivan, M., Cotter, A., & Hevey, D. (2004). Attachment styles and psychological profiles of child sex offenders in Ireland. *Journal of Interpersonal Violence, 19,* 228–251.

Marshall, W. (1989). Intimacy, loneliness and sexual offenders. *Behavioral Research and Therapy, 27,* 491–503.

Marshall, W. (1993). The role of attachments, intimacy, and loneliness in the etiology and maintenance of sexual offending. *Sexual and Marital Therapy, 8,* 109–121.

Marshall, W. (2005). Therapist style in sexual offender treatment: Influence on indices of change. *Sexual Abuse: A Journal of Research and Treatment, 17,* 109–116.

Marshall, W., Anderson, D., & Fernandez, Y. (1999). *Cognitive-behavioral treatment of sexual offenders.* London, UK: Wiley.

Marshall, W., Barbaree, H., & Fernandez, Y. (1995). Some aspects of social competence in sexual offenders. *Sexual Abuse: A Journal of Research and Treatment, 7,* 113–127.

Marshall, W., Bryce, P., Hudson, S., Ward, T., & Moth, B. (1997). The enhancement of intimacy and the reduction of loneliness among child molesters. *Legal and Criminological Psychology, 1,* 95–102.

Marshall, W., Burton, D., & Marshall, L. (2013). Features of treatment delivery and group processes that maximize the effects of offender programs. In J. Wood & T. Gannon (Eds.), *Crime and crime reduction: The importance of group processes* (pp. 159–174). New York, NY: Routledge.

Marshall, W., & Burton, S. (2010). The importance of group processes in offender treatment. *Aggression and Violent Behavior: A Review Journal, 15,* 141–149.

Marshall, W., Fernandez, Y., Serran, G., Mulloy, R., Thornton, D., Mann, R., & Anderson, D. (2003). Process variables in the treatment of sexual offenders: A review of the relevant literature. *Aggression and Violent Behavior: A Review Journal, 8,* 205–234.

Marshall, W., Marshall, L., Serran, G., & Fernandez, Y. (2006). *Treating sexual offenders: An integrated approach.* New York, NY: Routledge.

Marshall, W., & Mazzucco, A. (1995). Self-esteem and parental attachments in child molesters. *Sexual Abuse: A Journal of Research and Treatment, 7,* 279–285.

Marshall, W., Serran G., & Cortoni, F. (2000). Childhood attachments, sexual abuse, and their relationship to adult coping in child molesters. *Sexual Abuse: A Journal of Research and Treatment, 12,* 17–26.

Marshall, W., Serran, G., Moulden, H., Mulloy, R., Fernandez, Y., Mann, R., & Thornton, D. (2002). Therapist features in sexual offender treatment: Their reliable identification and influence on behavior change. *Clinical Psychology and Psychotherapy, 9,* 395–405.

Marshall, W., Thornton, D., Marshall, L., Fernandez, Y., and Mann, R. (2001). Treatment of sexual offenders who are in categorical denial: A pilot project. *Sexual Abuse: A Journal of Research and Treatment, 13,* 205–216.

Martin, M., Garske, J., & Davis, M. (2000). Relation of the therapeutic alliance with outcome and other variables: A meta-analytic review. *Journal of Counseling and Clinical Psychology, 68,* 438–450.

Maslow, A. (1954). *Motivation and personality.* New York, NY: Harper.

Maxwell, H., Tasca, G., Ritchie, K., Balfour, L., & Bissada, H. (2014). Change in attachment insecurity is related to improved outcomes 1-year post group therapy in women with binge eating disorder. *Psychotherapy, 51,* 57–65.

McCormack, J., Hudson, S., & Ward, T. (2002). Sexual offenders' perceptions of their early interpersonal relationships: An attachment perspective. *Journal of Sex Research, 39,* 85–93.

McGrath, R., Cumming, G., Burchard, B., Zeoli, S., & Ellerby, L. (2010) *Current practices and emerging trends in sexual abuser management: The Safer Society 2009 North American survey.* Brandon, VT: Safer Society Press.

McRoberts, C., Burlingame, G., & Hoag, M. (1998). Comparative efficacy of individual and group psychotherapy: A meta-analytic perspective. *Group Dynamics: Theory, Research, and Practice, 2,* 101–117.

Miller, S., Duncan, B., Brown, J., Sparks, J., & Claud, D. (2003). The Outcome Rating Scale: A preliminary study of the reliability, validity, and feasibility of a brief visual analog measure. *Journal of Brief Therapy, 2,* 91–100.

Milner, T., & Robertson, M. (1990). Comparison of physical child abusers, intrafamilial sexual child abusers and child neglecters. *Journal of Interpersonal Violence, 5,* 37–48.

Minnesota Board of Social Work. (2009). Minnesota Board of Social Work Practice Act, Minnesota Statute §148D.

Miner, M., & Munns, R. (2005). Isolation and normlessness: Attitudinal comparisons of adolescent sex offenders, juvenile offenders, and nondelinquents. *International Journal of Offender Therapy and Comparative Criminology, 49*, 491–504.

Miner, M., Robinson, B., Knight, R., Berg, D., Swinburne Romine, R., & Netland, J. (2010). Understanding sexual perpetration against children: Effects of attachment style, interpersonal involvement, and hypersexuality. *Sexual Abuse: A Journal of Research and Treatment, 22*, 58–77.

Miner, M., Swinburne Romine, R., Robinson, B., Berg, D., & Knight, R. (2016). Anxious attachment, social isolation, and indicators of sex drive and compulsivity: Predictors of child sexual abuse perpetration in adolescent males? *Sexual Abuse: A Journal of Research and Treatment, 28*, 132–153.

Mitchell, C. (2015). Resistant clients: We've all had them, here's how to help them. Retrieved April 2015 from https://www.psychotherapy.net/article/resistant-clients

Mohr, J., Gelso, C., & Hill, C. (2005). Client and counselor trainee attachment as predictors of session evaluation and counter-transference behavior in first counseling sessions. *Journal of Counseling Psychology, 52*, 298–309.

Moos, R. (1994). *Group Environment Scale: A social climate scale.* Palo Alto, CA: Consulting Psychologists Press.

Morgan, R., Ferrell, S., & Winterowd, C. (1999). Therapist perceptions of important therapeutic factors in psychotherapy groups for male inmates in state correctional facilities. *Small Group Research, 30*, 712–729.

Morris, J. (2014). Resistance and my favorite patient. *International Journal of Group Psychotherapy, 64*, 391–398.

Mulloy, R., & Marshall, W. (1999). Social functioning. In W. Marshall, D. Anderson, & Y. Fernandez (Eds.), *Cognitive behavioral treatment of sexual offenders* (pp. 93–109). Chichester, UK: Wiley.

National Association of Social Workers. (2008). *NASW code of ethics.* Washington, DC: Author.

Nitsun, M. (1996). *The anti-group: Destructive forces in the group and their creative potential.* London, UK: Routledge.

Orlinsky, D., Grave, K., & Parks, B. (1994). Process and outcome in psychotherapy— Noch einmal. In A. Bergin & S. Garfield (Eds.), *Handbook of psychotherapy and behavior change* (pp. 270–376). New York, NY: Wiley.

Overholser, J., & Beck, S. (1986). Multi-method assessment of rapists, child molesters, and three control groups on behavioral and psychological measures. *Journal of Consulting and Clinical Psychology, 54,* 682–687.

Parish, M., & Eagle, M. (2003). Attachment to the therapist. *Psychoanalytic Psychology, 20,* 271–286.

Prentky, R., Knight, R., Sims-Knight, J., Straus, H., Rokous, F., & Cerce, D. (1989). Developmental antecedents of sexual aggression. *Development and Psychopathology, 1,* 153–169.

Prescott, D. (2008). A group for integrating treatment lessons into daily life. *ATSA Forum, 20,* 1–9.

Proeve, M. (2003). Responsivity factors in sexual offender treatment. In T. Ward, D. Laws, & S. Hudson (Eds.), *Sexual deviance: Issues and controversies* (pp. 244–261). Thousand Oaks, CA: Sage.

Quirk, K., Miller, S., Duncan, B., & Owen, J. (2012). Group Session Rating Scale: Preliminary psychometrics in substance abuse group interventions. *Counseling and Psychotherapy Research, 13,* 194–200.

Reddon, J., Payne, L., & Starzyck, K. (1999). Therapeutic factors in group treatment: A consumers' report. *Journal of Offender Rehabilitation, 28,* 91–101.

Reimer, W., & Mathieu, T. (2006). Therapeutic factors in group treatment as perceived by sex offenders: A consumers' report. *Journal of Offender Rehabilitation, 42,* 59–73.

Rubino, G., Barker, C., Roth, T., & Fearon, P. (2000). Therapist empathy and depth of interpretation in response to potential alliance ruptures: The role of therapist and patient attachment styles. *Psychotherapy Research, 10,* 408–420.

Rutan, J., & Stone, W. (1993). *Psychodynamic group psychotherapy* (2nd ed.). New York, NY: Guilford Press.

Ryan, G., & Lane, S. (1991). *Juvenile sexual offending: Causes, consequences and correction.* Lexington, MA: Lexington Books.

Sauer, E., Lopez, F., & Gormley, B. (2003). Respective contributions of therapist and client adult attachment orientations to the development of the early working alliance: A preliminary growth modeling study. *Psychotherapy Research, 13,* 371–382.

Saunders, E., Awad, G., & White, G. (1986). Male adolescent sexual offenders: The offender and the offence. *Canadian Journal of Psychiatry, 31,* 542–549.

Sawle, G., & Kear-Colwell, J. (2001). Adult attachment style and pedophilia: A developmental perspective. *International Journal of Offender Therapy and Comparative Criminology, 45,* 32–50.

Sawyer, S. (2000). Some thoughts about why we believe group therapy is the preferred modality for treating sex offenders. *ATSA Forum, 12*, 11–12.

Sawyer, S. (2002). Group therapy with adult sex offenders. In B. Schwartz & H. Cellini (Eds.), *The sex offender* (Vol. 4). Kingston, NJ: Civic Research Institute.

Sawyer, S., & Jennings, J. (2014). Facilitating group-centered treatment groups for sex offenders. In M. Carich and S. Mussack (Eds.), *The handbook of sexual abuser assessment and treatment* (pp. 125–150). Brandon, VT: Safer Society Press.

Sawyer, S., & Prescott, D. (2011). Boundaries and dual relationships. *Sexual Abuse: A Journal of Research and Treatment, 23*, 365–380.

Scheidlinger, S. (2000). The group psychotherapy movement at the millennium: Some historical perspectives. *International Journal of Group Psychotherapy, 50*, 315–339.

Schwartz, B., & Cellini, H. (Eds.) (1988). *A practitioner's guide to treating the incarcerated male sex offender: Breaking the cycle of sexual abuse*. Washington, DC: US Department of Justice; National Institute of Corrections.

Seidman, B., Marshall, W., Hudson, S., & Robertson, P. (1994). An examination of intimacy and loneliness in sex offenders. *Journal of Interpersonal Violence, 9*, 518–534.

Seto, M., & Lalumiere, M. (2010). What is so special about male adolescent sexual offending? A review and test of explanations through meta-analysis. *Psychological Bulletin, 136*, 526–575.

Shorter Oxford English Dictionary (5th ed.). (2002). Oxford, UK: Oxford University Press.

Smallbone, S., & Dadds, M. (1998). Childhood attachment and adult attachment in incarcerated adult male sex offenders. *Journal of Interpersonal Violence, 13*, 555–573.

Smallbone, S., & Dadds, M. (2000). Attachment and coercive sexual behavior. *Sexual Abuse: A Journal of Research and Treatment, 12*, 3–15.

Smallbone, S., & Dadds, M. (2001). Further evidence for a relationship between attachment insecurity and coercive sexual behavior in non-offenders. *Journal of Interpersonal Violence, 16*, 22–35.

Smallbone, S., & McCabe, B. (2003). Childhood attachment, childhood sexual abuse, and onset of masturbation among adult sexual offenders. *Sexual Abuse: A Journal of Research and Treatment, 15*, 1–10.

Sribney, C., & Reddon, J. (2009). Adolescent sex offenders' rankings of therapeutic factors using the Yalom Card Sort. *Journal of Offender Rehabilitation, 47*, 24–40.

Stein, E., & Brown, J. (1991). Group therapy in a forensic setting. *Canadian Journal of Psychiatry, 36*, 718–722.

Stermac, L., & Quinsey, V. (1986). Social competence among rapists. *Behavioral Assessment, 8*, 171–185.

Stirpe, T., Abracen, J., Stermac, L., & Wilson, R. (2006). Sexual offenders' state-of-mind regarding childhood attachment: A controlled investigation. *Sexual Abuse: A Journal of Research and Treatment, 12*, 289–302.

Strauss, B., Burlingame, G., & Bormann, B. (2008). Using the CORE-R battery in group psychotherapy. *Journal of Clinical Psychology, 64*, 1225–1237.

Tasca, G., Balfour, L., Ritchie, K., & Bissada, H. (2007). Change in attachment anxiety is associated with improved depression among women with binge eating disorder. *Psychotherapy: Theory, Research, Practice, Training, 44*, 423–433.

Tasca, G., Cabrera, C., Kristjansson, E., MacNair-Semands, R., Joyce, A., & Ogrodniczuk, J. (2014). The Therapeutic Factor Inventory–8: Using item response theory to create a brief scale for continuous process monitoring for group psychotherapy. *Psychotherapy Research, 52*, 1–15.

Taube-Schiff, M., Suvak, M., Antony, M., Bieling, P., & McCabe, R. (2007). Group cohesion in cognitive-behavioral group therapy for social phobia. *Behaviour Research and Therapy, 45*, 687–698.

Thornton, D., Mann, R., & Williams, F. (2000). Therapeutic style in sex offender treatment. Unpublished manuscript, Offending Behavior Programming Unit, HM Prison Service, London. http://www.statisticshell.com/docs/factor.pdf

Tillitski, C. (1990). A meta-analysis of estimated effect sizes for group vs. individual vs. control treatments. *International Journal of Group Psychotherapy, 40*, 215–224.

Tingle, D., Barnard, G., Robbin, L., Newman, G., & Hutchinson, D. (1986). Childhood and adolescent characteristics of pedophiles and rapists. *International Journal of Law and Psychiatry, 9*, 103–116.

Tregaskis, D. (2000). Mix or match? Do adult abusers respond better to treatment in separate or mixed groups? Unpublished MSc dissertation, University of Birmingham, UK.

Tuckman, B. (1965). Developmental sequence in small groups. *Psychological Bulletin, 63*, 384–399.

Tuckman, B., & Jensen, M. (1977). Stages of small group development. *Group and Organizational Studies, 2*, 419–427.

Upper, D., & Flowers, J. (1994). Behavioral group therapy in rehabilitation settings. In J. Bedell (Ed.), *Psychological assessment and treatment of persons with severe mental disorders* (pp. 31–56). Philadelphia, PA: Taylor & Francis.

Ward, T., Hudson, S., & Marshall, W. (1996). Attachment style in sex offenders: A preliminary study. *Journal of Sex Research, 33*, 17–26.

Ward, T., Hudson, S., Marshall, W., & Siegert, R. (1995). Attachment style and intimacy deficits in sexual offenders: A theoretical framework. *Sexual Abuse: A Journal of Research and Treatment, 7*, 317–335.

Ward, T., Mann, R., & Gannon, T. (2007). The good lives model of offender rehabilitation: Clinical implications. *Aggression and Violent Behavior, 12*, 87–107.

Ward, T., McCormack, J., & Hudson, S. (1997). Sexual offenders' perceptions of their intimate relationships. *Sexual Abuse: A Journal of Research and Treatment, 9*, 57–74.

Ware, J., & Frost, A. (2010). A review of the use of therapeutic communities with sexual offenders. *International Journal of Offender Therapy and Comparative Criminology, 54*, 721–742.

Ware, J., Frost, A., & Boer, D. (2015). Groupwork in Australia: Working with sex offenders. In K. O'Sullivan, A. King, & T. Nove (Eds.), *Groupwork in Australia* (pp. 252–267). Sydney, Australia: Institute of Group Leaders.

Ware, J., Mann, R., & Wakeling, H. (2009). Group vs. individual treatment: What is the best modality for treating sex offenders? *Sexual Abuse in Australia and New Zealand, 2*, 2–13.

Weber, R. (2003). *Principles of group psychotherapy.* New York, NY: American Group Psychotherapy Association.

Wheelan, S. (1990). *Facilitating training groups: A guide to leadership and verbal intervention skills.* New York, NY: Praeger.

Wheelan, S. (1994). *Group processes: A developmental perspective.* Boston, MA: Allyn & Bacon.

Wood, E., & Riggs, S. (2008). Predictor of child molestation: Adult attachment, cognitive distortions and empathy. *Journal of Interpersonal Violence, 23*, 259–275.

Wood, E., & Riggs, S. (2009). Adult attachment, cognitive distortions, and views of self, others, and the future among child molesters. *Sexual Abuse: A Journal of Research and Treatment, 21*, 375–390.

Yalom, I. (1970). *The theory and practice of group psychotherapy* (1st ed.). New York, NY: Basic Books.

Yalom, I. (1975). *The theory and practice of group psychotherapy* (2nd ed.). New York, NY: Basic Books.

Yalom, I., & Leszcz, M. (2005). *The theory and practice of group psychotherapy* (5th ed.). New York, NY: Basic Books.

Yalom, I., Tinklenberg, J., & Gilula, M. (1968). *Curative factors in group therapy*. Unpublished manuscript, Stanford University, Stanford, CA.

Yates, P., & Ward, T. (2008). Good lives, self-regulation, and risk management: An integrated model of sexual offender assessment and treatment. *Sexual Abuse in Australia and New Zealand, 1*, 3–20.

About the Authors

Steven Sawyer, MSSW, LICSW, CGP
Mr. Sawyer is a Licensed Independent Clinical Social Worker and a Certified Group Psychotherapist. He is founder and president of Sawyer Solutions, LLC, a private clinical services and organizational consulting practice. In his clinical practice, he provides clinical and consultation services to individuals, families, and organizations. He currently serves as a consultant to Catholic religious orders on matters of sexual abuse prevention and management, provides clinical supervision services for the State of Minnesota, operates a treatment program for adults who have committed a sexual offense, manages a program for men who pay for sex, and provides individual, conjoint, and family therapy.

Over the past 30 years, he has been a founding board member and executive director of a nonprofit agency, a founding board member and past chapter president of the Minnesota Chapter of the Association for the Treatment of Sexual Abusers (MNATSA), and a past board member and chair of the Minnesota Board of Social Work. Mr. Sawyer is the recipient of the 2004 MNATSA Professional Service Award and the 1999 Mankato State University Social Work Alumnus of the Year Award.

Mr. Sawyer is an experienced public speaker who has given lectures and trainings locally and nationally to public and professional groups about sexual offender treatment and sexual abuse prevention. He has published articles and book chapters on a program for men who use prostitutes, sexual abuse in the Catholic Church, group therapy with sexual offenders, sexual dysfunction in sexual offenders, and sexual offender treatment program outcomes research.

Jerry L. Jennings, Ph.D.
Dr. Jennings is a clinical psychologist and award-winning screenwriter and writer. He has published more than 50 journal articles, book chapters, and books, including three clinical texts: *The Mindfulness Toolkit for Counselors, Teachers, Coaches and Clinicians of Youth* (2013); *Responsibility and Self-Management* (2007); and *Breaking the Silence*

of the Lambs (2014), which is a unique first-person forensic case study and clinician's memoir of the case of infamous sexual predator, Gary M. Heidnik. As Vice President of Clinical Services for Liberty Healthcare Corporation, he plays a major role in the development of innovative, best practices treatment programs in both facility and community settings for a diverse array of challenging adult and adolescent clinical populations, including felony ISTs, insanity acquittees, sexual offenders, SVPs, and individuals with intellectual and developmental disabilities and co-occurring disorders. Dr. Jennings is also dedicated to preserving and honoring the personal stories of Holocaust survivors and has published three memoirs on their behalf: *Stella's Secret* (2005), *I Choose Life* (2009), and *Darkness Hides the Flowers* (2011).